Industrial Relations in Africa

Also by Geoffrey Wood

INSTITUTIONS AND WORKING LIFE (*editor with P. James*)

TRADE UNIONS AND DEMOCRACY (*editor with M. Harcourt*)

CONTESTING PUBLIC SECTOR REFORMS (*editor with P. Dibben and I. Roper*)

THE ETHICAL BUSINESS: Challenges and Controversies (*with K. Mellahi*)

Industrial Relations in Africa

Edited by

Geoffrey Wood
Professor, School of Management, University of Sheffield, UK

and

Chris Brewster
Professor, Henley Management College, UK

© Geoffrey Wood and Chris Brewster 2007
Individual chapters © contributors 2007

All rights reserved. No reproduction, copy or transmission of this publication may be made without written permission.

No paragraph of this publication may be reproduced, copied or transmitted save with written permission or in accordance with the provisions of the Copyright, Designs and Patents Act 1988, or under the terms of any licence permitting limited copying issued by the Copyright Licensing Agency, 90 Tottenham Court Road, London W1T 4LP.

Any person who does any unauthorised act in relation to this publication may be liable to criminal prosecution and civil claims for damages.

The editors have asserted their rights to be identified as the editors of this work in accordance with the Copyright, Designs and Patents Act 1988.

First published 2007 by
PALGRAVE MACMILLAN
Houndmills, Basingstoke, Hampshire RG21 6XS and
175 Fifth Avenue, New York, N.Y. 10010
Companies and representatives throughout the world

PALGRAVE MACMILLAN is the global academic imprint of the Palgrave Macmillan division of St. Martin's Press, LLC and of Palgrave Macmillan Ltd. Macmillan® is a registered trademark in the United States, United Kingdom and other countries. Palgrave is a registered trademark in the European Union and other countries.

ISBN-13: 978-0-230-01366-7 hardback
ISBN-10: 0-230-01366-X hardback

This book is printed on paper suitable for recycling and made from fully managed and sustained forest sources. Logging, pulping and manufacturing processes are expected to conform to the environmental regulations of the country of origin.

A catalogue record for this book is available from the British Library.

A catalog record for this book is available from the Library of Congress.

10 9 8 7 6 5 4 3 2 1
16 15 14 13 12 11 10 09 08 07

Printed and bound in Great Britain by
Antony Rowe Ltd, Chippenham and Eastbourne

Contents

List of Tables	xi
List of Figures	xii
List of Contributors	xiii

1 Introduction: Comprehending Industrial Relations in Africa   1
Chris Brewster and Geoffrey Wood

Comprehending industrial relations, and industrial relations in Africa	1
The context – structural adjustment in Africa: deindustrialisation, informalisation and organised labour	2
The actors	4
Employers and employment in the informal sector	7
Individual national experiences and common trends	8
Conclusion	12

Part I   Country Studies from East and Central Africa   15

2 The Dynamics of Industrial Relations in Eritrea: 1991–2006   17
Fitsum Ghebregiorgis and Luchien Karsten

Introduction – the Eritrean Context	17
The historical development of trade unions in Eritrea	18
The parties	20
Employment relations	22
Industrial disputes	23
Civil society and citizenship behaviour	24
Conclusion	24

3 The Development of Industrial Relations in Kenya   28
George Hagglund

Introduction	28
The colonial era	28
The rise of Kenya's industrial relations system	31
Conclusion	37

4 Industrial Relations and the Social Partners in Kenya 39
Tayo Fashoyin

Introduction	39
The economy and labour market challenges	39
The legal framework for industrial relations	41
Trade unions and employers' associations	43
Collective bargaining, dispute resolution and the Labour Court	46
Tripartism, social dialogue and development	49
Conclusion	50

5 Industrial Relations in Malawi 53
Lewis Dzimbiri

Introduction	53
The country and context	53
Origins and present state of trade union movement: an overview	55
Independence and trade union movement	55
Industrial relations legislation	56
New labour policy	57
The Labour Relations Act 1996	57
Employment Act 2000	58
Present industrial relations practices	58
Conclusion	63

6 Contemporary Issues in Industrial Relations: Uganda 66
Joy T. Kirenga

Introduction	66
Uganda's historical context	66
Overview of the economy	66
Employment and employment trends	68
Legal framework	71
Employers and their organisations	71
Employees and their organisations	72
Current challenges in industrial relations in Uganda	72
The way forward	73

Part II Country Studies from Southern Africa 75

7 Industrial Relations in Conditions of Economic Stress: The Zimbabwe Case 77
Lloyd Sachikonye

Introduction	77

The economy: stupid!	78
Employment and the labour market	80
Industrial relations: legal framework, stresses and strains	81
An elusive social contract	83
Conclusion	85

8 Trade Unions and Neo-Liberal Reforms in Mozambique: The 'Hollowing Out of Industrial Relations'?   87
Edward Webster and Geoffrey Wood

Introduction	87
Unions and democracy: issues and challenges	87
The Mozambican political context	88
The economic context	89
Mozambican unions	90
Mozambican unions in practice	91
General issues	94
Conclusion	95

9 Labour Regulation in Namibia: From 'Colonial Despotism' to 'Flexible Taylorism'   98
Gilton Klerck

Introduction	98
Namibia under South African rule: migrants, masters and the gendarmerie state	100
Labour regulation in the first decade of independence: 'flexibility', globalisation and neo-colonialism	104
Conclusion	107

10 Industrial Relations and Employment Insecurity in South Africa: The Possibilities of Social Justice Unionism   111
Pauline Dibben

Introduction	111
The changing South African labour market, and the union response	112
The role of COSATU and employment legislation in South Africa	113
Defining 'Social Justice Unionism': a distinct concept	116
COSATU: a 'Social Justice Union'?	116
'Social Justice Union' in South Africa: a descriptive or normative analysis?	120
Conclusions: moving toward 'Social Justice Unionism' in South Africa	121

11 The Emerging and Changing Industrial Relations Landscape in Botswana — 125
Thabo Lucas Seleke

Introduction	125
Origins of trade unions in Botswana	125
Botswana's political economy	126
The Botswanan labour movement	127
Labour laws and the changing industrial relations landscape in Botswana	128
The 2004 Trade Dispute Act	130
Trade Union and Employers' Organisation Act	130
Challenges facing unions in Botswana	131
Conclusion	132

Part III Country Studies from West and North Africa — 135

12 Industrial Relations in an Emerging Morocco — 137
Mohamed Essaaidi

Introduction	137
The legal context	138
Labour rights and their application	140
Conclusions	145

13 The Development of Industrial Relations in Nigeria: 1900–2006 — 147
Sola Fajana

Introduction	147
Origin and development of trade unions	148
Evolution of industrial unionism in Nigeria	150
The trade unions: further reforms	151
Developments within labour centres	153
Union–state relations	155
Petroleum pricing and further reforms of trade unions	156
Industrial conflict	158
Future prospects and concluding remarks	160

14 Contemporary Industrial Relations in Nigeria — 162
Dafe Otobo

Introduction – the Nigerian context	162
The industrial relations system	164
Collective bargaining and wage bargaining in the public sector	166

Emerging issues in the public sector	169
Collective bargaining and wage bargaining in the private sector	171
Emerging issues in the private sector	173
Institutionalised conflict regulation: disputes, strikes and lockouts	174
Explanations of disputes and strikes	176
Institutionalised disputes settlement mechanisms	177
Concluding remarks: the state, globalisation and industrial relations	178

15 Industrial Relations in Ghana — 182
Garth Frazer

Introduction	182
A brief history of industrial relations in Ghana	182
The mechanics of industrial relations in Ghana	186
Unions and unionisation in Ghana	191
Trends in industrial relations in Ghana	193
Conclusions	195

16 Industrial Relations in Francophone Africa – the Case of Niger — 198
Richard Croucher

Introduction	198
History: dependence and independence	199
The economy: from national construction to impoverishment and dependence	201
SAPs: consequences for unions	202
Union responses, national and international	203
Conclusion	204

Part IV Trans-Continental Trends and Issues — 207

17 Organising the Informal Economy: Results and Prospects – the Case of Ghana in Comparative Perspective — 209
Richard Croucher

Introduction	209
Defining the informal economy	210
The informal economy: in need of extension or regulation?	210
Unions and the informal economy	211
Difficulties of unionising the informal economy	212
'Informal sector' organisation in Ghana	213
Conclusion	215

18 Cross-Continental Trends and Issues in Employment Relations in Africa — **219**
Frank Horwitz

Introduction	219
The role of government	221
Structural adjustment programmes	222
African organisations and trade union density	222
The State, collective bargaining and dispute resolution	224
Public sector industrial relations	225
Contemporary employment relations and labour markets	226
Analysis and conclusion	230
Index	235

List of Tables

5.1	Union growth in Malawi – 1999	59
5.2	Membership growth and decline in Malawian unions – 1995–99	63
6.1	Showing causes of strikes in the last 6 years	69
7.1	Key economic indicators – Zimbabwe	78
8.1	Method of appointing shop stewards	91
8.2	When were shop steward elections last held?	92
10.1	Summary of South African labour legislation – 1995–2003	114
10.2	Reliance on unions to protect interests, by tenure	117
10.3	Attendance at union meetings, by tenure	118
10.4	Engaging in collective action, by tenure	119
10.5	Party representation of workers, by tenure	120
13.1	Structure of unions – 1978–2006	151
15.1	Trade union membership of TUC affiliates in 2001	192
16.1	Changes in USTN revenue (in CAF)	203
18.1	Gross Domestic Product (GDP in US$ billion) and per capita GDP (US$) for selected African countries	220
18.2	Statistics on trade unions in selected African countries	224

List of Figures

4.1 Collective bargaining agreements and disputes,
    2000–2005   47
4.2 Strikes – 1996–2005   49
8.1 Estimated per cent of union penetration in respondents'
    workplaces   93

List of Contributors

Chris Brewster is a Professor at Henley Management College, Henley-on-Thames and University of Reading, UK.

Richard Croucher is a Professor and Director of Research at Middlesex University Business School, UK.

Pauline Dibben is Lecturer in Human Resource Management at the Management School, University of Sheffield.

Lewis Dzimbiri is Senior Lecturer, Faculty of Social Science, University of Botswana, Gaborone, Botswana.

Mohamed Essaaidi is a Professor at Abdelmalek Essaadi University, Tetuan, Morocco.

Sola Fajana is a Professor at the University of Lagos, Nigeria.

Tayo Fashoyin is Director of the International Labour Organization's Sub-Regional Office for Southern Africa.

Garth Frazer is Assistant Professor of Economics, Centre for Industrial Relations, University of Toronto, Canada.

Fitsum Ghebregiorgis is a Lecturer at the University of Asmara's Faculty of Business and Economics, Asmara, Eritrea.

George Hagglund is Professor Emeritus at the University of Wisconsin, Madison, USA and Visiting Professor, University of South Australia, Adelaide, Australia.

Frank Horwitz is Professor and Director of the Graduate School of Business at the University of Cape Town, South Africa.

Luchien Karsten is a Professor at the University of Groningen's Faculty of Organisation and Management, Landleven, Netherlands.

Joy T. Kirenga is the School Administrator in the Graduate School, Makerere University, Kampala, Uganda.

Gilton Klerck is a Lecturer at Rhodes University, Grahamstown, South Africa.

Dafe Otobo is a Professor at the University of Lagos, Nigeria.

Lloyd Sachikonye is Professor, Institute of Development Studies, University of Zimbabwe, Harare, Zimbabwe.

Thabo Seleke lectures in the Department of Political and Administrative Studies, University of Botswana, Gabarone, Botswana.

Edward Webster is Professor, Sociology of Work Programme, University of Witwatersrand, South Africa.

Geoffrey Wood is Professor at the School of Management, University of Sheffield, UK and Overseas Associate of the University of Witwatersrand, South Africa.

1
Introduction: Comprehending Industrial Relations in Africa

Chris Brewster and Geoffrey Wood

Comprehending industrial relations, and industrial relations in Africa

This book examines *industrial relations* (IR) in Africa. Africa is a huge continent with a rich endowment of resources that, in most countries, for a series of historical, economic and political reasons have not led to development and membership of the modern world. There are, of course, some existing and potential countries where significant progress has been made. For all these countries, however, a key resource remains the capability, commitment and deployment of their people in economic activity. The way that people are managed, their role in such management and the relationships between people and their representatives and their employers will be crucial factors in Africa's development.

Since Ben Roberts' (1964; Roberts and de Bellecombe 1967) studies on industrial relations in African and other developing commonwealth countries almost half a century ago, there have been very few attempts to collate existing knowledge about the continent into one volume.[1] Comparative studies of industrial relations have tended to concentrate on the developed world, especially Europe and, to a lesser extent now, North America and Japan (see, for example, Bean, 1994; Eaton, 2000). There have been far fewer studies of the developing world and almost none on Africa. However, there is a growing interest in the relevance of the African experience (see Chapter 17), with two volumes that provide significant coverage of *human resource management* on the continent, namely Budhwar and Debrah (2001) and Kamoche *et al.* (2003). This volume, presenting texts on many of the Africa countries, written by experts in, from or on those countries, attempts to fill the gap in research on IR across the continent. There is not space in a single volume to devote a chapter to each African country, and our analysis has been limited by the IR scholars that we know, or could find, were conducting primary research in the area. Hence, for example, whilst the book includes chapters from North, West, East, the Horn, and Southern Africa, there is only one chapter from the Mahgreb states and one from sub-Saharan Francophone

Africa. Two chapters are included on Nigeria and Kenya, given the relative importance of these countries on the continent, and their relative neglect in the international literature, especially when compared to the other continental great power, South Africa. Nonetheless, whilst it would need a second volume to cover the countries left out, this book provides a wider coverage of IR in Africa than previous texts.

We explore the situation across the continent, chapters examining both formal and informal arrangements and practices. In particular, we have been keen to encourage authors to explore the context of industrial relations: something we feel is crucial in all studies of the subject, but is certainly required for any serious understanding of the topic in Africa. Whilst the researchers writing here are based in many different continents, most of the contributors to this volume are African scholars based at African universities, or from that background, with many years research experience on their chapter topics. This has ensured that the contributions do not represent 'tourist research', but rather are the product of detailed primary research and knowledge.

This introductory chapter identifies the current economic context in Africa, and outlines the situation of the actors: the State, employers and trade unions. We also examine the crucial role played by the informal sector. We then introduce the chapters in the book and draw some preliminary conclusions.

The context – structural adjustment in Africa: deindustrialisation, informalisation and organised labour

The imposition of structural adjustment programmes (SAPs) – needed loan financing in return for neo-liberal reforms centring on radical reductions in the role of the state, marketed as mechanisms for economic recovery – in Africa in the 1980s proved devastating for the continent. Compelled into acceptance of these programmes, most tropical African governments were faced with the worsening, rather than the amelioration, of structural crises. By the close of that decade, it was already clear that the reforms had failed even on their own terms, with increasing debt, poor macro-economic performance, the collapse of education and health care systems, and an inability to meet the basic social needs of the bulk of the population (Naiman and Watkins, 1990).

Meanwhile, as George (1990) notes, currency devaluations and privatisations ensured foreign access to raw materials and infrastructure on discounted terms. Market saturation resulted in diminishing returns for African experts, whilst the stringent terms of SAPs restricted the resources available for diversification (George, 1990). Indeed, any stability attained was at a great cost in areas of domestic investment, even in terms of basic physical and social infrastructure (Mkandawire and Soludo, 2002). The effects of a continent-wide brain drain have been exacerbated by the demoralisation and debilitation of the civil service through ongoing downsizing, outsourcing, and universal vilification as corrupt (ibid.).

More recently, the poor track record of, and growing resistance to, SAPs has led to the IMF replacing them with Poverty Reduction Strategy Papers (PRSPs), supposedly better tailored policies, focused on the needs of individual countries, and incorporating local issues and concerns. Yet, PRSPs continue to denigrate the role of the developmental state – other than in terms of policing, patent protection, market access, and controlling the movements of peoples – and represent little in the way of improvement on SAPs (Zack-Williams and Mohan, 2005). In 2005, the major industrialised nations of the world promised to cancel the debts of the poorest; yet, in addition to 'ending' corruption, this relief remains contingent on further privatisation and the elimination of blockages on private investment (Willett, 2005).

As Hoogevelt (2005) notes, through modest reforms, adherents of neo-liberalism have been able to co-opt many of the concerns of groundswell campaigns in the West, such as 'Make Poverty History', through debt relief, a renewed commitment to basic education and health care, whilst retaining a commitment to the hollowing out of the developmental state, and the denigration of economic alternatives. Hence, it is hardly surprising that the campaigning musician-cum-entrepeneur, Bono, was able to state that Rupert Murdoch was one of his most helpful supporters (ibid.). In reality, there is more to Africa's economic reconstruction than further debt relief; ultimately the promotion of economic alternatives in Africa is contingent on indigenous associations, such as national labour movements. No country has successfully industrialised in the absence of an active developmental state, with the possible exception of Britain that was able to count on the captive market of India. Nor is there any indication that SAPs have had anything other than detrimental effects on the economic diversity of target nations.

The 'War on Terror' has further contributed to the closing off of economic alternatives. Developmental resources and aid have increasingly been directed in the support of full-scale military adventures, and low key conflicts; yet, neo-liberal policies have worsened domestic and economic tensions in many areas of the developing world, further fuelling violent conflicts, rather than underwriting future prosperity (Willett, 2005).

In practical terms, the effects of neo-liberal reforms on unions have been four fold. First, over two decades of under-spending on education at all levels (with the exception of a handful of southern African states) has eroded national skills bases, placing new-labour market entrants at a very much weaker position *vis-à-vis* their employers. Quite simply, increasing numbers of Africans lack access to basic – let alone technical – education, condemning them at best to poorly paid jobs. Lower skills profiles place employees in a very much weaker bargaining position. Secondly, the destruction of large areas of industry in the face of intense overseas competition and wholesale job cuts has greatly reduced the pool of potential union members. Large-scale job cutbacks have also taken place in the public sector in most African states. Again, the resultant rises in unemployment would weaken the bargaining position of those in jobs. Thirdly, significant currency devaluations have made for effective pay cuts; unions have had to devote a great deal of attention simply to slow the declining material conditions of members. Finally, the emasculation of the state has resulted in a inability to enforce labour laws effectively in many tropical African states.

The actors

The state

The state is 'a politically organised body of people occupying a definite territory and living under a government entirely or almost free from external control and competent to ensure habitual obedience from all persons within it – in other words, possessing external and internal sovereignty' (Anderson and Parker, 1964: 234). Governments represent the means through which states operate: they encompass the people and agencies designated to carry out the state's purpose (ibid., 235). Theoretically speaking, the government serves as an instrument through which the state serves its citizens. In reality, many tropical African states fail to fulfil these basic functions: some, such as the case of Somalia, fail to meet the basic prerequisites of a state at all. Nonetheless, most African states retain at least some functions of government, and, formally speaking at least, are engaged in the business of promoting social progress, even if their actual track record is patchy.

Conservatives blame Africa's endemic economic crises squarely on individual national governments on the continent. More sophisticated *theories of the failure of the state* again argue that the African state has failed to live up to the legitimate expectations and needs of their people (Hyden, 2002: 5). However, unlike neo-liberal conceptualisations, these theorists acknowledge that states can make a difference, and that human agency mediated by public institutions can provide the basis of general social progress and development (ibid.: 5). Theories of the failure of the state focus on the inability of the state to make peasants – and indeed, many of those working in the informal sector – comply with its interests; this is of real significance in Africa, where a very high proportion of employment is in the informal sector. Others argue that deeply embedded patronage networks make progress impossible (ibid.: 5).

In the field of industrial relations, states seek to regulate both the conditions under which labour power is sold, and how it is used (Edwards, 2002: 162). The former would encompass interventions such as social security, which would guarantee basic living standards, so that the supply of labour power is not totally dependent on the market (ibid.). With the exception of a small number of states – mostly in southern Africa – social security provisions on the continent tend to be either negligible or totally absent. This means that individuals are compelled to sell their labour power at any cost – and/or rely on extended, informal family based networks of support. The demands of the latter place great strains on those already in employment, and make having work inherently far more stressful than would otherwise be the case. Other ways the state can regulate the sale of labour power would be by imposing age limits on employment or through the operation of minimum wages. Again, across much of the continent, the hollowing out of government – as a result of both structural adjustment programmes and internal failings – has greatly weakened the capacity of governments to enforce the law in this area, whilst the continued ideological hegemony of neo-liberalism has emasculated the political will. Finally, enforcement of any type of labour legislation is at best patchy; most informal sector operatives are entirely beyond legal restrictions in this area.

The second area where the state may regulate the employment relationship is in the deployment of labour power (Edwards, 2002: 162). This would include union organisational rights, restrictions on working hours, health and safety legislation, employment protection, including anti-discrimination and anti-harassment measures, and formal grievance proceedings. Again, the general capacity of most governments on the continent to regulate these areas of the employment relationship remains weak and uneven; and, again, often entirely absent in relation to informal working.

During the early years of independence, most tropical African governments pursued active industrial policies, with a large role being accorded to parastatal enterprises. Traditional areas of industrial strength on the continent have included industries such as textiles, food processing and beverages, in addition to agriculture and mining. Many countries also developed a range of other industries, most notably motor components and assembly. IMF imposed neo-liberal reforms devastated most of these areas of activity, with the notable exception of beverages, reflecting the strength of national brands, strong distribution networks and the relative costs of shipping short versus long distances. Hasty and poorly conceived privatisations have been followed by wholesale asset stripping or cherry picking, both contributing to the ongoing shrinkage of formal sector work and employment: in very few cases have national governments been able to reverse the damage done.

Employers

Within Africa, private sector employers can be divided into three broad categories. Firstly, there are foreign owned multinational corporations (MNCs). Such companies may tailor their employment relations towards practices in their country of origin. Instances of the latter are relatively uncommon in tropical Africa, but can be found, *inter alia*, in South Africa's motor industry, where major German motor manufacturers have successful disseminated advanced cooperative production paradigms. Secondly, they may follow practices in the country of operation: this may result in subsidiaries basing their activities on cost-cutting, taking advantages of local institutional shortcomings to engage in higher levels of labour repression and/or pay very much lower wages (even in relative terms) than would be acceptable in their country of origin.

Thirdly, they may adopt a mixed model, reserving most senior positions for expatriates, consigning indigenous employees to relatively lowly paid positions.

A third cluster of employers are indigenous-owned firms, the overwhelming majority of which are small. In more developed southern African states, such as South Africa and Botswana, such firms tend to be governed in a manner similar to their counterparts in the developed world. However, in much of tropical Africa, the ownership of a large proportion of firms tends to be via extended families, with employment relations being acted out on patriarchal lines. Not only is capital accessed by personal networks, but also labour (c.f. Kimemia, 2000; Wood and Frynas, 2006). However, returns are often low and volatile, precluding such networks from moving beyond a basic subsistence and coping level, unlike their counterparts in the Far East (Wood and Frynas, 2006).

As Wood and Frynas (2006) argue, both pre-colonial and colonial societies left a legacy of paternalism in the workplace: this has led to the persistence of Taylorist (and pre-Taylorist) work systems, characterised by authoritarianism, fixed divisions of labour, limited and informal training (also a product of weak local training institutions), and low levels of participation and involvement. On the one hand, it could be argued that increased consumer pressures have forced indigenous firms linked to global commodity chains to upgrade their practices. On the other hand, it can be argued that, in the operation of such networks, labour standards continue to receive a low priority when compared to cost or quality concerns (Mellahi and Wood, 2002). Again, insecure tenure has become the norm in most tropical African states, compounded by wholesale job shedding as a result of SAPs.

Trade unions

In their classic account, Freeman and Medoff (1984) argue that unions enhance social efficiency. Whilst neo-liberals charge that they distort the operation of labour markets in the direction of monopoly, this is offset by the provision of voice mechanism, that allow employees to express concerns, and hence providing a basis for fairer, more equitable and sustainable employment relations – and indeed, raise social concerns of importance beyond the workplace. To this, Kaufman (2004) adds a third face: they offset the monopsony powers of the employer. The dominance of neo-liberal ideologies in setting government policies in Africa has generally resulted in the positive aspects of unionism being ignored; rather, through labour market deregulation, or more commonly, through poor enforcement of existing labour laws, unions have been forced onto the defensive, a process exacerbated by wholesale job losses in manufacturing and the state sectors continent-wide.

Yet unions can play a role of inestimable value on the continent. As agents of civil society, unions may serve – and in many African countries have served – as campaigners to promote democracy within the wider society, challenging authoritarian regimes, and providing a mechanisms for voicing a broad range of social concerns when formal political structures are moribund or semi functional (Wood, 2004b). They may also serve as guardians of hard-won democratic gains, and/or as partners in accommodations between competing interest groupings (ibid.). At the workplace, they have a vital role in deflecting employers away from low wage low skill production paradigms, and towards higher value added models; as employers are precluded from reaping gains accruing from labour repression, they are forced towards more cooperative labour relations paradigms, characterised by high wages and high skills (Wood and Glaister, 2006). Through combining country studies with general overviews, this book explores the current state of labour unions in Africa, and the prospects for revitalisation.

The events of the past two decades have not been wholly detrimental to unions. In most African countries, the immediate post-independence period saw a drift to one-party rule; the authoritarian political systems that emerged invariably subsumed any trade unions into little more than transmission belts for official policy. At the same time, ideological commitments to socialism or progress helped secure a range of basic employment rights, helping legitimise otherwise fragile political institutions.

The 1990s saw a dramatic return to multi-party democracy in many African states, after many years of single party rule (Southall, 2003: 142). As Southall (2003: 142) notes, whilst conservative accounts have argued that this largely represented the product of Western pressure in the aftermath of the cold war, there is little doubt that, in reality, internal forces played a central role in the reversal of authoritarian rule. Within many African countries – ranging from Kenya to Zambia – trade unions played a central role in protest movements that impelled democratic reforms (ibid.). However, in most cases they proved incapable of challenging the imposition of neo-liberal reforms once multi-partyism had been achieved. Even in South Africa, the Congress of South African Trade Unions has proved incapable of checking the imposition of market-driven policies, although it has proved somewhat more successful in checking an ambitious privatisation agenda.

Employers and employment in the informal sector

No discussion of industrial relations in Africa would be complete without pointing out the importance of the informal sector in the continent. The informal sector constitutes an important part of economic social life everywhere, particularly in developing economies. In Africa, the informal sector forms a major, perhaps the major, part of economic activity.

The exact nature and effects of the informal sector remains a subject of much contention. It has variously been seen as part of the creeping marginalisation of vulnerable labour market categories worldwide, a response to over-regulation, a cause and effect of inequality, a creative field of operation for the entrepreneurially minded or a survival strategy of last resort. The informal sector can be defined as economic activity based on small enterprises, an especially important survival strategy for the poor, when state social security is weak or non-existent (Martin, 2000).

There is a strong relationship between the size and scale of unregulated economic activity and social inequality; poverty is a major cause of informal sector activity (Rosser and Rosser, 2001). Informal sector operatives – especially larger operatives within the underground economy – have sometimes been depicted as latter day versions of the 'robber barons' of early capitalism who later turned into respectable philanthropists; as essentially productive capitalists fleeing rapacious officialdom (Rosser and Rosser, 2001). However, informal sector activity more commonly may represent a survival strategy of last resort, with 'negative feedback loops' (weakening regulatory machinery and a coterminous emasculation of state benefits) resulting in a vicious circle of exclusion (ibid.).

In contrast, it has been suggested that the lack of regulation contributes to the 'Brazilianisation' of an economy, with the inevitable pressures being downward rather than upward (*Financial Times*, 31/8/2000). If informal sector activity constitutes a large segment of an economy, this will invariably result in increased tax shortfalls, reduced social spending, and, hence, an increasing number of individuals being forced to turn to the informal sector for survival (Rosser and Rosser, 2001). This can result in the informal sector threatening to totally overwhelm the formal one (ibid.). In Africa, the proportion of informal jobs is ever-increasing; rather than the uniform pattern of progress depicted by modernisation theorists, it seems that development trajectories are polarizing, with a large proportion of the world's population being forced to turn to the informal sector for survival (Williams and Wildebank, 2000).

In summary, the key industrial relations issues emerging from the informal sector centre on its scale, its marginality, and the tenuous, dangerous and poorly rewarded nature of work. A growing proportion of African workers are confined to the informal sector: indeed, a case can be made that the typical employment relationship in Africa is in the informal sector. What makes it particularly complex is that many engaged in these activities are both workers and owners. This, and marginal and fragile livings, makes any attempt at unionisation extremely difficult; whilst there are politically powerful informal traders associations in many parts of Africa, these tend to have populist-reformist orientations, and often closer to political elites than the bulk of those employed in this area.

Individual national experiences and common trends

Any overview of the state of employment relations in such a vast and variegated continent as Africa must necessarily begin with caveats. Countries on the continent vary greatly in their stage of economic development. On the one hand, in most countries, the peasantry remains important, and the informal sector has become increasingly so, whilst the lifting of protective tariffs as part and parcel of structural adjustment programs has devastated large areas of industrial activity. On the other hand, there are vast differences in employment relations practice between failed and criminal states, and functional and stable multi-party democracies with growing economies. We have sought to illustrate this diversity through a range of country chapters, encompassing a wide cross-section of countries. However, space required certain omissions. Firstly, we have not concentrated on coverage of North Africa, because of the very different nature of political systems in that region, and its closer affinity with the Middle East. Secondly, our coverage of Francophone Africa is more limited; this reflects both the serious political crises experienced in some countries (e.g. Ivory Coast and DRC) and the limited nature of existing industrial relations research in others (e.g. Chad, Cameroon, Togo, Mali).

The book that you have in front of you has been written by country experts from a wide range of African countries. Section A consists of country studies from East and Central Africa, Section B, southern Africa, Section C, West and North Africa, whilst Section D covers issues of continent-wide relevance.

Part I: country studies from East and Central Africa

Chapter 2 – by Fitsum Ghebregiorgis and Luchien Karsten – explores the nature and extent of industrial relations practice in Eritrea. They examine the extent of free union activity, the role of collective agreements, and the relationship between industrial relations to civil society and citizenship behaviour. It is concluded that workplace conflicts tend to be resolved by dispute settlement mechanisms internal to the firm. On the one hand, industrial relations practice is based on Western practices centring on trade unions and collective bargaining. On the other hand, industrial relations in the country 'is characterised by the republican virtues owing to the active participation of Eritrean citizens in the country's rehabilitation and reconstruction process to promote economic growth and catch up with the world economy.'

In Chapter 3, George Hagglund examines the emergence of the modern Kenyan industrial relations system, as a product of trade offs between various interest groups. Kenyan industrial relations remains dominated by the needs of succeeding national governments, and their desire to exercise control over both unions and private sector firms; meanwhile the Kenyan economy remains in a highly precarious position, not conducive to stable long term employment relations. The companion Chapter 4, by Tayo Fashoyin, provides a more detailed account of the present state of play of Kenyan industrial relations, according special attention to the possibilities and prospects of tripartism in one of Africa's most important economies.

In Chapter 5, Lewis Dzimbiri looks at the changing nature of Malawian industrial relations over the past four decades: a central theme of his analysis is on the role of the state and donors in shaping industrial relations practice in that country. Whilst the labour movement was reduced to a subservient role during the Banda years, it regained a more independent role in the

1990s: at the same time, job losses during that decade as a result of structural adjustment programmes have posed new problems for Malawian trade unions.

In Chapter 6 on Uganda, Joy Kirenga examines the IR situation in one of the African countries that has suffered most from the fluctuations in global markets and exploitation by those outside the country. Making the point strongly that this is mainly a rural, subsistence, economy, she sets industrial relations within the country in context. The case has extra resonance for the editors as industrial action and associated riots almost stopped the author from completing the text in time and it was only through her considerable ingenuity and persistence that the chapter is here.

Part II: country studies from Southern Africa

Chapter 7, by Lloyd Sachikonye, looks at the Zimbabwean case: again a story of labour union activism and collective bargaining, mixed with extensive state intervention. The chapter explores the linkages between political crises, economic decline, and the volatility of present-day Zimbabwe industrial relations. Sachikonye concludes that the practice of industrial relations has been heavily – and adversely – affected by the combined processes of economic decline and state authoritarianism: 'any improvement in the climate of industrial relations will be bound up with economic and political reform on a democratic path.'

Chapter 8, by Eddie Webster and Geoffrey Wood, provides an overview of the state of Mozambican trade unions. It seeks to shed further light on the effects of structural adjustment and political liberalisation on unions and the practice of employment relations. Whilst focusing on the case of organised labour in a newly democratised developing economy, the dilemmas posed by a shrinking of employment bases in traditional areas of union activity, reduced security of tenure and *de facto* legal deregulation, and the need to reach out to highly marginalised categories of labour, are also shared by unions in many developed countries.

Chapter 9, by Gilton Klerck, evaluates the effects of the changing Namibian regulatory environment on firm level practices. Klerck concludes that a low-wage, low-skill, low-trust, numerically-flexible paradigm is becoming embedded in both industrial and work relations in that country. Furthermore, new technologies and work practices have contributed to widening the gap between more secure, skilled, core workers, and more vulnerable categories of labour.

Chapter 10, by Pauline Dibben, explores changes in employment regulation in South Africa, and the challenges facing organised labour in that country. She notes that whilst workers enjoy strong – and effectively enforced – protection from one of the most progressive bodies of labour legislation in the world, unions have battled to cope with wholesale job losses, and to make themselves relevant to the needs of those employed in the informal sector. Dibben goes on to explore the potential of alternative strategies for union organisation, to ensure that organised labour has the capacity positively to shape South Africa's future trajectory. In the following chapter, Thabo Seleke looks at industrial relations in Botswana. Despite being a multi-party democracy, unions have battled to secure political independence, and, until relatively recently, to act independently of government.

Part III: Country studies from West and North Africa

Chapter 12, by Mohamed Essaaidi, outlines the employment context and the framework of industrial relations in Morocco. A French-type civil law based system, formal legislation plays a very much greater role in determining the practice of employment and work relations than would the common law systems commonly encountered in Anglophone Africa. Yet, despite this key difference in employment regulation, the Moroccan industrial relations context has much in common with other countries on the continent: above all, the increasing importance of the informal sector, and the inability of employers and organised labour to reach and maintain legitimate and enforceable collective agreements.

Chapter 13, by Salo Fajana, outlines the development and the historical context of industrial relations in Africa's most populous state, Nigeria. The colonial legacy and the sometimes very depressing developments in government since that time provide a rich context, within which industrial relations has developed. The recent economic developments and the influence of petroleum on the state in general and industrial relations in particular are clearly outlined and the impact of the successive political developments on industrial relations are manifest. Chapter 14, by Dafe Otobo, goes into more detail on the current industrial relations scene in Nigeria, bringing out the role of the various parties and the impact of the successive acts of parliament and legal institutions on industrial relations in the country. As elsewhere in Africa, the public sector is both a politically charged factor in the economy in its own right and a more significant element of the picture of industrial relations than might be found in many developed countries. Detailed examples and case studies of strikes and other developments indicate the impact of industrial relations in the public sector in Nigeria.

In Chapter 15, Garth Frazer looks at industrial relations in Ghana. Despite the negative effects of wholesale redundancies in recent years, unions continue to have a significant presence in the formal sector, whilst there has been a general trend towards greater pluralism and the more professional handling of disputes, the latter trend being the converse to what has been experienced in many other countries on the continent.

The final chapter of the section explores the changing nature of industrial relations in a sub-Saharan Francophone African state, Niger. Despite differences in colonial experiences and legislative traditions, Richard Croucher notes that, in common with their counterparts in Anglophone African countries, unions in Niger have had to contend with membership declines as a result of wholesale job losses in the formal sector, which have followed on the imposition of structural adjustment policies. In turn, this has drained away union resources, resulting in the fragmentation of the labour movement. Whilst some efforts have been made to organise the informal sector, in practice, this has yielded mixed results.

Part IV: Trans-Continental trends and issues

In Chapter 17, Richard Croucher looks at central industrial relations issues in the informal economy in Africa. Any attempt to understand IR in Africa without understanding the role of the informal economy is bound to be extremely partial. Using the example of Ghana and Ghanaian experiences of organizing within the informal economy the results and prospects of these efforts are examined. Croucher argues that whilst there is little doubt as to the desirability of unionisation, it is hindered by limited union resources to defend members, especially as historically speaking unions have not been geared for this purpose. It is agued that unionisation has been most successful when founded on self-organisation, and when it has enjoyed state support.

Chapter 18, by Frank Horwitz, looks at trans-continental trends and issues. Horwitz identifies the key elements of employment relations in African emergent and transitional economies as colonial impact, nationalism, post-colonial state formation and crisis, structural adjustment, democratic reforms, and pressures for social partnership. This is followed by a more detailed look at employment relations problems and challenges in selected African states.

Conclusion

The global ascendancy of employer interests at the expense of organised labour following on the economic crises of the 1970s represents only one of many pressures recasting industrial relations in Africa. Neo-liberal reforms have had particularly adverse consequences on the continent, weakening the capacity of the state to enforce existing and new industrial relations legislation, and resulting in wholesale job-shedding in the formal sector. Whilst the spread of multi-partyism has allowed unions in many African countries to exert increasing independence, the latter still face difficulties both in relations with political parties, and in being relevant to what is, in most cases, the bulk of the workforce, informal sector workers.

Note

1. There are only four other collections with a continent-wide scope that deal explicitly with IR (as adverse to human resource management and related areas of management) – Damachi *et al.* (1979), Fashoyin (1992), ILO (1964) and Essenberg (1985). The latter is a short monograph, and the ILO collection the proceedings of a seminar.

References

Anderson, W. and Parker, F. (1964), *Society: Its Organization and Operation*. Princeton: Van Nostrand.
Bayart, J-F, Ellis, S. and Hibou, B. (1999), *The Criminalization of the State in Africa*. Bloomington: James Currey.
Bean, R. (ed.) (1994), *Comparative Industrial Relations*. London: Routledge.
Budhwar, P. and Debrah, Y.A. (eds) (2001), *Human Resource Management in Developing Countries*. London: Routledge.
Damachi, U., Seibel, H. and Tractman, L. (eds.) (1979), *Industrial Relations in Africa*. London : Macmillan.
Eaton, J. (2000), *Comparative Industrial Relations*. Cambridge: Polity Press.
Edwards, P. (2002), 'The State and the Workplace', in Kelly, J. (ed.), *Employers and the State – Industrial Relations: Critical Perspectives on Business and Management, Volume 3*. London: Routledge.
Fashoyin, T. (1992), *Industrial Relations and African Development*. New Delhi: IIRA/South Asian Publishers.
Financial Times (London).
Freeman, R. and Medoff, J. (1984), *What Do Unions Do?* New York: Basic Books.
George, S. (1990), *A Fate Worse than Debt*. New York: Grove Weidenfeld.
Hoogevelt, A. (2005), 'Postmodern Intervention and Human Rights', *Review of African Political Economy*, 106: 595–601.
Hyden, G. (2002), 'Rethinking the Study of African Politics', in Haines, R. and Wood, G. (eds), *Postmodernism in Africa*. Port Elizabeth: IPDR.
ILO. (1964), *Industrial Relations in Certain African Countries*. Geneva: ILO.
Jessop, B. (2001), 'Series Preface', Jessop, B. (ed.), *The Parisian Regulation School: Regulation and the Crisis of Capitalism, Volume 1*. Cheltenham: Edward Elgar.
Kamoche, K., Debrah, Y.A, Horwitz, F.M. and Muika, G.N. (eds.) (2003), *Managing Human Resources in Africa*. London: Routledge.
Kaufman, B. (2004), *Theoretical Perspectives on Work and the Employment Relationship*. Champagne Urbana: Industrial Relations Research Association.
Kimemia, P. (2000), 'An Overview of the Performance of the East African Economies Since 1985: Implications for the New Initiative on East African Co-operation', *African Sociological Review* 4, 1, 119–37.
La Porta, R., Lopez-de-Silanes, F., Shleifer, A. and Vishny, R. (2000), 'Investor Protection and Corporate Governance', *Journal of Financial Economics* 58, 3–27.
Martin, G. (2000), 'Employment and Unemployment in Mexico in the 1990s', *Monthly Labor Review*, 123, 11: 3–18.
Mellahi, K. and Wood, G. (2002), 'Desparately Seeking Stability: The Remaking of the Saudi Arabian Labour Market', *Competition and Change*, 6, 4: 345–62.
Mkandawire, T. and Soludo, C. (2002), 'Towards the Broadening of Development Policy Dialogue for Africa', in Mkandwire, T. and Soludo, C. (eds), *African Voices on Structural Adjustment*. Dakar: Codesria.
Naiman, R. and Watkins, N. (1990), 'Survey of the Impacts of IMF Structural Adjustment in Africa: Growth, Social Spending, and Debt Relief'. http://www.hartford-hwp.com/archives/30/111.html
Roberts, B. (1964), *Labour in the Tropical Territories of the Commonwealth*. London: G. Bell.
Roberts, B. and de Bellecombe, L Greyfie. (1967), *Collective Bargaining in African Countries*. London: Macmillan.
Rosser, J. and Rosser, M. (2001), 'Another Failure of the Washington Consensus', *Challenge*, 44,2: 39–50.

Southall, R. (2003), 'Africa', in Burnell, P. (ed.), *Democratization Through the Looking Glass*. Manchester: Manchester University Press.

Willett, S. (2005), 'Barbarians at the Gate: Losing the Liberal Peace in Africa', *Review of African Political Economy*, 106: 569–94.

Williams, C. and Wildebank, J. (2000), 'Beyond Employment: An Examination of Modes of Service Provision in a Depressed Neighbourhood', *The Service Industries Journal*, 20, 4: 33–46.

Wood, G. (2004a), 'Business and Politics in a Criminal State: The Case of Equatorial Guinea', *African Affairs*, 103: 547–67.

Wood, G. (2004b), 'Trade Unions and Democracy: Possibilities and Contradictions', in Harcourt, M. and Wood, G. (eds), *Trade Unions and Democracy*. Manchester: Manchester University Press.

Wood, G. and Frynas, G. (2006), 'The Institutional Basis of Economic Failure: Anatomy of the Segmented Business System', *Socio-Economic Review*, 4, 2: 239–77.

Wood, G. and Glaister, K. (2006), 'Innovative Managerial Strategies, Unions and Competitiveness: The Case of South Africa', working paper, School of Management, University of Sheffield, Sheffield.

Zack-Williams, T. and Mohan, G. (2005), 'Africa: From SAPs to PRSP', *Review of African Political Economy*, 106: 501–3.

Part I
Country Studies from East and Central Africa

Part 1

2
The Dynamics of Industrial Relations in Eritrea: 1991–2006

Fitsum Ghebregiorgis and Luchien Karsten

Introduction – the Eritrean context

Eritrea, with its 124,320 square kilometres and a population of about four million, is Africa's newest independent country, having formally achieved its independence from Ethiopia in April 1993. One of the African nations that were colonised by Western countries, Western colonial control was imposed on Eritrea for about 60 years. The modern economic history of Eritrea began in 1890, when the country first came under Italian occupation. During the next 100 years, Eritrea was under different successive colonial rulers: Italy (1890–1941), Great Britain (1941–52), imposed federation with Ethiopia (1952–61), and a colony of Ethiopia (1961–91) (GOE, 1996).

Three decades of fighting to achieve that independence have left Eritrea with a devastated infrastructure. The economy of the country has been decimated by 30 years of war, drought and inappropriate social and economic policies. There is no sector in the economy that has not been affected negatively by this trio of scourges, and the three decades of lost opportunity have made Eritrea one of the poorest nations in the world. As citizens of a new nation, the Eritrean people have been actively participated in the rehabilitation and development of the national economy. Tewolde (2002) noted that Eritreans have been heavily involved in the reconstruction programme under the umbrella of their respective organisations consistent with a systemic competitiveness perspective such as the National Confederation of Eritrean Workers (NCEW), the National Union of Eritrean Youth and Students (NUEYS), the National Union of Eritrean Women (NUEW) and the rural people through their local administrations. The participation of the people in the reconstruction and rehabilitation programme of the economic, social and institutional infrastructure was unprecedented and gave a jump-start to the economy of the country.

Agriculture has traditionally been the mainstay of the Eritrean economy with 70 per cent of the population engaged in agriculture as a means of subsistence. However, due to absence of rain for long periods and the slow growth or decline of agricultural export commodity prices, agriculture's contribution to gross domestic product (GDP) is low. The agricultural sector accounts for 18.7 per cent of GDP (2001 estimates), with the other significant sectors of industry contributing 22.3 per cent and services providing 59 per cent (CPR Unit, 2002). Modern industry started in the 1920s, when Italy began to build modern factories to meet the demands of Italian settlers. However, throughout the long period of colonisation, the Eritrean industrialisation process has subsequently been weakened (for instance, see Tseggai, 1981; Makki, 1996; Tewolde, 2002).

At liberation, the transitional government of Eritrea inherited from Ethiopia a socio-economic environment that was close to a standstill and an over-centralised system of administration; it inherited weak institutions and a civil service that needed to be developed from scratch because the civil service structure that evolved during colonial rule was designed primarily to serve colonial interests (World Bank, 1994; Tessema, 2005). Nevertheless, the government has undertaken several actions in order to make the Eritrean civil service efficient and effective. Under a comprehensive public sector strengthening programme, the government has implemented a large number of measures to rationalise institutions and has completed the process of streamlining the civil service reducing staff members by 34 per cent, down to 18,500 from over 30,000 (University of Asmara, 1997); and an improved salary scale was introduced to motivate the employees in order to work efficiently and to reduce systemic corruption (Tewolde, 2002).

This chapter investigates the extent of industrial relations in Eritrea. Specifically, the objective of this chapter is to examine the extent of free trade union activity and freewill membership of workers, the degree of dependence on collective agreements in determining labour conditions and labour disputes, industrial disputes and method of resolution and equal employment opportunity. Furthermore, the chapter tries to link industrial relations to civil society and citizenship behaviour.

This chapter has seven sections. The first section presents the historical development of trade unions in Eritrea followed by the industrial relations actors in section two. Section three looks at the employment relations. In section four, the equal employment opportunity act is described. The fifth section analyses the occurrence of industrial disputes and the mechanisms to resolve the disputes. Section six addresses the issue of whether and in what way industrial relations relates to the development of civil society and citizenship behaviour. Finally, section seven provides conclusions.

The historical development of trade unions in Eritrea

The trade union movement in Eritrea has its origins back in the Italian colonial period (1890 to 1941) and continued during the British administration (1941 to 1952). Specifically, the British administration introduced some liberalisation policies in terms of improved educational activities and freedom of association. The latter endangered the formation of many political parties, including those that agitated for the independence of Eritrea. During the British occupation, workers in Eritrean industries organised themselves to confront the segregated colonial employment system. Dock and railroad workers were the first to organise and strike, in particular, because they held strategic positions in the colonial economy that gave them an increased bargaining power. Killion (1997: 10) noted that 'in March 1949 a larger strike developed and the British Administrator was forced to call on Christian and Muslim religions "elders" to intervene with workers' representatives to negotiate a settlement and the men were persuaded to return to work only by their religious leaders'. The strike ended after 45 days with workers winning their demands for a salary increase based on equal-pay-for-equal-work, no overseas allowance for the Italians, progressive 'Eritreanisation' of skilled posts vacated by Italians, and medical and accident insurance. The outcome of such a successful action of transport workers inspired others to organise in a number of private, Italian owned industries to demand equality in pay and benefits. The first trade unions which were factory based emerged in late 1948 and later united to form the National Union of Eritrean Workers for Independence (NUEWI) on the 4 February 1952. The NUEWI was based on the principle of unity amongst all Eritrean workers, social justice for the citizens of the country and social justice for workers. The first 'Eritrean Workers Day' was celebrated on the 7 December 1952 (NCEW, 2002).

The erosion of Eritrea's political autonomy through the forced federation with Ethiopia in the 1950s catapulted the union movement into the leading force of the Eritrean nationalist movement (NCEW, 2003). Accordingly, trade union rights were withdrawn in 1957 and the NUEWI opposed to the abrogation of the rights of freedom of association; thereafter, leaders of the NUEWI were subject to harassment, intimidation and persecution. With the annexation of Eritrea by Ethiopia in 1961, legal trade unions ceased to exist and the confederation's office was closed. As a result of brutal repression, harassment, intimidation and the total closure of the office of the confederation, the majority of the leaders and many more workers started to flee the country and joined the armed struggle for independence, which begun in September 1961 and others remained in exile (ibid.). Eritrean workers sought employment in the Middle East, Europe and North America. The Eritrean workers in the diaspora organised themselves into unions and held their first meeting in Germany in 1970 (NCEW, 2002). Then workers' representatives held a meeting in the liberated areas of Eritrea in 1979 and founded the National Union of Eritrean Workers (NUEW). The NUEW had a membership of over 20,000 workers at the end of the war in 1991. After liberation in May 1991, through the initiatives of employees' factory-based unions reorganised, and according to Proclamation No. 8/1991, a national workers' confederation emerged.

The post-independence period has been noted for several developments. Between 1992 and 1997, the country achieved economic growth of 7 per cent on average annually. The political economy of Eritrean industry and service sector radically changed. Private enterprises developed in many areas. There was a great deal of privatisation, with much manufacturing, hotels and other property, which was nationalised in the colonial regime of Ethiopia passing into private ownership. Unfortunately, a new round of border conflict with Ethiopia (since 1998) has reversed much of the progress that the country had been making.

The parties

The state

After Eritrea's liberation, the Transitional Government restructured the labour administration system through the Transitional Labour Law of 1991 with a view to providing better services. Although the objectives and targets were admirable, the required facilities and manpower capabilities could not adequately accomplish the desired tasks. Realising that there were inadequacies, the Ministry of Labour and Human Welfare (MLHW) embarked on the idea of encouraging the establishment of private employment agencies. To this end, in 2001, Labour Proclamation of Eritrea No. 118/2001 was issued, repealing and replacing the former proclamation and all other related laws. The new labour law was ratified to attract foreign investment and it gives managers a free hand to hire and fire workers.

Although the Eritrean state claims that it plays a neutral third party role, the state still has influence on industrial relations. In particular, with the recent mass privatisations the role of the state as employer is diminishing and the state's interest in intervening in industrial relations is expected to decline, but taking into account the current political stalemate with Ethiopia, industrial relations in Eritrea are often politicised, in some cases for several reasons. Firstly, the state regards itself as the guardian of workers and their welfare. Secondly, the state has assumed the primary role in economic development and has viewed itself as the main force of economic and market stability. Furthermore, through state-created institutions such as the zonal or regional labour court tribunals, the government prescribes the interests of employees and employer organisations to be protected. However, employers and unions exercise certain degrees of freedom to negotiate terms and conditions of employment.

The unions

A union is a collective organisation of wage-earners for the purpose of maintaining and improving working conditions, promoting their economic interests, reasonably autonomous from the state and employers and is essentially a voluntary association (Bamber and Peschanski, 1996). After independence for Eritrea, membership of unions became voluntary. During the mid-1990s, there was an important change in the trade union reorganisation process: the NUEW organised its Fourth National Congress, which led to the establishment of the NCEW with a new and independent structure to protect the rights and benefits of employees. At this Congress, taking into consideration the sheer complexity of having members located abroad, it was decided that membership in the NCEW would be limited to workers residing in Eritrea. The NCEW is an umbrella for firm-based trade unions. The confederation includes five federations, classified according to the type of industry and nature of business. Currently, there are 230 factory-based unions with over 23,000 members throughout the country, representing over 80 per cent of the total workforce (Ghebregiorgis and Karsten, 2006).

Since its inception, the NCEW has been engaged in a number of activities, which include: restructuring and introducing a democratisation process into unions; organising new members; participation in dispute settlements; campaigning for the establishment of a labour court; organising educational and training programmes; and organising the informal sector. In particular, in order to achieve its main objectives and to promote harmonious industrial relations, the NCEW has proposed the establishment of a tripartite structure with the Department of Labour and Employers' Federation.

Modern industrial relations are new to many Eritrean managers and union leaders. The major employer of the unionised workforce is the government. The experiences of the large workforce in industrial relations were shaped by the former Ethiopian military dictatorship. Hence, to promote modern and harmonious industrial relations in the country, the NCEW in co-operation with international labour organs such as the International Labour Organisation (ILO), International Confederations of Free Trade Unions (ICFTU), LO-Norway, LO-Denmark and American Centre for International Labour Solidarity (ACILS) organised major industrial relations conferences.

Furthermore, the confederation has developed a model of collective agreement and has actively supported its affiliates (shop based unions) in negotiations with their employers taking into account the financial and administrative capacity of the respective organisations, the nature of the job, the level of productivity and operations (NCEW, 2002). Collective industrial relations in Eritrea operate through agreements between a single employer and a union. Details of the industrial relations are worked out through negotiations at firm level. Collective agreements are normally enterprise agreements that are specific and detailed with regard to pay and work arrangements. In the collective agreements, obligations of unions and employers are clearly distinguished. Membership of factory-based unions is free and the unions enlisted all categories of employees excluding top management because unions are said to represent the interest of all workers. Each member is required to pay one per cent of his/her monthly income as a membership fee. Of this one per cent, half of it is directly deposited with the firm's trade union to be used as a working capital and the remaining half is the contribution of the firm's trade union to NCEW. Unions are provided with offices and other facilities inside the organisations except in rare cases such as in multinational companies. In most organisations, employers co-operate with unions to automatically deduct membership fees from the employee's salary. In addition, workers through their union leaders are represented in the recruitment (management) committee. In accordance with the collective agreement, unions have the right to protect the legal rights of workers from employers (management) violations regarding promotion, unjustified dismissals, discipline, unpaid overtime work and public holidays, physical disability (hazard) and salary deduction for justified absenteeism etc. The unions have to agree on the dismissal or punishment of workers. Grievance procedures are regularly used and where necessary, unions oppose managerial decisions.

The employers

The Employers' Federation of Eritrea (hereinafter referred to as the 'Federation') was established in the late 1960s that operated for a short period only. A year after the Ethiopian military regime overthrew the Emperor of Ethiopia in 1974; the Federation was officially informed it was to be dissolved. Thus, since 1975 the Federation ceased to exist. With the liberation of Eritrea, employers commenced to participate in tripartite consultations. In 1996 an eleven member Committee was set up through the initiation of the MLHW in order to prepare the necessary grounds for the establishment of an employers' organisation (EFE, 1998). Accordingly, the committee prepared a draft Constitution and held several discussions regarding matters of interest to employers with concerned government bodies and the ILO. Among its main aims are: cooperate with government bodies and the NCEW for the development of the Eritrean economy and its human resources; safeguard and promote the interests of employers regarding international relations; facilitate and promote joint consultations among members; follow up and update members on existing laws and practices of labour; inform members about the activities of government bodies and related legislative organs which may affect or tend to affect the interest of the employers in industrial relations; upon the request of members advise, guide or assist on any industrial dispute or problems affecting industrial relations; act as the industrial organisation representing Eritrean employers on matters coming within the scope of the ILO.

The Federation is a part in a tri-partite relationship between the government, national labour union and employers. The objective of this tri-partite agreement is to establish a harmonised relationship between employees and employers in order to promote productivity and investment on fair employment terms. Although the Federation deals with unions and is involved in training and labour market related issues, it doesn't determine pay systems because in most cases pay is centralised by the Central Personnel Administration (CPA).

Employment relations

Employment relations in Eritrea have undergone major change after independence. As employees are free to join factory-based unions, base unions are also free to join the workers' confederation. Laws and regulations were developed in order to ensure fair employment practices and to promote harmonious industrial relations and human relations at work. According to the Labour Proclamation (2001) employees' associations may be established in an enterprise where the number of employees is twenty or more. The labour law aims at fair employment practices and gives employees the rights to strike for collective bargaining purposes and the rights to fair labour practices. The labour law seeks to promote employee participation in decision making through workplace forums and employee consultation. It provides for simple procedures for the resolution of labour disputes. In addition, the employment law provides for the establishment of the First Instance Labour Court and the Labour Relations Board.

The First Instance Labour Court has first instance jurisdiction on, amongst others, suits involving labour disputes except a labour dispute involving the termination of the contract of employment of an employees' association leader. Similarly, the Labour Relations Board have jurisdiction on labour disputes relating to unfair labour practices; collective labour disputes; and a suit involving the dismissal by an employer of an employees' association leader. Proclamations are usually regulations to guide employment policies in the public and private sectors, and Eritrean organisations are expected to conform to these guidelines when designing human resource management practices such as recruitment, selection, training, payment systems and structures and when developing industrial relations policies.

The labour law urges enterprises to provide reasonable terms and conditions of work and ensure industrial health and safety. The law on Collective Agreements and Contracts established procedures for negotiating collective labour agreements between unions and enterprise employers (managers). Union representatives act on behalf of members to negotiate with managers (employers) on issues regarding working conditions, unfair dismissal, training, disciplinary action, pay, etc. Employers are obliged to share work-related information as much as possible to minimise conflicts and to facilitate collective bargaining processes, and to make every effort to help employees understand the interpretation and application of the provisions of collective agreements and work rules. Furthermore, they are obliged to meet with the employees' representatives semi-annually to evaluate the collective agreement, unless the collective agreement provides for a lesser period. Equally, employees are obliged, *inter alia*, to implement instruction given by the employer based on the terms of employment contract and work rules.

Nevertheless, there is a tendency that employment relations is shifting to work place cooperation because the NCEW and shop floor unions urge employees to be disciplined and work hard to improve labour productivity.

Industrial disputes

In post-independence Eritrea there are relatively few industrial disputes. However, there exist some individualised verbal expressions of dispute such as absenteeism, permissions and working conditions. Although legally there is freedom to strike, Eritrean industrial relations is very peaceful. On the one hand, it could be that industrial relations in Eritrea is relatively matured since conflict is settled (prevented) at an early stage. On the other hand, much could be owed to the hard-won independence because employees in general, and union leaders in particular, refrain from engaging in strikes, specially in this difficult political period with neighbouring Ethiopia. There is a concern among the employees that their independence may be threatened, if they engage in strikes or disputes.

Civil society and citizenship behaviour

The Eritrean struggle for freedom has created a strong national identity and self-reliance. This has intensified an attitude of loyalty to and cooperation in firms which are reflected in the industrial relations. Industrial relations are part of an economy and the economy itself cannot be isolated from either the state or the society. Together they shape a civil society which is the historical product and result of an all embracing process of differentiation between power in the state and the division of labour in the economy. It also gives rise to an autonomous legal sphere to govern civil life. The civil society's fundamental purpose is to construct relationships between social institutions and people that give meaning to the terms civility and community (Waddock, 2001). In Eritrea, the sense of civility and community has developed quite strongly.

We may say that Eritrea has in its recent history strongly promoted the design of citizenship in its own way. Republican virtues can certainly be noticed in Eritrea and reflect themselves in the industrial relations. Categories like respect for orderly structures, loyalty to protect communities and volunteer extra effort for the common good as well as participation entailing an active and responsible involvement in community self-governance can be traced in Eritrean organisational settings and characterise Eritrean industrial relations (cf. Dyne and Graham, 1994; Mamdani, 1996).

Conclusion

In Africa, as in most developing countries, industrial relations systems have developed together with a move from colonisation to independence. Also, as in many African countries, the labour movement in Eritrea played a vital role in the liberation struggle. The working class joined hands with nationalist movements and the labour unions to create the Eritrean liberation fronts. During the colonial times, particularly between 1950s and early 1960s, the trade unions were strong in confronting segregated colonial employment policies and winning employees' demands. Nevertheless, the continued persecution, repression and intimidation of union leaders by Ethiopian rulers finally forced the workers' confederation and its affiliated shop-based unions to be closed.

After independence, a different industrial relations emerged in Eritrea driven by the need for national institutions, free market economic policy and privatisation. The emphasis on collective industrial relations was facilitated by the government intervention (MLHW) in industrial relations by providing legal prescriptions. Industrial relations fulfilled the function of providing employees with a collective voice, and unions with the means to establish terms and conditions of employment policies at enterprise level. The NCEW lay down general principles, leaving the details of collective agreement to be worked out through negotiations at the organisation level. Furthermore, the government effectively involved employers and unions in consultations in the formulation of labour policies through their participation in tripartism. Besides, employers' demand that the new labour law would ensure a favourable working environment in the country and completely change the labour market.

Employment relations in Eritrea provides for the establishment of standards of employment. These conditions cover from employment contract to termination. The employment relations aim to give effect to constitutional rights allowing employees the right to organise and the right to strike. Employers also have the right to form and join employers' federations (associations), and prevent workers from working by way of a lockout for the purpose of collective bargaining. Nevertheless, employers and shop-based unions emphasise workplace cooperation to increase productivity and remain competitive in the market place. The NCEW also believes that the enterprises should be financially strong in order to fulfil and protect employees' interest. In furtherance, the regulations contained in the Labour Law prohibit unfair discrimination against employees on several grounds including disability, gender, pregnancy etc. However, it should have explicitly included discrimination against HIV/AIDS testing, which is one of the significant issues threatening the African continent in general, and the workforce in particular.

Although industrial relations in Eritrea is not characterised by disputes, conflict resolution is achieved most of the time through dispute settlement mechanisms internal to enterprise such as conciliation at the work place and in some instances at the labour court. For reasons we have discussed, it seems that industrial relations in Eritrea have used many Western concepts such as trade unionism, freedom of association, collective bargaining and tripartism, and trade union registration. Also, it has been noted that Eritrea's industrial relations appear to include a hybrid of patterns of both business coordinated market economies and uncoordinated liberal market economies. Furthermore, it appears that the Eritrean industrial relations is characterised by the republican virtues owing to the active participation of Eritrean citizens in the country's rehabilitation and reconstruction process to promote economic growth and catch up with the world economy.

References

Bamber, G. J. and Peschanski, V. (1996), 'Transforming Industrial Relations in Russia: a Case of Convergence with Industrialised Market Economies?', *Industrial Relations Journal*, 27, 1: 74–88.
CPR Unit (2002), 'Conflict and Labour Markets in Manufacturing: The Case of Eritrea', *Social Development Report Dissemination Notes*, World Bank.
Dyne, L. Van and Graham, J. W. (1994), 'Organisational Citizenship Behaviour: Construct Redefinition, Measurement and Validation', *Academy of Management Journal*, 37: 765–802.
EFE (1998), *Employers' Federation of Eritrea Constitution*. Asmara.
Ghebregiorgis, F. and Karsten, L. (2005) *Employee Reactions to Human Resource Management and Performance in a Developing Country: The Case of Eritrea* (under review).
Ghebregiorgis, F. and Karsten, L. (2006), 'Human Resource Management Practices in Eritrea: Challenges and Prospects', *Employee Relations Journal*, 28, 2:144–63.
Ghebregiorgis, F. (2006) 'Western Models and African Realities: Human Resource Management and Performance in Eritrea'. PhD Thesis, University of Groningen, the Netherlands.
Government of Eritrea (GOE) (1991), *Transitional Labour Law*. Number 8/1991. Asmara.
Government of Eritrea (1996), *Eritrea's Export Sector: Constraints and Prospects*. Asmara.
Government of Eritrea (1997), *The Constitution of Eritrea*. Asmara.
Government of Eritrea (2001), *The Labour Proclamation of Eritrea*, Proclamation No. 118/2001, Vol. 10/2001, Number 5. Asmara.
Katz, M.B. (2001), *The Prize of Citizenship, Redefining the American Welfare State*. New York: Metropolitan Books.
Killion, T. (1997), 'The Eritrean Workers' Organisation and Early Nationalist Mobilization: 1948–1958', *Eritrean Studies Review*, 2, 1: 1–37.
Makki, F. (1996), Nationalism, State Formation, and the Public Sphere: Eritrea 1991–96, *Review of African Political Economy*, 23, 70: 475–97.
Mamdani, M. (1996), *Citizen and Subject, Contemporary Africa and the Legacy of Late Colonialism*. Princeton: Princeton University Press.
Marshall, T.H. and Bottomore, T. (1992), *Citizenship and Social Class*. London: Pluto Press.
Ministry of National Development (2005), *Consumer Price Index*, State of Eritrea.
NCEW (1994), *The Constitution*, NCEW Legal Department. Asmara.
NCEW (2002), *Reports on Trade Unions in Eritrea*. Asmara.
NCEW (2003), *Collective Bargaining and Agreements*, NCEW Legal Department. Asmara.
Silva, S. (1997), 'The Changing Focus of Industrial Relations and Human Resource Management'. Paper presented at the ILO Workshop on Employers' Organisations in Asia-Pacific in the Twenty-First Century.
Skinner, Q. and Strath, B. (2003), *States and Citizens*. Cambridge: Cambridge University Press.
Tessema, M. (2005), 'Practices, Challenges and Prospects of HRM in Developing Countries: The Case of Eritrean Civil Service'. PhD Thesis, University of Tilburg, the Netherlands.
Tewolde, M. (2002), 'Market-Oriented Policy Changes and Manufacturing Performance: The Case of Eritrea', PhD dissertation, University of Tilburg, the Netherlands.
Tseggai, A. (1981), 'The Economic Viability of an Independent Eritrea', PhD Thesis, University of Nebraska.

University of Asmara (1997), *Implementation Plan of the Eritrean Human Resource Development Plan*. Asmara.

Waddock, S. (2001), 'Integrity and Mindfulness: Foundations of Corporate Citizenship', *Journal of Corporate Citizenship*, 1: 25–37.

Whitley, R. (1999), *Divergent Capitalisms: the Social Structuring and Change of Business Systems*. Oxford: Oxford University Press.

World Bank (1994), *Eritrea-Options and Strategies for Growth*, Vol. 1. Washington, DC.

3
The Development of Industrial Relations in Kenya

George Hagglund

Introduction

The present industrial relations system of Kenya is a result of an amalgam of various interest group needs, British Colonial Office policies, and the efforts of other countries interested in the creation of an industrial relations model that was compatible with their own system. In the early years it was the European colonial settlers who had the greatest impact on how native Africans were treated. Over a period of six decades, the British Colonial Office strove with varying degrees of success to mediate between the Europeans and the Africans. By the 1940s, the Cold War would define the shape of the industrial relations system to evolve after Kenya gained independence. The United States, as well as other major powers participated in the development of a system that matched their ideas and interests

The colonial era

Post-World War I developments

The period following World War I was a period of great economic expansion, increased European settlement and successful attempts by settlers to see that native wages remained low or were cut still further. There were some offsetting attempts by the British government to remind the Colonial Government of Kenya that the League of Nations called for a trusteeship role in labour matters for the Kenyan Colonial Government but little heed was taken.

The International Labour Organisation (ILO) and the British Labour Party began exercising some oversight over colonial activities in several countries, including Kenya. The growing presence of British corporations who had little concern for settler opinions also moderated attitudes toward native Africans, since labour costs were not necessarily their primary focus. There was a growth in the number of white settlers moving onto the land, and this led to demands for reducing the size of native reserves and giving the land to settlers, which tied in to the old settler idea that reducing the size of the reserves would make it easier to recruit workers for their activities since the reserves could not provide enough land for the needs of a growing population. Settlers again raised their objections to any liberalising of the terms and conditions of employment for native workers, but in spite of their complaints, the Ordinance was amended to require the Principal Labour Inspector to check workplaces, housing, rations, water and medical equipment and he was given powers to prosecute with the Chief Native Commissioner's permission (*Master and Servants Amendment Ordinance*, 1919). However, the Resident Natives Ordinance was drafted to increase the rates of hut and poll taxes (ibid.), which worked to the detriment of Africans.

Also in 1919, the Native Authority Ordinance was amended to provide for paid compulsory labour for state purposes. Along with this change were issued circulars to 'strongly encourage' recruitment of native labour. Not only men, but women and children were to be encouraged to go out and engage in paid work, and Chiefs and elders were reminded that it was their duty to encourage all unemployed men to go out and work on plantations. There were protests against these policies expressed by 'compelling' workers to leave home to work for settlers on farms and plantations, but their opinions did not carry the day (Clayton & Savage, 1974). The first sign of organised protest came in 1922, when Asian skilled and semi-skilled workers struck the Railway. The Railway broke the Railway Artisan Union by taking action against its leadership and eventually forcing through a 10 per cent cut in wages. While the Sikhs who made up the skilled workers had internal solidarity, they did not enjoy the support of the working community as a whole, since they were themselves an elite compared to the African workers who were less skilled and earned far less money. And the Indian workers were just learning how to bargain, attempting to use the Indian Association to negotiate on their behalf, and failed to enlist the support of other Asian employees. It was a necessary first step toward organising a labour movement that would pay off later.

The Great Depression

During the decade before the depression, native Africans had been decimated by disease and famine, while the settlers pushed passage of laws and ordinances that gave them greater control over the native work force, their movements, and who they worked for. The native reserves had diminished in size, and as the birth-rate climbed in the mid to late 1920s, there was no longer enough farming land for them to sustain their families. African workers were growing more desperate and their standard of living had fallen to historical lows.

By 1930 Kenya was greatly affected by the world-wide depression.

It was the Asian workers who first began to organise what would later become a union movement. In the 1920s they set up associations to protect what they had managed to garner in terms of wages and conditions. They fell in between the European elite and the Africans at the bottom of the heap. In 1931 they first tried the picket line as a bargaining tactic with six contractors serving the Railway and had some moderate success in that the wage cut precipitating the strike was eventually rescinded (*East African Standard*, 1922).

By the mid-1930s the first pioneer of organised labour had arrived on the scene; his name was Makhan Singh, born in India and arrived in Kenya in 1927 where his father took a job on the Railway. His father was later dismissed for helping to set up and lead the Railway Artisans Union which was broken in its first strike. Perhaps it was his father's unfortunate experience that led him to take a left-wing stance that later led him to join the Indian Communist Party. Also influential on Makhan Singh was the political outlook of Sikhs back in India: ideals including humanitarianism, egalitarianism, and freedom. While Sikhs shared these values with the Communists, they did not accept the party's atheism (Patel, 2006). Makhan Singh was sympathetic with the political orientation of the Communist bloc labour federation, the World Federation of Trade Unions (WFTU) and later in his career he expressed strong opposition to the Western Bloc's trade union confederation, the International Confederation of Trade Unions set up by the ILO. He was not the only one – some of the later African union activists were also persuaded to adopt the same ideology (Goldsworthy, 1982).

Singh's was a strongly egalitarian outlook, and he became involved by 1934 in what was called the Indian Trade Union. It was inspired by Indian railway employees but the leadership tried to extend its membership to other Indian workers, including the building trades, with limited success. The Railway workers had lost their permanent status and benefits as a result of cutbacks, and they were trying to get their losses back. In 1935 it was re-created as the Labour Trade Union of Kenya with Makhan Singh as its secretary. While aspiring to organise all workers, it continued to be mainly Indian in makeup. Singh's organising platform centred on securing the 8-hour day and a minimum wage of 200 shillings a month, along with full sick pay, eighteen days of paid local leave and four months long service leave after four years of service. The leadership wanted to abolish overtime and piece work, and daily wages to be replaced by weekly or monthly payments. The union under Singh's leadership also sought to help members with a long list of grievances. The workers at that time were mainly interested in wages and hours (Clayton & Savage, 1974).

A high point in Singh's trade union career was a strike against 6 firms in 1937. By this time Singh's union had been re-named the Labour Trade Union of East Africa (LTUEA), paying respect to increases in trade unions in Kenya's neighbouring countries. The strike dragged on for a couple of months with some violence and arrests of strikers. Eventually the government intervened and forced a settlement, and the workers gained the 8-hour day, a wage increase, and reinstatement of fired workers (Patel, 2006).

That strike in turn led to the passage of the Trade Unions Bill in the Legislative Council in July 1937, which led to the appointment of a registrar of trade unions and recognition of unions as legal organisations (Zarina Patel, 2006).

The task of the registrar was to set up a framework whereby unions could be recognised or de-registered by law.

In 1939 a general strike was called in Mombasa by the LTUEA. For the first time, Indian and African trade unionists got together in collective action. The union demands included a significant wage increase, regulation of working hours and conditions, health care, annual leave, and old age pensions. Makhan Singh played a vital part in the joint union leadership which probably marked him in the government's perceptions as a left-wing troublemaker and agitator. It would take action to neutralise his influence some years later.

In 1940, Makhan Singh returned to India where he immediately became involved in trade union activities that led to his arrest. He was released from prison in 1942 but put under house arrest and other forms of detention that lasted until January 1945. He returned to Kenya later that year but was under a cloud from then on, with the government trying to find a pretext to send him back to India (Zarina Patel, 2006).

Another General Strike in Mombasa in 1947 succeeded in awakening workers' consciousness to trade unionism, but the effects were not lasting. Makhan Singh played no significant part in the strike, and from then on, was busy trying to keep himself from being deported back to India where he knew he would not be welcome. The last strike in which he participated was in 1952, when his own union kicked him out on the grounds that he was an employer (Goldsworthy, 1982)

In 1950 the government closed in on Makhan Singh, and succeeded in deporting him to northern Kenya where he remained in detention for eleven and a half years. By the time he returned, Kenyan independence had been achieved, peace had been made with the British, and he was shut out of a significant role in the new African-dominated government. A chapter on left-wing trade unionism in Kenya was over. Any likelihood that the government to come would be dominated by socialists died with Singh's incarceration.

Makhan Singh was a proud man, who would not ask the Kenyatta government for a job in the new government once it was formed. However, the government did not act to include him in government, in spite of appeals from some of Makhan Singh's supporters (Zarina Patel, 2006).

The rise of Kenya's industrial relations system

At the time when Africans' interest in trade unionism was beginning to blossom, a young African Sanitary Inspector began to get interested in politics and eventually in trade unions. Born in 1930, his early experience as an inspector gave him access to European premises and helped him develop a relaxed manner of dealing with them that would stand him in good stead later in his career. He quickly joined the Nairobi African Local Government Servants Association (NALGSA) and within a short time was vice-president. Early in his career Tom Mboya decided that his career should begin in the field of worker organisations rather than within the political arena of the Kenya African Union, at that time controlled by Jomo Kenyatta (Goldsworthy, 1982).

From 1951 on, Mboya's career rocketed. He learned about Kenya's labour laws, how to build a union, and was ready to move on. He received considerable financial support from the Americans. By 1952 Kenyatta had been arrested by the Colonial Government and detained as a suspect in the Mau Mau rebellion. The acting president of the Kenya African Union, Kenyatta's political organisation, appointed Mboya as Director of Information for the party. Mboya lost no time in using his inside role to get himself promoted to acting treasurer in charge of the Party's funds. On the trade union side, he moved his union (NALGSA) into the Kenya Federation of Trade Unions, and by late 1953 Tom Mboya was General Secretary of the KFTU. By May 1955 Mboya had managed to get rid of his opponents and managed to change the name of the re-assembled federation to the Kenya Federation of Labour (KFL). He had demonstrated to all that he was cool, intelligent, meticulous in preparing for meetings, worked hard, and was a good negotiator. He also demonstrated that he was not a revolutionary although he was a strong nationalist and a ruthless leader when it came to fighting those in the labour movement and in the Party who opposed his objectives (Goldsworthy, 1982).

What was the role of the trade union movement in the fight for freedom and eventual independence? Tom Mboya and his allies wore two hats during the early struggle for freedom – they operated from a trade union base, but tended to pursue their nationalists goals as politicians rather than trade unionists. Mboya was concerned that too close a relationship between the trade union movement and their political goals might lead to a backlash against the unions, so he used his position in Parliament to explicate his goals regarding the new government (Goldsworthy, 1982).

Mboya in government

Kenya's industrial court system dates back to 1962, when Tom Mboya left his union post to become the country's first Minister of Labour after the British colonial government was dismantled and a new government was formed. Mboya's ascendance to the Ministry subsequently led to a conference of employer, union, and government representatives who drafted and signed the *Industrial Relations Charter* in October of 1962. Among the six areas defined in the Charter, there was a system for dealing with industrial disputes, intended to deal with a wave of strikes that plagued Labour Minister Mboya earlier in 1962.

Mboya and the other leaders of his time pondered about having a system of compulsory arbitration of disputes but decided against it. Instead, they chose a compromise between the British and American dispute resolution systems – a voluntary submission of disputes to the permanent justice of the Industrial Court, with powers to render final and binding awards within the defined limits set forth in the law (as amended from time to time) (Mboya, 1963). The final system resembled the Industrial Commission of Australia.

Mboya was the favourite candidate of the American and the British trade union movements, having had training and orientation in the collective bargaining and industrial jurisprudence system in both countries (Collins, 1990). He was a far-sighted individual, sensing the need for industrial justice and avoidance of damaging strikes that could hurt Kenya's fledgling formal economy. At the same time, he strongly supported the idea of workers having the right to form and join unions of their choice with the power to bargain with employers. He also recognised that organised labour had a responsibility to help build Kenya's position in the world through economic development (Mboya, 1963). But at the same time, he ruthlessly put down his political opponents and by 1964 had purged left-wing trade unions from leadership positions and did the same thing within KANU, the merged political party (Goldsworthy, 1982). These actions ultimately led to the formation of a single-party system after he was assassinated in 1969.

How was the Kenya Federation of Labour pulled into supporting economic development as opposed to simply looking after the interests of its members? Because Mboya and his colleagues had associated themselves completely with the militant Nationalist movement which preceded formation of the government. Once in power, Mboya was faced with a larger constituency which included employers and government, and he helped create a dispute resolution system which took their interests into account. The compromise was important, the new government needed some level of support from the White community of Kenya. In spite of weaknesses and divisions within the Kenyan trade union movement, Mboya's broad views on the form of industrial relations and dispute resolution prevailed. He continued an investigative and reporting function within the Labour Department and at first settled on the Joint Disputes Commission, created in 1961, to hear disputes voluntarily submitted to that body (Clayton & Savage, 1974).

It should not be assumed that Mboya inflicted his sole will on Kenya in 1962. Both the Kenyan Federation of Labour and the Federation of Kenyan Employers had influence on the final draft of the Industrial Relations Charter and subsequent passage of the Trade Disputes Act of 1964 which ultimately led to the formation of the Industrial Court that same year (Clayton & Savage, 1974).

Amendments to the Trade Disputes Act

Under the amended Trade Disputes Act of 1964, arbitration tribunals, boards of inquiry, and an Industrial Court were established. The original law called for a President appointed by the Chief Justice with four 'independent' assessors, two persons representing employers and two persons representing workers. In an amendment later that year, the employer and worker representatives were increased from two to five in anticipation of a heavy workload (Cockar, 1981). Years later the number of judges was increased from two to five (Amwayi, 2006).

The key position under the Kenyan system is the President of the Industrial Court, since the President, after consultation with the assessors appointed to hear particular cases, makes the final and binding decision. The assessors are required to sign the decision but they do not vote. The first President of the Industrial Court was Saeed Cockar, who presided for over 25 years with no assistance. A second Judge, Charles P. Chemmuttut, was appointed to the Industrial Court around 1990 to deal with the increased workload. President (Judge) Cockar's influence on the policies and operation of the Industrial Court has been profound since the earliest days (Mills, 1986). He for many years controlled collective bargaining settlements and industrial relations policy in Kenya by virtue of his position on the Court.

Because the Industrial Court was a near-instant success in reducing labour strife, fine-tuning legislation was passed in 1965 which set up procedures for settling disputes, limited secondary strikes, lockouts, mandatory binding arbitration by the Industrial Court in 'essential services' disputes, and gave unions mandatory check-off of union dues if agreed-to by the Minister for Labour. Thus, there was to be voluntary arbitration in non-essential services and compulsory arbitration in essential services, i.e., electricity generation and distribution or transport (Cockar, 1981). Another major change in the dispute resolution mechanism occurred in 1971, when the Industrial Court received authority to return dismissed or suspended employees to their jobs and to rule on disputes involving allocation of work or recognition of unions. The Industrial Court felt that it did not have the authority to reinstate employees or to order back wages paid in their original charter. In addition, the amended version of the Trade Disputes Act of 1971 required the Ministry of Labour to see that the parties participated in pre-arbitration fact-finding and conciliation procedures (Cockar, 1981). How important the latter issue was in terms of Court proceedings will be discussed in a later section.

Another amendment to the 1971 version of the Act was quite significant. It stated that the Court was required to respect any guidelines or other directives relating to wage and salary levels, and any other conditions of employment ordered by the Minister for Finance. This in effect required the Court to cap wage increases in awards at whatever level was authorised by the Government (Cockar, 1981). The amendment assured employers that wage levels in Kenya could not exceed increases in gross national product or inflation, and unfortunately committed workers to continuation of the sub-standard wages they had been working for under colonial rule and built into the system a permanent labour cost advantage for employers.

The effects of the 1971 amendments to the Trade Disputes Act were a draw as far as labour and employers were concerned. In theory, workers had a greater chance to be returned to their jobs if unjustly dismissed, and employers were assured that the Court would cut back excessive wage and benefit settlements to whatever guidelines were produced by the Ministry of Finance. Unions gained mandatory check off-of dues which made them financially viable on a continent where persuading impoverished workers to pay dues would be impossible under normal circumstances. However, the likelihood of an employee being returned to his or her job remained remote; the Court rarely ordered reinstatement of a worker who was unfairly dismissed (Hagglund, 1994).

National well-being and the Industrial Court

From the beginning, the Industrial Court regarded itself as the guardian of the country's economy and its ability to compete in world markets. With or without the 1971 amendments to the Act, the Court was from the beginning sensitive to the effect of increased labour costs on employers and the nation. And since the Court had the power to suspend and/or amend contract settlements and issue awards which became legally binding contracts, it actively intervened when it felt that the parties, and especially the unions, were imposing settlements which were not in the national interest. It set upon itself the responsibility of gauging the effect of contract settlements and awards on prices of products, creation of jobs, and attraction of outside capital for industrial development. In short, it was acting as an extension of conservative private enterprise and *laissez-faire* economic theory modified to the extent that it recognised unions' rights to exist and negotiate on behalf of their members.

Guidelines for contract awards

To direct itself, the Court set up four fundamental concerns to be applied when reviewing contract disputes, as follows (Cockar, 1981).

- 'The basic needs of the workers or the family budget (the basket of goods); movements in the cost of living.'
- 'Wage comparisons, i.e., wages paid in other industries & places.'
- 'Money, i.e., the financial position of the employer, the ability or inability to pay.'
- 'Productivity increase, if any, i.e., the workers efforts in increasing the productivity of an enterprise (hard to measure).'

Judge Cockar then went on to add as a fifth concern, 'The effect of a wage award on the employment situation in the country and on the price of the products of an undertaking, that is, its effect upon consumer purchasing power and employment.' Kenyan producers have faced tough price competition since the cutting back of protective tariffs in the 1990s.

The significance of the last guideline in a developing country cannot be underestimated, and it is clear that the Court took on a very important role as guardian of Kenya's economic viability. How it used the guidelines was to have a significant impact on employers and workers.

One of the problems with applying guidelines of the type described is getting solid information which allows the Court to make a rational decision. In an arbitration hearing, the parties present whatever information they are capable of providing which supports their case, and much depends upon the abilities of the parties presenting the case and available government data.

To illustrate the way the Court functioned, in 1993 seven cases involving contract terms were docketed with the Industrial Court out of the 65 decisions reviewed. Wage increases varied widely, apparently affected by the Court's perception of the current economy, the ability of the employer to pay an increase, and the nature of the union's original proposal. Since there were long delays in getting the case to a hearing, all of the cases were initially argued by the parties before devaluation occurred in 1993. Two or three unions came to the hearing with higher demands than those presented to the employer, usually arguing increases in costs of living, or the company had dramatically increased the prices of their products, to support their case. It was not easy to determine the guidelines on which the Court relied in individual cases, although they appeared to give special attention to the apparent economic condition of the employer involved.

One unfortunate feature of contract awards imposed by a third party is a continuing inability of the parties to reach accord on their own, preferring the 'easy out' of placing the responsibility for contract terms on an outsider. The Australian system, which was one of the models for the Kenyan Industrial Court, reported the same problem and in 1996 changed its system in order to encourage enterprise bargaining and a more competitive business environment (Mills, 1986). The complaint is that this type of system contributes to continuing immaturity of the parties to an agreement, since they never have to assume final responsibility for their actions.

Since all collective agreements must be registered with the Industrial Court, it has enormous power with regard to final terms and conditions. If in the opinion of the Court the parties have violated one or more of its guidelines, it has the power to set aside its terms and substitute new ones. This authority enables it to review salary increases, even though these may have been jointly agreed-to by the parties, and substitute its own judgment as to what is right and proper by sending the agreement back to the parties for further negotiation (Cockar, 1981).

On 27 July 1994, over one year after devaluation occurred, the Minister of Labour announced that wage guidelines were relaxed and the Industrial Court could award compensation (increases) up to 100 per cent (*The Standard*, 1994). This was the first official recognition by the government of the hardships worked on trade union members by the 1993 devaluation of the shilling. The Minister went on to say that workers could also negotiate additional productivity improvement pay, and that unions were not required to wait for the termination of their current two-year agreements before asking for pay increases. This statement illustrates the control that the government exercised over the labour market and unions.

Worker rights under the law

As of 2003, worker rights had changed very little over the past 20 years. Workers are free to join the union of their choice, or can register a new union with as few as seven members if there is no union already available for them to join.

There are about 42 unions representing about 600,000 members, about one third of the formal labour force sector. Further information on the present state of the Kenyan labour movement is provided in Chapter 4.

Conclusion

The Industrial Relations system of Kenya was set up and was functioning shortly after Kenya formed its first national government. The trade union movement has the right to bargain with employers, and negotiate agreements which are then approved by the Industrial Court. Europeans have little influence over the system except insofar as they can exercise their interests through collective bargaining. COTU is the major national labor organisation, but most grievances and contracts are handled at the local level. Teachers are still outside of COTU and their wage increases and terms of reference are subject to government intervention.

After Independence, Kenya promoted rapid economic growth through public investment, encouragement of smallholder agricultural production, and provided incentives for private industrial investment. Gross domestic product (GDP) grew by an annual average of 6.6 per cent from 1963 to 1973. Agricultural production grew by 4.7 per cent annually during the same period, stimulated by redistributing land. Between 1974 and 1990, Kenya's economic performance declined due to inappropriate agricultural policies, inadequate credit, and poor international terms of trade which contributed to the decline in agriculture. Kenya's inward-looking policy of import substitution and rising oil prices made Kenya's manufacturing sector uncompetitive. The government began a massive intrusion in the private sector. Lack of export incentives, tight import controls, and foreign exchange controls made the domestic environment for investment even less attractive.

From 1991 to 1993, Kenya had its worst economic performance since independence. Growth in GDP stagnated, and agricultural production shrank at an annual rate of 3.9 per cent. Inflation reached a record 100 per cent in August of 1993, and the government's deficit was over 10 per cent of GDP. As a result of these combined problems, bilateral and multilateral donors suspended programme aid to Kenya in 1991.

In 1993, the Government of Kenya began a major programme of economic reform and liberalisation. A new minister of finance and governor of the central bank undertook a series of measures with the assistance of the World Bank and the International Monetary Fund (IMF). As part of this programme, the government eliminated price controls, import licensing, foreign exchange controls, and privatised a range of publicly owned companies, reducing the number of civil servants and introduced conservative fiscal and monetary policies. From 1994 to 1996, Kenya's real GDP growth rate averaged just over 4 per cent a year.

The current modest economic recovery is a great improvement when compared to Kenya's abysmal performance in the 1990s. While the macro-economic framework has been stable, a set of deep-seated, inter-related 'micro' challenges continue to impede faster growth. The include dilapidated road, rail and port systems, over-regulation, widespread graft, insecurity, high-cost and poor quality power and telecom services, and overall economic governance that is erratic. All of these continue to make Kenya a risky and high-cost business environment and therefore an unattractive place to invest.

Over Kenya's history since the Protectorate was set up in 1894, the industrial relations system has been changed to meet the needs of the times. The industrial relations system, however, has changed little during the past 16 years and continues to operate under laws that have changed little since 1971.

References

Amwayi, J. E. (2006), *e-mail message*, Nairobi, 23 Sept. 2006
Clayton, A. and Savage, D.C. (1974), Government and Labour in Kenya, 1895–1963. London: Frank Cass.
Collins, R. (1990), *Eastern African History*. New York: Markus Wiener Publishing.
Cockar, S. R. (1981), *The Kenya Industrial Court: Origin, Development and Practice*. Nairobi: Longman Kenya Ltd.
East African Standard, 21 Nov. 1922.
Goldsworthy, D. (1982), *Tom Mboya: The Man Kenya Wanted to Forget*. Nairobi: Heinemann.
Hagglund, G. (1994), *Proceedings*, Caribbean Conference on Industrial Courts, Port of Spain, Trinidad, 28–30 Nov. 1994
Master and Servants Amendment Ordinance, Ord 27 of 1919, *E.A.P. Gazette*, 22 Oct. 1919. Nairobi.
Mboya, T. (1963), *Freedom and After*. Boston: Little, Brown & Co.
Mills, M. (1986), 'Mechanisms for Labour Harmony: Dispute Resolution in the Industrial Courts of Kenya and Zambia', New Jersey Institute of Technology, 323 King Boulevard, Newark, NJ 07102, August 1986.
Ord 1 of 1915, *E.A. P. Gazette*, 26 Jan. 1916
Patel, Z. (2006), *Unquiet: The Life and Times of Makhan Singh*, Zandgraphics, Nairobi.
The Native Followers Recruitment Ordinance, Ord 29 of 1915, *E.A.P. Gazette*, 8 Sept. 1915. Nairobi.
The Native Registration Ordinance, Ord 15 of 1915, *E.A.P. Gazette*, 19 May 1915. Nairobi.
The Standard, 'Govt Reviews Salary Rules', Nairobi, Kenya, 27 July 1994. Nairobi.
U.S. Department of State (2004), *Country Reports on Human Rights Practices for 2003*. Washington: US Government Printing Office.

4
Industrial Relations and the Social Partners in Kenya

Tayo Fashoyin

Introduction

The post-independence industrial relations policy in Kenya was a radical shift from the repressive colonial labour policy that targeted the nascent anti-colonial pro-independence labour movement. The 'new' policy recognised the legitimate role of trade unions in nation-building, but through a progression of coercive and corporatist policies that assured labour compliance with government political and development agenda. In effect, these policies reflected considerable influence by government in the management of the labour movement led by the Central Organisation of Trade Unions (COTU). Government coercive tendencies reached a peak with the brief forced-affiliation of COTU to the ruling political party Kenya African National Union (KANU), which also exercised considerable influence in the management of COTU and its affiliated unions (c.f. Ananaba 193).

This chapter argues that the industrial relations system in Kenya evolved as a result of a commitment to sound industrial relations by introducing a body of labour laws on employment relations, collective bargaining and dispute resolution that assures social stability and supports the country's industrial development. Despite the ups and downs of the political and economic development in Kenya, the overall thrust of the industrial relations policy has been in pursuit of social partnership.

The economy and labour market challenges

Kenya's economy experienced dramatic development soon after independence in 1963, with impressive growth occurring in modern industrial manufacturing, agriculture and tourism (EIU 1994). The 'miracle decade' of 1963–74 saw the average real growth rate of about 7 per cent. The industrial 'take off' was evidenced by an impressive manufacturing value added of 9 per cent, which represented a sharp contrast to industrial development in comparable economies in Africa. However, economic growth was short-lived, as growth soon decelerated and the country experienced economic decline or stagnation from the mid-1970s through to the 1990s. The long spell of economic decline was briefly interrupted in the late 1980s and early 1990s following the introduction of a new development agenda with support from the World Bank and International Monetary Fund programme to liberalise the economy, involving among others the abolition of import licensing, decontrol of interest rates and a reduction of the bloated civil service workforce (Government of Kenya 2000).

This policy thrust appeared to have momentarily improved the economy. The GDP grew at 4.3 per cent in 1990, but fell to 2.3 per cent and to 0.4 per cent respectively during 1991 and 1992. Inflation was briefly kept under control but by 1996 it had started an upward trend. Moreover, overall economic performance did not seem to respond to the reform and so the growth rate was not sustained throughout the 1990s (ibid.).

The lack of sustained commitment to economic reform, coupled with political instability contributed in no small way to the failure of the policies to stimulate the growth of the economy. Towards the end of the 1990s inadequacies in the infrastructure, such as energy and water shortages and bad road networks, contributed to the stagnation of the Kenyan economy. With these complex economic problems taking place concurrently with political liberalisation, which had brought about multi-party democracy after more than 30 years of one-party rule, the Kenyan economy was in the throes of multiple socio-economic problems. However, in this present decade, there is evidence of economic recovery. Real GDP growth rose by 5.8 per cent in 2005, up from 4.9 per cent in 2004, with estimated sustained growth during 2006–2007 (Government of Kenya 2006). The growth sectors are tourism, agriculture, transport and communication, and construction.

The behaviour of the labour market in Kenya during the present decade has reflected this continuity in the development effort, and has also been influenced by global pressures and domestic liberalisation policies. A key strategic response, in so far as the labour market is concerned, was a return to the founding principles of industrial relations in the country, based on tripartism. Inevitably industrial relations outcomes have reflected the ups and downs of economic performance, particularly on their impact on actors.

A disaggregation of the employment figures explain the structure of employment in the country. In the modern wage employment sector, for example, from a base of nearly 1.5 million employed people in 1995, a steady increase brought employment to over 1.8 million in 2005, representing an increase of 20 per cent over the decade (ibid.). The private sector segment of this employment figure was about 1.2 million in 2005, or 64 per cent of modern sector employment. This growth, while demonstrating the upturn of the economy, nevertheless masks the fact that the informal economy, or *Jua Kali*, as it is known in Kenya, is the main source of employment growth in the country, as in most labour markets in Africa. Thus, from a base of about

2.6 million informal operators in 1995, employment in the informal economy rose to 6.4 million in 2005, reflecting a phenomenonal growth of 146 per cent during the decade. It is therefore instructive where the prospect for employment and livelihood lies in the country. As will become evident later, the application of labour market regulations, institutions and processes that might help improve the quality and substance of employment in this crucially employment generating sector, and the vital role of trade unions in helping to improve the job quality and rights of workers, is still very marginal.

The legal framework for industrial relations

Constitutional guarantee for the rights of workers to freedom of association are provided in section 80(1) of the Constitution of Kenya. As in most jurisdictions, constitutional provisions of this kind are hardly enough to fully realise the protection of rights at work. Hence Kenya, like most countries, has put in place the legal foundation of industrial relations comprising a body of labour laws covering wide-ranging issues of employment relations, wages and wage councils, dispute resolution, occupational safety and health, workmen's compensation, and trade union and employers' organisations. The voluntary tripartite agreement, Industrial Relations Charter (IRC), is an important complement to the labour code in the country. It incorporates, for example, ILO's standards on freedom of association and organisational rights of workers and unions, and strongly reinforces tripartism and social dialogue in the industrial relations practice. With respect to the management of industrial disputes, a key innovation in the amended Trade Disputes Act of 1971 was the introduction of an Industrial Court, thus offering a further step in the dispute resolution system. I will return to this issue later.

Finally, as part of the government's quest for rapid industrialisation, it introduced the export-processing zones act in 1990, enabling foreign investors to set up business with substantial protection, including the exception of such businesses from provisions of the labour laws. For example, unions were not allowed to operate in the protected zones, thus effectively denying the right of workers to join unions which meant there was no avenue for them to raise disputes over unfavourable conditions of service. Although both the trade unions, with support from the ILO supervisory system and oftentimes the Federation of Kenya Employers (FKE), have argued against this protection, it was only in recent years that government has agreed to remove the protection. With the support of the ILO, the affected laws have been revised to bring businesses in the zones under the effective coverage of the labour laws, although the proposed revisions are yet to be approved by the government.

The labour code was generously applied in periods of industrial growth, from independence through to the beginning of the 1980s. Thus all workers, including civil servants were allowed to organise and engage in collective bargaining. However, faced with deteriorating economic and political conditions, and intensified trade union agitation and protests in several sectors, noticeably in the relatively peaceful public service, the liberal application of labour laws soon proved unsuitable to the government. In 1980, the Union of Kenya Civil Servants, one of the earliest unions in the country, having been established in 1959 as a bargaining agent for all eligible civil servants, was disbanded. Government's argument was that the union's members were management people, who were however free to form a non-bargaining staff association. Again in 1992, strikes by university teachers and non-academic staff over poor conditions of service were broken and the respective unions disbanded, but members were encouraged to join their respective professional associations. Union rights were reinstated only in 2004, after the un-relenting advocacy and pressures from labour, backed by pressure from the ILO.

Further changes in the legal framework, in the context of restrictive application of the laws during increasing economic difficulty in the 1990s saw the government unilaterally amend the job security provisions in the Trade Disputes Act. In 1994 the Minister of Finance took the extraordinary step of introducing, in the Finance Bill to Parliament, amendments to both the Regulation of Wages and Conditions of Employment Act and the Trade Disputes Act. The amendment moved redundancy issues from the latter law to the former, the implication being that businesses were thus given a free hand to undertake enterprise restructuring, while their obligation was only to *inform* but not to *report* the proposed measure to the labour ministry as required under the Act. In terms of the labour relations process, this fundamental legislative change meant that disputes arising from enterprise restructuring, which was subject to negotiation through the dispute resolution machinery, became a purely employment issue, limiting the employer's obligation to the payment of legally binding redundancy benefits. The unilateral move by government in failing to consult with the sector ministry responsible for labour market issues, and the equally appalling neglect of the tripartite Labour Advisory Board was disheartening and an affront to the status and image of the established industrial relations institutions and processes in the country.

One outstanding provision of the IRC is its unequivocal preference for an industrial union structure that allows one union per sector. This policy was ostensibly made to overcome the problem of union multiplicity and proliferation common to most African countries, and so promote unity and effectiveness in the advancement of workers interests. However, as will be explained later, the union structure that emerged in the 1960s soon turned out to be inadequate to sustain this structural arrangement.

The anomalies of the previous years of compromise in the legal framework may now be arrested, through a recent tripartite effort to update the laws and streamline them with international labour standards. Under the proposed amendments, significant provisions are made to address some of the shortcomings that appear to weaken unions' internal administration, their ability to organise freely and provide service to members. Significant also is the severe restriction placed on the powers of civil court to adjudicate on internal trade union issues, while labour issues are to be taken to the Industrial Court, and an Appeals Labour Court to be introduced. These measures are likely to restore the dignity of the industrial relations system, as opposed to the role of civil courts that often do not recognise the non-legalistic merits of the employment relationship. The passage of the proposed reform into law will also obviate a long-standing argument of government for failing to ratify the crucially important ILO Convention No. 87, on the freedom of association and the right to organise. However, the five (5) pieces of reform bills that emerged through the tripartite committee continue to await government consideration and passage since April 2004, and appear to have stalled.

Trade unions and employers' associations

The COTU and workers' unions

The COTU is the voice of labour in Kenya, representing about 40 industrial (general) unions with estimated total membership of about 300,000 in 2005. These membership figures mask the fact that far more organised and unorganised workers are not officially represented by COTU. For example, the large teachers union, with a membership of nearly 200,000, and the newly re-registered unions in the civil service and tertiary education are not members in the COTU. Among the unorganised workers, the *Jua Kali* in the large informal economy are not organised or formally represented by the labour centre, although it claims to speak for them. On the basis of available data, the organised workforce represents less than a third of the formal wage employment in the country, or a union density of about 30 per cent.

The structural organisation of the unions has its foundation in the historic principle of one union per industry, instituted by the non-legally binding tripartite charter, the IRC. But most unions have not followed this structural arrangement. Rather, they have been operating as general unions, recruiting members from several sectors, without regard to clearly defined industrial boundaries. One notable example is the Kenya Union of Commercial, Food and Allied Workers, KUCFAW, which organises workers across a number of sectors, such as banking and finance, food, retail trade, shipping and security services. Partly as a result of this laxity in applying the principle of one union one industry, and partly as a result of agreements and the unions' role in the bipartite sectoral negotiations and tripartite wages boards the area of union impact is much broader than their actual membership representation (Fashoyin *et al*. 2006). However, the extent to which this possibility is real is a function of the effect-iveness of labour inspection by the labour ministry.

Another consequence of union organising beyond the narrowly defined industrial sectors was the failure of several unions to fully represent the multiple interests of their general-purpose membership, resulting in inevitable internal divisions and ultimately membership splits. For example, during the decade of the 1990s, no less than 3 groups broke away from the KUCFAW to form separate unions.

The spate of splinter unions has been distracting, sapping the energy and resources of the affected unions and thereby weakening their voice at the industrial and enterprise levels. This was hardly unexpected, given the unwieldy structure of such unions and their incapacity to effectively represent the employment problems facing the various groups they claim to represent. This division in unions has clearly weakened the solidarity among workers and role of unions in labour–management relations across the country. Weakness arising from the failure to effectively service the various interests within them, coupled with political ambition of rival union leaders, have drawn the attention of other actors outside the labour field, seeking to fill the opening unavoidably created by internecine rivalries. This point will be dealt with later. At the same time, it will be an exaggeration to suggest that the 'industrial union' principle has been jettisoned or completely broken down. On the contrary, the recent amendment in the IRC was intended to relax the industrial union policy, for example by allowing the formation of unions in clearly identifiable sectors. In this context, both the government and employers have supported COTU in underscoring the merits of maintaining the principle as they are in the long-term interest of labour in the country.

The FKE and employers

Most employers in the medium and large enterprises category are members of or affiliated to the Federation of Kenya Employers (FKE), which is the main employers' voice on labour market issues in the country. The FKE operates through its 9 sectoral groups and 6 affiliated trade associations across the country. According to the FKE report for 2005, membership was 2,358, made up of 1,442 direct members and 96 members of affiliated associations (Federation of Kenya Employers 2005: 12). This represented a declining trend that started in 1996 when a membership of 2,995 fell by 21 per cent by 2005. The membership decline coincided with the downturn of the economy, and that led to extensive contractions in industrial output, leading to business closures and retrenchments of the workforce. Available evidence suggests that while the larger enterprises were contracting, the SMEs were in fact increasing, both in number, size and industrial outputs (c.f. Machuka et al., 2004).

For a long time membership of the federation was limited to the relatively large enterprises and multinationals, but with growing decline in the number and scope of operation of such firms, and a corresponding increase in the number and strategic importance of the small and medium enterprises, the FKE has oriented its membership recruitment strategy beyond its traditional source for membership. While this effort is yet to cover the large proportion of SMEs in the country, the federation represents a growing number of businesses in this category, most often through the latter's membership of industrial associations and occasionally by direct membership. Today FKE sources indicate that about 40 per cent of its membership belongs to the small and medium enterprises.

Therefore, it was hardly surprising that in seeking to strengthen their voice in the broader economic policy issues and to enable business to present a united voice, four key business organisations (the Kenya Association of Manufacturers, Kenya National Chambers of Commerce and Industry and the East African Association – largely the foreign investors from Britain and North America – and the FKE), made a declaration to reaffirm their commitment to dialogue in the Joint Industrial and Commercial Consultative Council in December 2000 (Federation of Kenya Employers, 2005). To achieve this unity of purpose, the four organisations announced in the same declaration the establishment of a loose body, known as the Kenya Business Consultative Forum, as a lobby group to present employers' views to government on various policy issues of interest to them. However, the forum barely took off, due to organisational and financial shortcomings, but also prevailing mutual suspicion might have contributed to the collapse of this initiative. Nevertheless, as confirmed to this author in an interview in September 2006, the need for joint forces continue to be felt by the business community and led them once again to found the Kenya Business Council in 2002. Regrettably, this body failed to make significant impact as a result of a weak resource base. As confirmed during the interview with this author, this new body has followed the same path as the previous efforts, and left the business groups disunited in presenting one voice on critical business and national issues.

The challenge from other actors

In the decade beginning from the mid-1990s both the trade unions and the employers' bodies were confronted by the challenge posed by other social actors, notably the non-governmental organisations (NGOs) and the civil society organisations (CSOs) who had entered the terrain traditionally reserved for the labour market actors, and in some way operated in a destabilising manner. At enterprise level, union leaders and employers frowned at the appearance of other actors in the domain of collective bargaining. A bemused Kenyan delegate told the International Labour Conference in 2002 that consumer organisations 'are demanding that NGOs be involved in collective bargaining and negotiations, contrary to our tripartite agreement, which gives trade unions the right to be the sole negotiators or negotiating bodies for determining the terms and conditions of employment of their members' (ILO, 2002). The challenge from other actors may appear to be a transient phenomenon, but it has raised fundamental issues of union responsiveness to membership services, and the role of public policy and partnership in longer-term industrial relations practice in the country.

As the foregoing analysis suggests, the appearance of other actors in industrial relations has been slow in coming, and the outcome of complex internal and external forces, too complex an analysis to be undertaken in this chapter.

Only a summary of the issues can be attempted here. The sources of the challenge include (1) the structural deficiency that allows sectoral unions to recruit beyond industrial boundaries, leading to the inevitable failure of such unions to provide adequate services to their widely disparate membership; (2) the inability of some union leaders to provide effective leadership in strategy and service to their members, the latter including failure to deal with workers' work-related grievances. In the case of employers, try as the FKE may, it has not been able to speak effectively for small and micro enterprises, which are generally unorganised. Seeing this outlet, the NGOs and CSOs seized this opportunity.; (3) the anomaly created in public policy which precludes union activity in protected areas such as the export processing zones (EPZs) and (4) failure of unions to organise critical sectors, notably the fast growing horticulture industry.

Others explanations are the observed predilection of development partners to support NGOs and CSOs, especially on issues such as human rights, governance and people-oriented causes, which have created attractive sources of employment and fund-raising. This external influence of the development agencies is also evident in the preference of stakeholders such as the International Financial Institutions for parallel private sector institutions. A notable example is the Kenya-Private Sector Alliance (KEPTA) established in 2003, which brings together several business organisations, NGOs and CSOs. This body had the blessing of the government and support from donors, but organisations such as this have a tendency to undermine traditional business institutions.

In summary, it can be argued that the involvement of other actors has led the tripartite partners, particularly the labour and employers' organisations to appreciate the critical need for internal cohesion in changing environment. They also recognise the broader context of industrial relations, the potential added value of other actors, their complementarity and mutually reinforcing roles.

Collective bargaining, dispute resolution and the Labour Court

Collective bargaining is an old tradition in Kenya. Today over 200 collective bargaining agreements (CBAs), at both the sectoral and enterprise levels are made annually across industry in the country. Estimates suggest that these agreements cover about 1.5 million direct beneficiaries. However, the area of impact of CBAs could be considerably larger because, as previously stated, sectoral collective agreements or the tripartite industrial wage councils' awards have a way of influencing wage decision of businesses that are not directly involved in the collective bargaining exercise. At the same time, it needs to be borne in mind that the coverage of collective agreements still represents a small fraction of wage earners, estimated at more than twice the size of modern sector wage employment in 2005. In fact, as shown in Figure 4.1 the

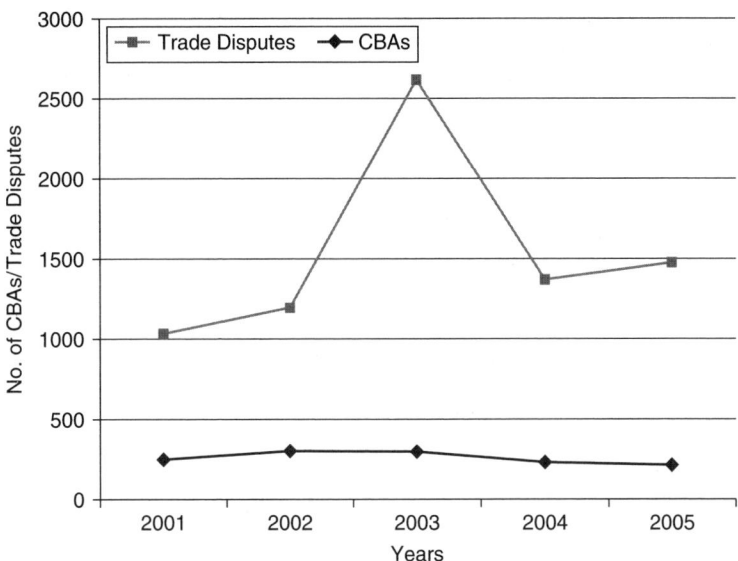

Source: Ministry of Labour and Human Resource Development, Nairobi.

Figure 4.1 Collective bargaining agreements and disputes, 2000–2005

number of collective agreements during the last four years has fallen considerably owing to a number of factors, including declining industrial activity, reluctance of some employers to recognise unions and bargain with them, and the absence of trade union activity in the protected export processing zones. Thus, the number of CBAs in 2000 represented just one half of the agreements that were signed in 1998 (Fashoyin, 2001). The exceptionally large number of CBAs and trade disputes recorded in 2003 was connected with the major political development that brought an end to the Moi era and the democratic rapture that accompanied the election of President Kibaki.

Collective bargaining takes place at the industry and enterprise levels. Industry level bargaining, at one time the preferred level at which negotiation took place, has become unpopular, as economic difficulties have induced enterprises to push for decentralised bargaining. In this way employers have a free hand to negotiate on a number of key areas, such as wages and compensation, productivity and work methods at the enterprise level. The new orientation allows enterprises to respond more speedily and efficiently to global pressures. Industry bargaining is today confined to a few industries such as tea plantations, agriculture, banking, engineering and mining. The FKE provides technical support for their members, and through this ensure that the dignity of industry level CBA is preserved by ensuring that key elements of the industry agreement are preserved. In contrast, COTU is not involved in enterprise level bargaining, leaving this role to its affiliates, who very often lack the manpower and financial resources to negotiate multiple individual agreements with employers.

The industry agreement is generally believed to establish minimum standards, but in enterprises where the union has no strong presence or where the employer is unwilling to engage in negotiation, the minimum standards in the CBA have tended to be the applicable rates and conditions. Bear in mind however that the majority of workers are outside the direct cover of CBAs, especially the micro, small and medium enterprises. This presents two important observations. First, as a recent study shows (Fashoyin *et al.*, 2006), while several small firms are not unionised, the wages and other conditions they give have broadly been responsive to existing provisions. Generally, the minimum standards that might have been established in the employment law, industry CBAs or the standards that are periodically set at the tripartite industry Wage Councils or those prescribed by General (Wages) Order, are applied.[1] The second is that as demonstrated in the study, wages in unionised SMEs are significantly superior to those in non-union enterprises, although the overall labour relations were not always as good as in non-union enterprises (Fashoyin *et al.*, 2006).

Disputes settlement

The legal foundation for resolving labour disputes is the Trade Disputes Act. The IRC limits its role in this area to intra-union disputes. In so far as disputes in labour relations are concerned, the law assigns a considerable role to the labour ministry and the industrial court, to which appeals can be made when the machinery of the ministry or tripartite adjudication is not satisfactory to any of the disputing parties. In some cases, some disputes, such as those in the essential services, are referred directly to the industrial court.

As the law and practice in the area of dispute management indicates, there has been a general downward trend in the incidence of strikes, and person-days lost during the last 10 years, as shown in Figure 4.2. In 2000 there were 41 strikes involving 17,794 workers and 51,171 person-days-lost. In 2005, the respective figures were 17 strikes involving 9,393 workers, reflecting a number of realities in labour relations practice in the country. These include the relative efficiency of the dispute resolution machinery, the imprudence of going on strike, particularly in a difficult economic environment, coupled with the relative weakness of workers in relation to the employers. One may recall, for example, the extraordinary decision of government in 1994 to give a free hand to business to address redundancy issues without any role for workers or their union.

A major threat to the dispute resolution machinery and sustainable social dialogue processes in Kenya is the failure of the labour ministry to fully play its leadership role in industrial relations, particularly in ensuring that

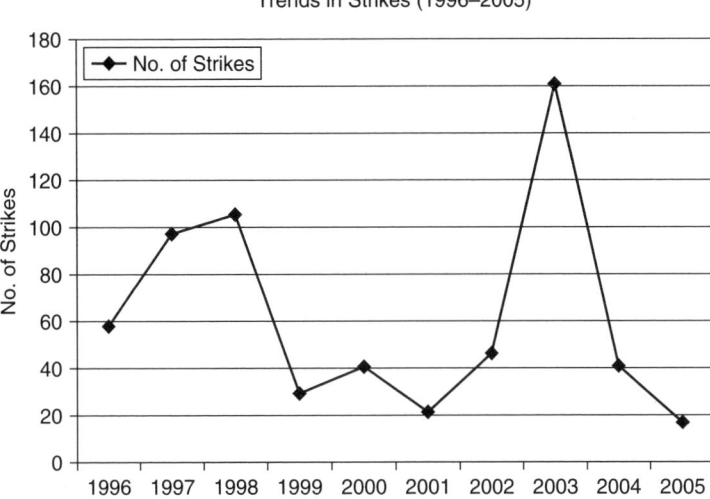

Source: Ministry of Labour and Human Resource Development, Nairobi.

Figure 4.2   Strikes – 1996–2005

institutions such as the National Tripartite Negotiating Committee are able to meet regularly to discuss pressing issues. This shortcoming is demonstrated by the recent disagreement between unions and employers in the tea industry over the failure of the latter to follow the provisions of the CBA as they relate to the introduction of new technology. Management's unilateral introduction of planting machines led to a strike action, which required the labour minister to make a stay of action order on both sides while a tripartite committee investigated the dispute. Rather than facilitate this committee, the labour ministry curiously authorised management to recommence the use of the machines to the consternation of the workers.

The Industrial Court

A full discussion of the role of the Industrial Court is provided in Chapter 3.

Tripartism, social dialogue and development

The commitment of the government and the social partners to tripartite cooperation represents the long-held belief that through this process, social stability can contribute to national development. As a result of this principle, all sides have from the onset embraced an industrial relations system that allows the use of consultative mechanisms for resolving industrial problems (Iwuji, 1979; Henley, 2000; Kamoche, 2000). It is true that not all the processes had been consistently used over the years, but the return to tripartite cooperation during periods of adverse economic conditions in the 1990s reaffirmed the usefulness of tripartite cooperation. Of particular significance was the enlargement of the space for tripartism beyond the labour ministry by including other government departments. This approach acknowledges the usefulness of going beyond the confines of the labour market.

The foregoing perspective led to a return to the National Tripartite Consultative Committee, a purely labour relations forum that was largely ignored for most of the 1980s and early 1990s. While the committee had been useful in dealing with labour relations issues, its reactivation in the mid 1990s took its founding objective more seriously. Thus article b (1) of the Industrial Relations Charter empowers the committee to deal with 'matters affecting the economy in general and employment matters in particular'. In other words, while dealing with labour law reform, the committee should undertake an assessment of the implication of the law for the economy and the labour market. Discussion of this kind usually involved officials of other government departments, and had facilitated discussions of wide-ranging national issues, including energy supply and water shortages, both of which led to extensive industrial contraction and retrenchment in the late 1990s, the establishment of a productivity centre and the formulation of a national employment policy. In the labour relations arena, the committee has dealt with the reactivation of the unions in the public service, extension of the labour code to the export processing zones, intra-union disputes and the role of the civil courts in industrial relations processes (Fashoyin, 2001: 25).

At a higher level, the social partners have also engaged in tripartite plus consultation in the Joint Industrial and Commercial Consultative Committee (JICCC,) which was established 1997, at the pinnacle of the economic crisis, as a multi-stakeholders forum for addressing critical economic issues, propose solutions and ensure implementation (ibid.: 25–7). This body, comprising some 50 stakeholders – including on the government side, ministries of finance, industry, agriculture, labour, transport, energy and local government. On the business side were the FKE, manufacturers association, chambers of commerce, and bankers and insurers associations. The workers were represented by COTU, embodying the broad consensus among the working people. With signs of economic recovery, the JICCC is regretfully becoming less active; nevertheless its establishment demonstrates how social dialogue can help bring multi-stakeholders together to deal with critical national issues that impact on the operation of the labour market.

Conclusion

The government of Kenya and the social partners continue to see industrial relations as an important instrument for achieving economic and social stability necessary for national development. The manifestation of this is the readiness of the tripartite partners to institute an industrial relations framework that gives each actor space to influence labour market governance through meaningful voice on broader issues of economic and social development. In spite of the deteriorating economic difficulties of the 1990s and the earlier part of the present decade, the tripartite partners had exercised the courage to go back to the founding principles of joint effort to address sectoral and national economic difficulties.

There are of course threats to a sustained social dialogue process. Trade unions and employers need to take concrete measures to strengthen their internal cohesion that prepares them for effective engagement on labour market and broader economic issues. The need for internal cohesion is a key to creating effective synergies and cooperation with other social actors to help strengthen the voice of labour both in the labour market and overall economic policymaking. Such orientation would help labour and employers' organisations to assert their influence on labour issues, within the overall national context. It will most probably help to avert the involvement of unhelpful external interventions from opportunistic actors.

The challenge of other actors highlights two significant phenomena. The first is an awakening call to trade unions, employers and indeed the labour ministry that any blemish created in their responsiveness to day to day industrial relations practice will create room for other actors to fill-in the opening, with potentially undesirable consequences. The second is the opportunity, often ignored, of the usefulness of partnership and collaboration with other actors whose expertise or value-added could significantly contribute to, or enhance the role of the tripartite partners in industrial relations. This perspective is particularly relevant to the trade unions which need such partnerships to redress the representational deficit, created by the triple difficulty of membership decline, recruitment difficulties and wavering appeal of unions in a changing labour market. Partnership of this kind is equally important to the employers' association and indeed the labour ministry, to enhance their influence in the policy-making arena.

Note

1. Evidence, however, suggests that of the more than 10 Wage Councils across industry, only one – the General Wages Advisory Board – which prescribes the General (Wages) Order is functioning effectively and has broad application in the unorganised enterprises in the country.

References

Ananaba, W. (1979), *The Trade Union Movement in Africa*. London, C. Hurst,
Economist Intelligence Unit (EIU) (1994), *Kenya 1993/94. Country Profile*. London

Fashoyin, T. (2001), 'Kenya: Social Dialogue and National Development'. InFocus Programme for Social Dialogue, Labour Law and Labour Administration, ILO, Working Paper No. 3. Geneva.

Fashoyin, T. (2006), 'Employment Relations and Human Resource Management in Small Firms: An African Perspective', *Issues Paper No. 23*. Harare: ILO Sub-Regional Office for Southern Africa, Harare.

Fashoyin, T., Sims, E. and Tolentino, A. (2006), *Labour–Management Cooperation in SMEs – Forms and Factors*. Geneva: ILO.

Federation of Kenya Employers (2005), *Annual Report and Financial Statements*. Nairobi.

Government of Kenya (2000), *Economic Survey*. Nairobi: Ministry of Planning and National Development.

Government of Kenya (2006), *Economic Survey*. Nairobi: Central Bureau of Statistics

Henley, J. (2000), 'Management in Kenya', in Warner, M. (ed.), *Management in Emerging Countries*. London: Thomson Learning.

International Labour Office (2002), *Proceedings of the Resolution Committee of the 90th Session of the International Labour Conference*. Geneva: ILO.

Iwuji, E. (1979), 'Industrial Relations in Kenya', in Ukandi G. Demarche, H., Seibel, D. and Trachtman, L (eds), *Industrial Relations in Africa*. London: Macmillan

Kamoche, K. (2000), *Sociological Paradigms and Human Resources: An African Context*. Aldershot: Ashgate.

Kenya Employers (2000), 'Press Statement on Kenya's Economic Revival', released 15 December 2000. Nairobi.

Machuka, S., Onkunya, J., Chune, N. and Omolo, J. (2004). 'Labour-Management Partnership in Small and Medium Enterprises: The Case of Kenya'. Geneva: ILO.

5
Industrial Relations in Malawi
Lewis Dzimbiri

Introduction

This chapter examines industrial relation in Malawi over a period of more than four decades. Central to the analysis is the role of the state and the international donor community in shaping Malawi's industrial relations since independence. The role of the labour movement shifted from a vibrant to a docile one during move from the colonial period to the country's independence as a one-party state, then again to a more buoyant role during the return to multiparty democracy in the 1990s. The chapter starts with the political and economic context of the country before examining the origins and present state of trade unions in Malawi. It also discusses industrial relations legislation and present industrial relations practices. These include freedom of association, collective bargaining, disputes resolution and the right to strike.

The country and context

Situated in Southern Africa and bordered by Zambia, Tanzania and Mozambique, Malawi, called Nyasaland under British colonial rule during the period 1891–1963, covers 118, 500 sq. km. A small landlocked country with a population of 12 million, Malawi was a member of the federation of Rhodesia and Nyasaland (Malawi, Zambia and Zimbabwe) between 1953 and 1963. The Nyasaland African Congress (NAC) formed in 1944 to agitate for independence called Hastings Kamuzu Banda, then practising medicine in Ghana, to lead the independence struggles. The arrival of the charismatic Banda was the beginning of the end of colonial administration in Malawi (Pike, 1968). Malawi gained independence under Banda on 6 July 1964 before becoming a republic and one-party state in 1966. For three decades, Malawi was ruled by a dictatorial Malawi Congress Party government until it became transformed into a multiparty democracy in 1994. Intense human rights repression and overall, poor governance[1] created a great deal of discontent with the one-party regime. The landmark Catholic Bishops' letter of 8 March 1992 was highly critical of the existing social, political, cultural order and general economic decay, abuse of human rights and low wages and called for political reforms (Dzimbiri et al., 2000). The withholding of non-humanitarian aid by donors to secure tangible and irreversible evidence of transformation in basic human rights weakened the state's grip on power and allowed voluntary pressure groups to agitate for political and economic reforms. The outcome of the 1993 national referendum, declared free and fair by the international community, returned Malawi to a multiparty state (Dzimbiri, 1994). The 17 May 1994 General Election saw the defeat of Banda's MCP and the success of Muluzi's United Democratic Front (UDF). In 1999, the Muluzi's UDF government entered its second term of office. In 2004 the same UDF took over Government under Bingu wa Mutharika as president in a third multiparty elections. In 2005, due to intra-party conflict and the need to extricate himself and pursue his zero tolerance policy on corruption without inhibitions, Dr Mutharika left the UDF and formed his Democratic People's Party.

The Malawian economy is agriculture-based and depending on climatic conditions, agriculture accounts for more than one-third of GDP and over 90 per cent of export earnings. It employs nearly half of those in formal employment, and directly and indirectly supports an estimated 85 per cent of the population. The country's staple crop is maize, although tobacco is by far Malawi's largest export, followed by tea, cotton and sugar; mineral resources are poor.

In response to economic crisis, Malawi was forced to embark on a World Bank and IMF Structural Adjustment Programme in the early 1980s. The growth rate further declined in the 1990s because of fluctuations in the smallholder agricultural sub-sector. Economic growth rate declined from 4.1 per cent per annum in 1989 to -12.4 per cent in 1994 and -3.1 per cent in 1998 (Chipeta, 1999). The formal sector, which includes those in estate agriculture and the formal industrial sector, absorbs 13 per cent of the economically active (NSO, 2001:10).

Real wages have declined since the 1960s. Malawian workers experienced continued erosion of standards of living from the 1980s through into the 21st century. According to Chipeta (1999: 38), the consequence has been a fall in workers' living standards, rising incidence of malnutrition among children and adults, an increase in malnutrition-related diseases and deaths, decreasing morale and low productivity among workers. In 1994, the Government formulated the 'poverty alleviation policy' – as a strategy for improving the living standards of the people through free primary school education, adult literacy programmes – and to address environmental degradation, infant mortality, overpopulation and the spread of HIV/AIDS (GoM, 1995a). In late 2000 Malawi was approved for relief under the Heavily Indebted Poor Countries (HIPC) programme (GoM, 2004). The IMF and the World Bank continue to urge the Government to control expenditure, privatise public corporations, liberalise the economy and remove subsidies.

Origins and present state of trade union movement: an overview

The development of an organised labour movement was the product of a series of strikes against poor wages and working conditions by teachers, night soil workers, domestic servants and rail workers during the 1940s in Blantyre (McCracken, 1998). The Transport and General Workers Union (TGWU) was the first registered union in 1949 and this was followed by the Commercial African Trade Union (CATU) in 1952. In 1954, the Nyasaland Railway Workers Union (NRWU) was formed. The Trades Union Congress of Nyasaland was formed in June 1956. 1956 to 1963, saw the formation of many more unions. By independence in 1964, Malawi had 19 trade unions with a membership of 4,763 (Ministry of Labour, 1969). However, the need for independence shaped the functioning of trade unions during the colonial period. As workers associated poor working conditions with foreign government and employers, they felt that they had a duty to join nationalist politicians who agitated for independence. Workers organised political strikes in collaboration with nationalist politicians in support of independence struggles on the assumption that economic benefits – in the form of higher wages and good conditions of employment – would emerge with political independence (Wood, 1992). Between 1947 and 1963, there were 247 strikes recorded by the Department of Labour.

Independence and trade union movement

When Malawi became independent from Britain in 1964, she soon drifted to single party rule: a one-party constitution was adopted in 1966. It was during the one-party period that an authoritarian state emerged. An attack by six cabinet ministers on President Banda's domestic and external policies six weeks after the 6 July 1964 independence celebrations led to the President clamping down on his opponents.

In the run-up to independence, the trade union movement had already experienced a number of setbacks. The first involved the Malawi Congress Party (MCP) changing its position *vis-à-vis* workers' interests. With signs in 1960 that Britain was ready to end its rule, MCP's attention focused on encouraging unity and socioeconomic development at the expense of workers' interests. Trade unionists saw MCP's concept of unity as tantamount to absolute trade union subordination to the MCP (McCracken 1988) and this widened the gulf between the labour movement and government.

After independence, labour controls continued, as the independent regime assumed the characteristics of the colonial authority: violent repression combined with a highly centralised system of governance, which bore hard on the labour movement. The Government's negative attitude towards unions stemmed from the assumption that the unions' demands would push up production costs and that industrial action would disrupt production and reduce profits. Political leadership in turn influenced management systems at the workplace: managers were dictatorial, one-way communication prevailed as directives were issued from above. Workers could not negotiate wages and conditions of employment. The Employers' Consultative Association of Malawi – formed in 1956 as the Nyasaland Employers' Association – remained on very good terms with the Government throughout the one party period owing to the apparent workplace compliance brought about by the Government's labour policy: control on unionism, absence of collective bargaining, suppression of the right to strike, and a low wage policy were all to the advantage of employers.

By the end of the 1980s, the trade union movement was so docile that an observer could have concluded that there were no trade unions at all. Out of 19 trade unions at independence, 5 remained on paper – the Malawi Railways Workers Union, the Building Construction, Civil Engineering and Allied Workers Union, the Transport and General Workers Union, the Local Government Workers Union and the Plantation and Agriculture Workers Union. They were 'on paper' because they held no meetings, conducted no elections, although at times leaders benefited from seminars and workshops funded by the state. As the following sections will demonstrate, this harsh industrial relations climate changed in the early 1990s.

Industrial relations legislation

Throughout the one-party period, the state used the Trade Unions Act 1958, the Trade Disputes (Arbitration and Settlement) Act of 1952 and the Employment Act 1964 as the major industrial relations legal framework. One of the key problems to this framework was that it restricted freedom of association through the empowering of the Registrar of Trade Unions to control the formation and registration of trade unions, operation and financial management of the unions, international affiliation and assistance to trade unions from international trade union fraternity. Collective bargaining was never spelt out in the Trade Unions Act 1958. Reliance was put on Wages Advisory Councils and Wages Board created under the Minimum Wages (Miscellaneous Provisions) Act 1964 to determine wages and conditions of service but Government's Low Wage Policy of 1968 made these councils and board mere talking shops. The exclusion of collective bargaining in the Trade Union Act 1958 had created a gap in the legal framework and prevented the development of bargaining experience among workers and employers. There was also severe control of the right to strike as there was no clear framework for strikes in non-essential services. Essential services were severely restricted in the Trade Disputes (Arbitration and Settlement) Act 1952. The Ministry of Labour was under-funded and poorly staffed to the extent that it could not afford to inspect workplaces to check minimum standards of service including wages, or review legislation which became obsolete as economic and social conditions kept on changing. The massive strike waves of 1992–93, amidst international pressure for good governance, observance of human rights and accountability, led to major reforms in industrial relations legislation.

New labour policy

Growing pressures from the shopfloor forced the state to rethink its industrial relations policies: in 1993 the state published a new policy on collective bargaining and trade unions. It formally promised to encourage the right to organise and engage in collective bargaining and affiliation to international organisations and to support employers and workers' education programmes and the training of union leaders. The encouragement of freedom of association and non-victimisation in employment and the provision of the necessary legal framework and administrative arrangements for freedom of association and collective bargaining were other facets of the new policy. Unlike the one-party constitution which did not make any provision for labour rights, the 1995 National Constitution, enshrined human rights provisions that supported independent trade unions. Section 13(l) provided for the peaceful settlement of disputes through negotiation, good offices, mediation, conciliation and arbitration. Section 31 gave the right to fair and safe labour practices, fair remuneration, the right to form and join trade unions or not form or join trade unions, fair wages and equal remuneration for work of equal value and the right to withdraw labour.

The Labour Relations Act 1996

The enactment of the Labour Relations Act (LRA) 1996 to 'promote sound labour relations through the protection and promotion of freedom of association, the encouragement of effective collective bargaining and the promotion of orderly dispute settlement conducive to social justice and economic development' represented a further step to reform. This Act signified a major transformation by making adequate provisions to enhance freedom of association, collective bargaining, dispute settlement and the right to strike. It prohibits discrimination on grounds of race, colour, nationality, ethnic or social extraction, religion, political opinion, language, sex, marital status, family responsibilities, age, disability, property or birth. Unlike the previous Act the Registrar's power to control union formation and operation is limited. The Registrar cannot cancel the registration of a trade union at his own volition unless at the request of the organisation itself or by an order of the Industrial Relations Court (IRC). The LRA gives unions' freedom to receive external funding and to spend monies on activities without the authority of the Registrar of Trade Unions although trade unions are required to send annual audited accounts to the Registrar. The right to strike was confirmed by the 1995 Constitution.

Employment Act 2000

Individual employment rights are now embodied in the Employment Act 2000. It incorporates employment principles enshrined in the 1995 constitution and the ILO conventions. One significant provision is that the EA applies to all employees including those in Government, public authority or corporation (s.2), unlike the previous Act that applied to the lowest paid employees only. The Act prohibits discrimination in recruitment, training, promotions, terms and conditions of employment, termination of employment and termination on grounds of race, colour, sex, language, religion, and political or other opinion. The Act is clear on hours of work, overtime, payment of wages, annual leave, and maternity leave, disciplinary procedure, dismissals and remedies for unfair dismissal. While the employer has the power to summarily dismiss an employee on grounds of misconduct, lack of skill or any other reason, an employee has a right to lodge his grievance with the IRC for 'unfair dismissal' or 'unfair labour practices' with the burden of proof resting with the employer. The balance of power created by the EA has reduced the powers of employers and the state and enhanced workers' power. While in the past the state could dictate labour-related issues for employers and employees to comply, and employers could change the 'rules of the game', the EA empowers workers to challenge the employer's right to manage.

Present industrial relations practices

In assessing the current industrial relations practices key issues to be examined include freedom of association and trade unions in the 1990s and beyond; collective bargaining, dispute resolution and the right to strike.

Freedom of association: trade unions in the 1990s and beyond

The resurgence of the labour movement after three decades of dormancy needs to be understood against the background of the wider impact of the 1992–93 strike waves following the transition to plural politics. Against the background of positive state policy in industrial relations, through the encouragement of trade unions and collective bargaining that came with the 1993 policy on trade unions and collective bargaining, a process of worker self-organisation and renewal started. In October 1993, the Trade Union Congress of Malawi (TUCM) organised a Commonwealth Trade Union Council funded workshop aimed at resuscitating the labour movement. On 27 June 1995 the TUCM was legally registered under the name Malawi Congress of Trade Unions (MCTU). By the end of 1994 the Ministry of Labour had registered twelve private and public sectors unions (the existing five and seven new ones).

The number of registered unions increased from 12 to 19 during 1994–99. Table 5.1 shows union membership by 1999.

Table 5.1 Union Growth in Malawi – 1999

Name of Trade Union	Date registered	Membership		Density (%)
		Actual	Potential	
MCTU	27-6-95	17 unions	20 unions	
CSTU	23-1-95	2,000	45,000	4
TUM	1-2-95	35,000	50,000	70
CWU	1-2-95	200	1,000	20
CIWU	1-2-95	10,000	30,000	33
SPAWU	1-2-95	500	12,000	4
HFCWU	9-2-95	5,000	15,000	33
LGEU	9-2-95	1,200	12,000	10
TGWU	1-2-95	3,000	10,000	30
BCCEAWU	17-3-95	20,000	40,000	50
RWU	24-2-95	1,200	1,800	67
PAWU	14-2-95	9,000	200,000	4
TGLSSU	14-2-95	1,800	30,000	6
EMWU	15-4-98	284	800	36
CSBTU	21-4-98	na	na	na
ESCOM	21-4-98	1,600	2,000	80
TTAWU	21-4-98	na	na	na
MHCWU	9-11-98	na	na	na
MPTCWU	26-11-98	3,500	5,182	68

Source: Dzimbiri (2002).

By 2000 the Congress for Malawi Trade Unions (COMATU), a second labour federation and an MCTU breakaway, brought the total number of trade unions to 21 (Ministry of Labour, 2000); by 2005 there were 25 unions with a total membership of 119,230.

Employers Consultative Association of Malawi (ECAM)

The Employers' Consultative Association was created in Malawi as a reaction to the growth and development of trade unions in the country. During the one party period it was called the Employers Consultative Association of Malawi (ECAM) and its role has been to function as a representative of the employers in tripartite meetings with Government and trade unions; as an information bureau; to train employers in collective bargaining, dispute settlement and interpret labour laws to its members; and to represent its members at international level. During the one-party period, the association spoke the same language with the Banda regime because the industrial peace that reigned was good for employers. The repression of the labour movement was to their advantage. ECAM held seminars and workshops for its members during the one-party period: it was one of the better organised actors in industrial relations throughout the one-party period. During the transition to a multiparty state, when worker militancy erupted amidst political changes, ECAM, like the Government of Malawi, was taken unaware because it had not developed the skills required to negotiate with workers due to a long period of industrial peace. It simply issued a statement asking its members to resolve disputes with employees amicably and quickly in the interest of the nation.

Collective bargaining

The political system that existed between independence and 1991 prevented workers from demanding improvements in wages and conditions of employment. Laws of detention without trial and the sudden disappearance of dissidents scared workers and employers. Following the labour law reforms of the 1990s, the LRA made provisions for enterprise and sectoral level bargaining as long as a 20 per cent membership threshold has been attained (s.25). Where an employer refuses to recognise a trade union, the latter can appeal to the IRC, if the employer is the Government or a public corporation; or to the Secretary for Labour for private sector employers/employees. Where the 20 per cent threshold is not possible, a union or an employer association could apply for the establishment of an Industrial Council which is composed of employer and employee representatives to negotiate wages and conditions of employment, establish dispute resolution machinery and develop an industrial policy for the industry concerned. The need for parties to negotiate in good faith, produce written and duly signed collective agreements, the legal enforceability of collective agreements, submission of copy of collective agreements to the Registrar and disclosure of information by parties to the negotiation as entrenched in the LRA have the potential to enhance collective bargaining and the protection of workers' and employers' interests. However, employers, through the Employers Consultative Association, have vehemently protested the 20 per cent threshold as undemocratic and pro-worker. It is worthy noting that collective bargaining has on the majority of cases occurred only after workers have gone on strike. In other words, rather than being the last resort after all effort have failed, the strike is the precursor of collective bargaining. One reason offered by the majority of workers is employers' delaying tactics in handling workers' grievances – the strike is meant to demonstrate that workers are serious. There have been a lot of gains in terms of wages and conditions of employment resulting from the rise of collective bargaining.

However, public sector reforms that have been going on since the liberalisation of the economy have placed constraints on the scope of collective bargaining. Fiscal discipline by the government as part of IMF and World Bank sponsored reforms has meant that any bargaining process in the public sector has to take account of the imposed restraints on the national budget. At the eve of the New Year in 1996 for example, the President announced a 25 per cent salary increase across the entire public service, only to be frowned upon by donors who threatened to withdraw of funding if the salary increase was implemented. To the embarrassment of the Government, the said salary increase was postponed to April the following year, and subsequently it was never implemented. The feeling of helplessness by both employees and their employer in collective bargaining in the midst of IMF conditionality have been aptly captured by a local musician, now a member of Parliament, Mlaka Maliro, who in his music, queries the government whether its constituency is the IMF or the people that voted it into power. This is a reaction to the tendency by the Government to listen more to the IMF than to the grievances of its own citizens and employees. Retrenchment, occasioned by privatisation of public enterprises, has reduced not only the membership of trade unions in many sectors, but has also cautioned workers from demanding better conditions of employment and higher wages when there are few employment opportunities left. For example, out of the 42 public enterprises privatised by 2002, about 48,000 jobs were lost against 30,000 new jobs created. Union leaders are even more concerned because they are more vulnerable to selective retrenchment.

Disputes resolution and the right to strike

The procedure for settling disputes and taking industrial action are articulated in sections 42–54 of the LRA. There is a need for either party to report any dispute to the Secretary for Labour (PS) who arranges for conciliation and mediation after voluntary procedures have been exhausted. The PS has to be satisfied that the dispute settlement procedures established in the collective agreement have been exhausted, unless both parties have decided to waive those procedures. If one party to the dispute is the Government (including a public authority or a commercial enterprise in which the Government has an interest), the parties shall agree on the conciliator. Where parties are unable to agree on the conciliator, the Industrial Relations Court shall designate an independent arbitrator on application by either party. The dispute shall be resolved within 21 days otherwise it shall be designated an 'unresolved dispute'. In such cases, the secretary for labour or either party to the dispute shall apply to the IRC for determination if the matter involves essential services or the interpretation of statutory provision or any provision of the collective agreement or contract of employment. But if the matter involves interest disputes, and is deemed unresolved, either party can apply to the IRC for determination or give at least 7 days' notice to the PS that they intend a strike or lockout. The LRA provides procedures for a strike or lockout in case a dispute is unresolved and prohibits strikes in essential service.

It was not until the transition to multiparty democracy that the tremendous awakening of the labour movement really took place: large-scale strikes erupted, starting at David Whitehead & Sons Textile Company on 5 May 1992. As Van Donge (1995: 230) noted, 'the fabric of society seemed fundamentally shaken by riots resulting from industrial unrest in Blantyre and Lilongwe'. In the first two weeks of May 1992, 66 strikes were reported and over 50 people were killed by the police as they opened fire to restore law and order. Public and private sector organisations participated in the various waves of strikes that characterised Malawi in the 1990s. The biggest single employer of over 136,000, the civil service, experienced two big strikes that paralysed the country's health, education, transport and other services. Teachers, nurses, junior doctors, custom officers, and clerical officers all went on strike at different times demanding increases in salaries, allowances, overtime payments and general improvement in conditions of service, removal of arrogant managers and protesting at Government maize and petrol prices. Between 1992 and 1999, the *Daily Times* reported of 90 strikes (Dzimbiri, 2002). 54 organisations that reported only 4 strikes for the 1966–91 period reported 75 strikes involving 70,000 workers and 400,000 days lost (ibid: 133). Official records, which did not include 50 strikes including many in the civil service, show that there were 300 strikes involving 270,000 workers and 800,000 days lost compared to 182 strikes, 19,000 workers involved and 27,000 days lost during the 1966–91 period. Thus, the 1992–99 decade experienced a much greater amount of strike activity on all counts compared to the three decades of the one-party period-one and half times the numbers of strikes, 13 times as many workers involved and 28 times as many days lost. Strikers did not just demand improved wages and conditions of employment. They also demanded the removal of senior managers and challenged or defied employers' and Government dismissal threats. Some challenged Government policy on privatisation and maize prices and refused to meet middle managers and demanded to meet the State President or Vice President. Many of these strikes were without warning, used as economic weapons and were political instruments.

Redundancies and union busting

Anti-union behaviour in the form of victimisation of union leaders, refusal of time-off for union activities, refusal of access by unions to workplaces by employers, divide and rule tactics are some of the issues unionists have raised in recent years. Retrenchment is one of the dangers unionists were exposed to. A union leader is the first person to be retrenched. Anti-union attitudes have negatively impacted on the prospects of unions. For instance, out of the 11 unions the Ministry of Labour's study analysed, 6 were declining as shown in Table 5.2.

While some unions are gaining members, others are losing. BCCEAWU and PAWU are examples of the latter case. State officials viewed membership decline as a product of many factors, such as members' loss of faith due to failed strikes, reluctance to pay union fees, poor leadership, financial constraints, travel problems to meet members, and the alliances some union leaders made with opposition politicians. Unionists viewed the decline as the result of the state's 'hide-and-seek' and 'divide-and-rule tactics' (Dzimbiri, 2004). While these could be genuine explanations for low membership in some unions, the gains shown in the other unions within the same period require other explanations.

Table 5.2 Membership growth and decline in Malawian unions – 1995-99

Name	Estimated no. 1995	Estimated no. 1999	Rise(+)/decline(−)
CSTU	2000	800	−1200
TUM	30,000	35,000	+5,000
TGWU	3,000	6,500	+3,500
LGEU	1,200	1,100	−100
CIAWU	1,000	6,000	+5,000
SPAWU	1,000	6,000	+5,500
HFPCWU	500	5,000	+4,500
RWU	1,2000	800	−400
BCCEWU	20,000	2,000	−18,000
PAWU	9,000	2,000	−7,000
TLSWU	1,800	1,000	−800

Source: Ministry of Labour (2000: 13) – recalculated.

Conclusion

Industrial relations in Malawi witnessed a major transformation in the 1990s following political and economic transformation of the country. Many labour rights that were lost during the one-party era were recovered. Freedom of association, collective bargaining, dispute resolution and the right to withdraw labour are rights Malawian workers have gained in recent years. Nonetheless, the government faces of the challenge of reconciling economic development dictates, and neo-liberal calls for competitiveness and efficiency, with demands by the international community for human rights and good governance. Inevitably, the state wishes to attract private sector investment, which, in the Malawian context is most forthcoming when costs of production – in reality, mostly wages – are low, and there is industrial peace.

Industrial relations reforms in the 1990s stemmed from the political reforms that led into the transition from the one-party to a multiparty state. This major state transformation was possible as a result of international pressure and in particular the withholding of Malawi's non-humanitarian aid and calls for democratic reforms. Since 1989 the World Bank has abandoned its previous purely economistic interpretations of African crisis and advocated instead good governance, gender equality, decentralisation of power, human rights, the need to check corruption and the involvement of local people in decision-making (Ihonvbere, 2000). The consequence of this pressure led to the 1993 national referendum and the 1994 general election that in turn led to the formal creation of a multiparty state in Malawi. The one-party state was not subjected to pressures for good governance and democratic reforms for close to three decades. Human rights violations such as detention without trial, forced donations to the president, murder of dissidents, repression of freedom of speech and association, which Amnesty International documented (1993), did not lead to an international outcry at the time. One reason for this had been Malawi's capitalist and pro-western stance during the Cold War period; Western capitalist nations saw Malawi as a good ally. Like other authoritarian Africa states which received international financial support despite human rights violations (Ihonvbere, 2000), Malawi continued to receive financial aid from the donor community. The fact that such a position was maintained for three decades suggests that the international community indirectly helped the creation of a status quo in the role of the state in industrial relations. By reacting to human rights violations and imposing economic sanctions, the Western donor community facilitated the breakdown of an authoritarian one-party state and the creation of a multiparty state and therefore a new industrial relations regime. The question we cannot answer yet, but is crucial, is how far the externally-induced changes in Malawi have become institutionalised and can be sustained in practice. There are numerous examples of failures of democracies in Africa as evidenced by arguments over electoral results, voting along regional lines as the case of the 1994 and 1999 general elections in Malawi (Patel, 2000) which also resurfaced in the 2004 elections; lack of tolerance for dissenting views, and suppression of labour rights. These are symptomatic of deep-rooted problems, which would continue to confront democracy, human rights and therefore, pluralistic industrial relations in Malawi and some parts of Africa.

Note

1. Detention without trial, repression of basic freedoms, politically motivated murder of dissidents, forced party card sales, forced attendance at MCP meetings, gifts to the head of state, and the punitive role of youth league wing of the party in the rural and urban areas.

Bibliography

Amnesty International (1993), *Malawi: Preserving the One Party State – Human Rights Violation and the Referendum*. London: International Secretariat.
Chipeta, C. (1999), 'The Malawian Economy Under the First Multiparty Government', *Southern African Political Economy Monthly*, 12: 5, 36–43.
Dzimbiri, L. (1994), 'The Malawi Referendum Elections of 1993', *International Journal of Electoral Studies*, 13, 3: 228–34.
Dzimbiri, L. Ngware, S. & Ocharo, R.M.(2000), *Multipartism and People's Participation: Multiparty Democracy in Kenya, Malawi, and Tanzania*. Dar-es-Salaam: TEMA Publishers.
Dzimbiri, L. (2002), 'Industrial Relations, the State and Striker Activity in Malawi', unpublished PhD dissertation, Keele University, UK.

Dzimbiri, L. (2004), 'Trade Unionism under the one-party and Multiparty Political Systems in Malawi', *Malawi Journal of Social Science*, 18. 17–33.

GoM, (1995a), *Policy Framework for Poverty Alleviation*. Lilongwe.

GoM, (2004), *Malawi Economic Growth Strategy*. Lilongwe: Government Press.

Ihonvbere, J. (2000), 'Politics of Constitutional Reforms and Democratization in Africa', *International Journal of Comparative Sociology* 41:1, 9–26.

McCracken, J. (1988), 'Labour in Nyasaland: An Assessment of the 1960 Railway Workers' Strike', *Journal of Southern African Studies* 14: 2: 279–90.

Ministry of Labour, (1969), *Report of the Ministry of Labour 1963–1968*. Lilongwe.

Ministry of Labour, (2000) *Human Rights and Employment Report*. Lilongwe. Otanez, M. (1995), *Labour and Democratisation in Malawi*. MA thesis, Institute of Social Studies, The Hague.

Patel, N. (2000), '1999 Elections in Malawi: Challenges and Reforms', in Ott, M., Phiri, K. and Patel, N. (eds), *Malawi's Second Democratic Elections: Process, Problems and Prospects*. Blantyre: CLAIM.

Pike, J.G. (1968), *Malawi: A Political and Economic History*. London: Pall Mall Press.

Van Donge, J. (1995), 'Kamuzu's Legacy: The Democratization of Malawi or Searching for the Rules of the Game in African Politics', *African Affairs*, 94: 227–57.

Wood, T. (1992), 'Bread with Freedom and Peace: Rail Workers in Malawi, 1954–1975', *Journal of Southern African Studies*, 18:4: 727–38.

National Statistical Office of Malawi (NSO) (2001), Malawi, Statistics. Lilongwe:

6
Contemporary Issues in Industrial Relations: Uganda

Joy T. Kirenga

Introduction

Arguably, there has been more turbulence in Uganda in issues affecting industrial relations than in many other countries. Events during and since the colonial era have been dramatic and often bloody and continue to affect the lives of ordinary Ugandans. As a result, the country has an industrial relations system that is, in effect, a 'work in progress' rather than an established system. The discussion in this chapter will examine the historical and economic context as well as the effects of structural adjustments and privatisation on the experience and practice of the main players. Finally, we discuss the way forward.

Uganda's historical context

Uganda was a British Protectorate until independence in 1962. Since then, Uganda has gone through a number of political upheavals, including military government. These have brought insecurity. There has been civil war in the northern part of the country, where civilians have lived either in the bush or protected camps for the last 20 years. The dynamic historical and socio-economic changes in Uganda have affected the labour situation and labour relations. Issues include minimal employment, high unemployment rates, and low wages compared to the cost of living. Poverty among the working people has become widespread all over the country since the 20-year old war has claimed millions of people and billions of shillings.

Overview of the economy

The agricultural sector forms the cornerstone of the Ugandan economy. It accounts for about 40 per cent of the total Gross Domestic Product (GDP), over 70 per cent of total exports, and about 80 per cent of employment. Eighty five per cent of Uganda's population of 22 million live in rural areas and depend mainly on agriculture for their livelihood (Fashoyin, et al.: internet). Coffee has historically been Uganda's main business. In 2001, it was estimated that majority of households depended on coffee as an important or the only source of cash income. Most Ugandans now in the age bracket of 45–60 years managed to get basic or even better education only because their parents had coffee as their source of cash income: coffee was booming. It is a different story now.

Uganda's economy has great potential; it is endowed with significant natural resources including copper and cobalt. The country enjoyed a strong and stable period in the years approaching independence in 1962. On top of agricultural products, there were valuable minerals, especially copper, discovered at Kilembe in Western Uganda. In 1967 Uganda and the neighbouring countries Kenya and Tanzania joined together to form the East African Community (EAC) with the aim of creating a common market and sharing the cost of transport. Uganda registered impressive growth rates for the first eight years after Independence.

The economy deteriorated under the rule of President Idi Amin Dada from 1971 to 1979. Amin's militaristic government had ill chosen economic policies and aimed to eliminate the Asians who had previously managed the economy. Amin gave all Asians with British passports 90 days in which to leave the country; and added that those who dared to remain, 'would be sitting on fire!'. Ugandans, who had no experience in running businesses, took over the shops and other enterprises, while military officers became Managing Directors of important enterprises like the Coffee Marketing Board. Within a few years, those businesses were no more. This had a severe impact on employment patterns and industrial relations. All active people started getting money through the *'magendo'* (the black market), characterised by smuggling coffee to the neighbouring countries, especially Zaire and Kenya. Uganda's years of political turmoil left the country with substantial loan repayments, a weak currency and high inflation rates.

The Museveni regime, which came into power from 1986, put in place an Economic Recovery Programme (ERP) with the aim of achieving a stable and steady macro-economic framework. This was meant to promote growth by providing an enabling environment for private sector investment. The National Agricultural Research Organisation (NARO) aimed at strengthening research in agriculture leading to a unified extension system. The extension system ensured technology transfer to small-holder farmers. This was successful: the agricultural sector registered a remarkable recovery with annual growth rates ranging from four to ten per cent between 1986 and 1999.

The government also negotiated a policy framework paper with IMF and started implementing policies designed to restore price stability and producer incentives through proper price control and re-allocation of public sector work. Inflation reduced from 54 per cent in 1995–96 to 5.1 per cent in 2004. However, in spite of registering remarkable achievements in the agricultural sector, there were, and still are, constraints in marketing infrastructure, finance and environmental degradation. International markets for Uganda's traditional export crops have become much more competitive; and yet Uganda has limited world markets prospects for its food crops.

Uganda's economy being predominantly based on peasant agriculture, most Ugandans work outside the monetary economy, and also outside paid employment. Industrial relations needs to be set in the context that there are very low levels of paid employment.

Employment and employment trends

The number in paid employment is limited, especially with regard to jobs in industry. Even amongst waged employment, the agricultural sector (particularly sugar and tea estates and flower production) contains many of the major employers in the country. The big agricultural estates operate with a core staff of permanent workers, using seasonal/casual workers as need arises. Most industries and services in Uganda depend on the agricultural sector. Uganda is endowed with a favourable climate conducive for agriculture, and most wage earners are able to survive, in a country where official wages have fallen below the cost of living, because they have access to land where they or their extended families can raise food crops.

Multinational Enterprises (MNEs) in the country, especially in the agricultural sector, have contributed to the promotion of employment opportunities and the reduction of poverty in Uganda. MNE plantations have not only provided significant direct employment in rural areas, but have helped to sustain the livelihoods of many thousands of other workers through indirect employment as well. It seems that now, however, MNEs are turning towards the casualisation of labour.

In Uganda strikes are used often, especially among the plantation workers where they burn plantations of sugarcane whenever the employer fails to improve their wages and conditions of work. The agricultural sector experienced a high incidence of industrial unrest, in particular in the 1990s with the greatest number of working days lost to strikes in 1996.[1] High on the agenda amongst the causes of dispute is, commonly, workers' demands for higher wages, a reduction in excessive work, and poor and inadequate quantities of meals provided to the manual workers in the sugar plantations. Table 6.1 highlights some examples.

The government is the largest single employer through its civil service and medical and education services. Though independent organisations, trade unions are expected to abide by government regulations, right from the formation of workers' organisations and during their operations.

The government determines which trade union should be officially recognised in case of any competition in a new multi-partism system in Uganda. Uganda has been called to appeared before the ILO Committee of Experts, signifying that all is not well with industrial relations. In 2004, for instance, a case was taken against Uganda by the International Textiles, Garment and Leather Workers Federation (ITGLWF), in which the company TRI-STAR[2] mistreated and dismissed staff without notice.

Table 6.1 Showing causes of strikes in the last 6 years

Year	Organisation	No. of staff	Reasons
2000	1. Century Bottling Company, Cocola Nakawa	Unskilled and skilled 90 people	1. Management's refusal to attend to workers problems within 2 weeks as earlier agreed
	2. Century Bottling Company	Same (150 people)	2. Breach of agreement by not victimising workers
	3. Cable Corporation Ltd. Lugazi	66	3. No overtime paid Unfair dismissal of Branch Chairperson by management Pay increase
	4. Cable Corporation		
	5. Rwenzori	Same as above 400 people	Pay raise Protest against Graduate tax deductions and lack of protective wear
2001	Moyo District Health workers	284, skilled and unskilled workers	Delay for salaries Failure to pay Failure to access pay roll
	Mweru/Nakigira Tea Estates Kakira Jinja	Unskilled	Wages increase
	M/S Windsor Lake Victoria Hotel	70 semi and skilled workers	Dismissal of one shop steward and 2 other persons external influence so salary increases for 2 years
	Nakigira Tea Estate (Entebbe Wakiso District)	200 unskilled	Demand for wages increase
2002	1. Kinyara Sugar Works Ltd Masindi	420 unskilled	Introduction of Pay as you earn (PAYE)
	2. M/S Energo (U) Ltd Ntungamo-Rukungiri Road Construction	300	Demand to be allowed to join the Union
	3. Kinyara Sugar Works	600 unskilled and skilled	Introduction of 4 shifts without consulting workers
	4. Kinyara Sugar Works	450 unskilled and skilled	Protest against Graduated Tax assessment
	5. Uganda Fishnet Ltd, Kla	46 unskilled	Delayed negotiations and terminal benefits

(Continued)

Table 6.1 (Continued)

Year	Organisation	No. of staff	Reasons
2003	Apparels Tri-Star (U) Ltd, Kla	1,200 semi skilled and unskilled workers	Dismissal of staff Refusal of workers to join trade union Working long hours Unfair terminals and no benefits paid Communication breakdown between workers and personnel officer
2004	1. Energo (U)Ltd.Ntungamo	120 both skilled and unskilled	Violation of CBAs Refusal to confirm workers on probation
	2. Ug. Fishnet Ltd. Kla	60 semi and unskilled	Non promotion of protective gear
	3. Tororo Cement Industries Ltd. Tororo	(1232 workers) Senior, skilled and unskilled	Management refused to honour earlier agreement on payments of arrears Lack of welfare policy Casualisation of labour Failure to implement CBA
2005	Uganda Railways Corporation, Kla	Skilled	Payment of consolidatied salary Factor of 1/500 in pension payment
	Makerere University	300 day one and 900 day two (both skilled and unskilled)	Demand for pay raise paid to Academic staff by government

Source: Strikes Register in Ministry of Labour and Employment.

Legal framework

The Commissioner for Employment, Labour and Industrial Relations is charged with the responsibility of enforcing legislation. The constitution of the Republic of Uganda, gives full freedom of association and the right to strike through Articles 29 and 40. The government has also shown good will towards freedom of association even for traditional public services employees, who were originally not allowed to form trade unions. The current government's policy is to accord a voice to workers by allowing representation in the Uganda Parliament, with five workers representatives under the 'marginalised group' category.

There are general legislative statutes that establish minimum standards for working conditions in the country. Such conditions are set out in the Employment Act; the Trades Disputes (Arbitration and Settlement) Act; the Factory Act, 1964; the Trade Unions Decree 1976; and the Workers Compensation Act, 2000. Uganda recently (2006) ratified the Freedom of Association and Protection of the Right to Organise Convention, 1948 (No.87), and the Collective Bargaining Convention, 1949 (No.89). There was a fear that Convention 89 would encourage multi-partyism. Between 1986 and 2006, Uganda had been operating under the 'one umbrella' system of government. In February 2006 Ugandans were able to elect their leaders under multi-party politics and the Convention was ratified.

Uganda's labour laws have been obsolete for many decades. It is only recently that, after going through extensive reviews for more than ten years, some bills have become operational. The labour laws that do exist in relation to protection of employees have not been fully effective with regard to application and compliance, since the economic forces have long overridden the labour legislation (Ssekaana, 1998).[3] One good example is the so-called Minimum Wage, enacted in 1984. The lowest paid person should earn a monthly salary of Ugandan Shillings 6,000 (at the end of 2006, the dollar exchange rate was 1,810); but it has fallen into abeyance. The lowest annual pay in public service at the end of 2006 was Ugandan Shillings 60,000. In organisations where trade unions have negotiated salaries the pay is slightly more. Most people in paid employment in Uganda live below the poverty line.

Employers and their organisations

The Federation of Uganda Employers (FUE) is the umbrella organisation of employers. FUE's membership includes the public and private sectors and non-governmental organisations (NGOs). FUE carries out training programmes within the sector in order to improve industrial relations, reduce exploitation and safety hazards. Key among the functions FUE provides to its members are representation on questions of economic and social policy; guidance on employment relations; training; specific assistance on small enterprise and entrepreneurship development; and training on HIV/AIDS in the world of work.

Certain minimum standards of wages and conditions are a must if the organisation has to recruit and maintain labour, as well as to sustain 'morale'. The employer must balance retaining the workers in employment with the cost of doing so. That naturally means that workers' jobs are always at the mercy of economic condition of a given country. For example, Mukwano Industries have even refused to recognise trade unions in their organisation. Most employers are not bothered with good working conditions even though there is an argument that good working conditions are important for labour absorption and retention by any organisation (Kiguundu, 1998).

Employees and their organisations

The first trade unions in Uganda, in 1939, were more political vehicles/platforms than workers' representative organisations. There was only one national centre, the National Organisation of Trade Unions (NOTU), affiliating the 21 unions. Currently there are two national Centres, the new one being the Confederation of Free Trade Unions (COFTU), which affiliates 4 of those unions. The economic and political crisis of the 1970s reduced membership. Even though the constitution allows for formation of trade unions in the workplace, many managers tend to isolate key members of the trade unions. Some Ugandan institutions, even educational ones, have discouraged staff who hold diplomas and degrees from joining or participating in the union; arguing that trade unions are for low level staff. The guidelines for electing a University Council Workers Representative (2006–2011) state that only intermediate (eg filing clerk) and group employees (eg cleaners or cooks) are eligible to stand as candidates for the National Union of Educational Institutions. This is a effort to ensure that they are composed of semi-illiterate staff who will not manage to negotiate with or challenge management.

Current challenges in industrial relations in Uganda

In Uganda both trade unions and government centres of power, which are responsible for dealing with conflicts, are weak. There is no functional Industrial Court in the country. The industrial court's operations are seasonal: there are always excuses that, for example, there is no President of such a court.

- **Inadequate funding**: The Ministry of Labour and Employment, which is directly involved in industrial relations issues, is poorly funded. Inadequate resources provided to the Ministry prevent it putting in place inspection committees to ascertain the quality of the working environment.
- **Conflicts**: There are numerous conflictual situations between employer/employee; the Uganda Medical Workers Union and the Teachers Union are often locked in conflict with government over pay and allowances.

- **Union to union conflict:** The conflict between COFTU and NOTU has even split the Uganda Government and Allied Workers' Union, with each centre having one arm of the same union. Conflicts at the unions' national centre, or between unions, undermines the solidarity of the workers' cause. In-house fighting is a weakness that employer and government can exploit.
- **Threat of investors:** Investors in the country are reluctant to recognise Uganda laws, denying their workers the right to organise and join a trade union. Investors have even contributed to unemployment in Ugandans by importing cheaper labour. In the recent shake-up of Uganda Railways, where the old Ugandan management was overhauled, 'the old' were replaced by staff from South Africa, the new owners. Several other staff members in technical positions were laid off, which is typical of investors.
- **Unemployment:** The current high rate of unemployment has psychologically affected both the employed and the unemployed. Those who have jobs fear to lose them and, hence, accept poor working conditions. They fear to participate in union activities, hence reduction of union membership. Some even fear to taken their annual leave!

These challenges are aggravated by an assumption by employers/investors that liberalisation policy gives them the liberty to restructure labour costs and downsize staff, so as to improve on the efficiency and competitiveness of an industry.

The way forward

Identifying any way forward for industrial/ labour relations in Uganda is difficult because of a variety of unpredictable factors. First, as this chapter is written, factories are closing because of the limited amount of hydro-electric power countrywide, as a result of low water levels. As if that was not enough, high power tariffs were set arbitrarily (Daily Monitor newspaper).

Second, in 2006 Kenya and Uganda handed over their 110 years old railways operations to a joint venture led by South Africa's Sheltam Trade Close (Daily Monitor newspaper). The Uganda Railway workers Union was among the first trade unions in the country. These recent changes means that they will be expecting cuts in jobs – which will increase unemployment and poverty.

There may be some hope. The longstanding and outdated labour laws were revised in 2005 and are now operational. All stakeholders are hoping that such laws will be sustainable, especially the Compensation Law that required employers to pay a lot of money in the case of an accident.

The new Minister for Gender, Labour and Social Development is down-to-earth about ensuring that there is harmony amongst the stakeholders of industrial relations. The Commissioner for Labour, Employment and Industrial Relations agrees and adds that there should also be clear implementation of labour laws, which should no longer be ignored.

There is a need for a government policy in which attention should be paid to manpower development to train human resource core of the country with a national policy of salary /wages which should depend on ones educational qualifications, in order to avoid big gaps between employees of the same qualifications in different institutions, a problem in the country, leading to frequent strikes.

Notes

1. http://www.ilo.orgpublic/english/employment/multi/download/wp93.pd/search Uganda (p.10)
2. CASE No.2378 (GB.294/7/1) p.273
3. Ssekaana, M.(1998): Adequqcy of Labour Laws in the Employeer and employee Relations in Uanda (p.3.)

Bibliography

Armstrong, M.(2001): *Human Resource Management Practice*. Kogan Page, London
Hyman, R. (1975): *Industrial Relations a Marxist Introduction* Macmillan, London
internet:http://www.referenceforbusiness.com.encyclopedia/inc.inte.industrial-Relations.htm/
Kiggundu, D. (1998): *Employment Potential and Manpower. Retention for Small Scale Enterprises in Kampala* (dissertation unpublished)
Salamon, M.: (1998) *Industrial Relations Theory and Practice 3rd edition* Prentice Hall Europe, London .pg 3
Scott, R. (1966). *The Development of Trade Unions in Uganda*. East African Publishing House. Nairobi.
Fashoyin, T. et al *(Multinational enterprises in the planation sector:Labour relations, employment, working conditions and welfare facilities (*http://www.ilo.org/publis/english/employment/multi/download/wp93.pdf)
(http://www.ilo.org/public/english/multi/download/wp93.pd//search Uganda www.state.gov/r/pa/ei/bgn/2963.htm
Daily Monitor Newspaper of 3rd Nov.06 p.4
Selwyn, N (1996) *Law of Employment* 9th Ed. Butterworths, London.
Obeng-Fosu, P. (1991): *Industrial Relations in Ghana. The Law and Practice*. University Press. Accra.
The Constitution of Uganda 1995
Gonsalves, R. (1974) *The Politics of Trade Unions and Industrial Relations*. PhD thesis, Faculty of Social and Economic Studies of the Victoria University of Manchester (unpublished)
Kirenga, J. (1997) *Women's Participation in Trade Unions in Uganda: Case of National Union of Educational Institutions (NUEI)* Diploma in Labour Studies Dissertation, Ruskin College, Oxford. (unpublished)
Ogaram, D.: (2005): *The Role and Function of Government in Industrial Relations: How it performed since Independence:* A paper presented at Ndejje University, Saturday 08 October, 2005. (unpublished)
Ssekaana, M.(1998): *Adequacy of Labour Laws in the Employer and Employee Relations in Uganda*. Bachelor of Laws Dissertation, Faculty of Law, Makerere University, (unpublished) p.3
Lutwama, J.(2004) *Constraints to Employment Growth in the Formal Manufacturing Sector in Uganda*. Masters in Arts Dissertation, Economic Policy and Planning (EPP) of Makerere University. (unpublished)

Part II
Country Studies from Southern Africa

7
Industrial Relations in Conditions of Economic Stress: The Zimbabwe Case
Lloyd Sachikonye

Introduction

The industrial relations systems in Southern Africa have been categorised into three broad levels of development (Fashoyin, 1998). The first category is represented by the comparatively advanced industrial relations system in South Africa, a system that is a reflection of its relatively sophisticated economy. The second category comprises the industrial relations systems in countries such as Zambia and Zimbabwe in which workers have enjoyed a relatively longer history of freedom of association and right to collective bargaining. According to this view, in the third category are countries such as Botswana, Lesotho, Malawi, Mozambique and Namibia whose industrial relations systems have, until recently, remained relatively underdeveloped. In general, however, there appeared to be positive trends in the manner in which industrial relations were evolving in the region in the late 1990s (ibid.).

This Chapter has a narrower focus: it assesses the state of industrial relations in one of the countries with a history of labour union activism and collective bargaining but also one of extensive state intervention in the sector (Phimister and Raftopoulos, 1997; Sachikonye, 1998)). More pertinently, the Chapter attempts to show a link between the conditions of deepening economic stress and the volatility that has characterised Zimbabwe's industrial relations during the past 8 years. Uniquely amongst countries in Southern Africa, the country has suffered prolonged economic decline that has had a direct effect on employment patterns and industrial relations. The Chapter addresses this linkage and assesses the possible medium to long-term impact on industrial relations institutions, and more generally on relations between the state, organised business and labour. The political economy framework enables a more perceptive understanding of the linkage between changes (especially decline) in the economy and shifts in the political base towards entrenched authoritarianism. This largely explains the politicisation of industrial relations issues and economic struggles that have occurred as a consequence, as the Chapter will argue.

The economy: stupid!

The state of its economy has a profound effect on a country's industrial relations. But how has Zimbabwe's economy fared during the period 1997 to 2005? This period is one during which the economy has lurched from crisis to crisis and witnessed severe contraction. In particular, the economy shrank by about 30 per cent between 2000 and 2004; this GDP decline should be set against average growth rates of about 3 per cent in 2003 in other Southern African countries. This followed from a huge deficit and devaluation in 1997 as a result of politically inspired unbudgeted spending for war veterans. The deficit also accumulated as a consequence of the country's military intervention in the Democratic Republic of the Congo (DRC) between 1998 and 2001. It was estimated that, while it lasted, the intervention cost US$30 million per month. A hastily and poorly coordinated land reform that commenced in 2000 not only undermined the agricultural base but had ripple effects throughout the economy and society.

In 2004, manufacturing declined by about 9 per cent and was expected to decline by a further 5 per cent in 2005. Many companies have closed and thousands of jobs lost in the sector over the past 5 years. Table 7.1 summarises key economic indicators.

Zimbabwe's exports have fallen by about 70 per cent since 2000 as a result of the overall gloomy macroeconomic climate (Games, 2005). During the same period, employment is estimated to have shrunk by 20 per cent, investment by 50 per cent and capacity utilisation by 55 per cent. The knock-on effects of endemic shortages of fuel and electricity include the problem of capacity underutilisation. While foreign exchange earnings from merchandise were about US$3.1billion in 1996, it slumped to US$1.4 billion in 2003.

This is the economic background against which an assessment of the country's industrial relations will be made below. Here it is also important to insert the political factor into this wider background.

The period from the late 1990s marked a watershed in Zimbabwean politics to the extent that the ruling elite became more determined and self-confident

Table 7.1 Key economic indicators – Zimbabwe

	1997	1998	1999	2000	2001	2002	2003
Real GDP %	1.4	0.8	−4.1	−6.8	−9.5	−14.7	−14.0
Inflation	18.9	31.7	58.5	55.9	71.9	133.2	600
Budget deficit (%)	−8.2	−5.5	−7.7	−24.1	−8.2	−13.8	−14.0
Domestic debt (US$bn)	13.4	44.2	77.6	162.1	194.1	345.8	590.9
Foreign debt (US$m)	4117	3841	3285	3614	3180	4503	–
Export growth	−2.9	−20.9	−01	−14.3	−28.3	−10.3	−5.3

Source: Kanyenze (2004).

in advocating and pursuing its 'entitlement' to the national economic cake. First, it argued that it was 'entitled' to receive compensation for its participation in the liberation struggle that had culminated in independence in 1980. The War Victims Compensation Fund was the state fund set up for this purpose in the early 1990s. There was corruption in its disbursement and the seeds for conflict with the war veterans, who felt marginalised in the share-out, were sown during this period. Second, another catchword was 'economic empowerment', and this provided rationale for acquisition of white commercial farms through what were euphemistically termed 'farm invasions'. The ruling elite sought to engage in 'accumulation through dispossession' without incurring costs such as offering compensation to the evicted farmers. Third, other conduits of self-enrichment included state contracts as well as 'project funds'. As one economist observed, project money was also disbursed at the ruling party's rallies to attract votes at the 2000 and 2002 elections (Kanyenze, 2004). These flows of these tax-payers moneys ensured the deterioration of the budget deficit thus further accentuating the economic crisis. Summing up elite accumulation during this period, one analyst observed that after 1997 wealth acquisition took on a more rampant character; as the economy unravelled, it provided opportunities for those who wished to extract rents more openly than before (Davies, 2005). For instance, the management of the foreign exchange market provided quick returns to those who had access to foreign exchange.

The self-aggrandisement by the elite had a direct effect on the levels of corruption in both the public and private sectors. The 'rule of law' was spurned while violence became a feature of election campaigns in 2000 and 2002. Coercion was used an instrument of settling wage disputes by a state-sponsored labour federation, the Zimbabwe Federation of Trade Unions (ZFTU) in 2001. This period had also witnessed the emergence of a strong opposition movement; formed in 1999, it contested the 2000 election and won almost half of the directly elected seats. The labour movement, organised under the auspices of the Zimbabwe Congress of Trade Unions (ZCTU), was the backbone of this opposition front.

However, while economic mismanagement by the ruling elite explains the poor economic record, an external factor has also contributed to the crisis. The implementation of a structural adjustment programme (SAP) in the early 1990s contributed to weakening some of the foundations of the economy. Although the outcome of the SAP may have been different if it had been fully implemented, the reality was that the impact on some sectors contributed to the beginnings of de-industrialisation while social service cutbacks deepened poverty (ZCTU, 1996; Sachikonye, 1999; Bond and Manyanya, 2001). An assessment of industrial relations therefore needs to situate them in this broader framework of authoritarianism, patronage, corruption and persistent opposition to it. In the next section, we turn our attention to how employment and industrial relations have been shaped by this economic and political environment.

Employment and the labour market

On attainment of independence, Zimbabwe was one of the few states in Sub-Saharan Africa with a diversified economy resting on a relatively sophisticated industrial base. Formal sector employment was considerable by African standards. About 10 per cent of the population of 13 million was employed in the 1990s. Given an economically active population of 5.9 million, the formal sector thus accounted for about 25 per cent of the employed population. As we will see, the larger proportion of the economically active population has been absorbed into the informal sector. By 1999, the number of persons employed in the formal sector was estimated at 1.5 million or about 12 per cent of the population. During the 1990s, the annual average increase of new jobs was 18 000. This was clear evidence of very slow job growth in the formal sector of the economy. Nevertheless, despite the sluggish growth, new jobs continued to be created in agriculture and the services sector, especially finance, insurance and real estate. But significantly there were declines in the manufacturing and construction sectors, a process that accelerated from 2000 onwards. Another sector that registered a decline was public administration where the number of jobs dropped from 95 000 in 1991 to 71 000 in 1996.

In the period 2000 to 2004, there has been a further contraction in formal sector employment. As we have already observed, the largest decline has been in commercial agriculture (about 60 per cent) followed by manufacturing (about 20 per cent) and mining. The contribution of these sectors to the economy has also plummeted during the past four years.

The few sectors where employment growth has been buoyant are the services sector and the informal sector. Finance and distribution have been the fastest growing amongst the services. But it is the informal sector that has experienced the greatest surge in growth, a trend that began in the 1990s. It is a sector that has absorbed most of the workers that were laid off in such sectors as manufacturing and commercial agriculture. Because of ease of entry into the sector, those who were unable to obtain jobs after school and other long-term unemployed people have sought to earn a living in this sector. These two factors – the lack of formal sector employment opportunities and an increase in the demand for informal sector products and services – explain the expansion of the sector (Grimsrud, 1998). Despite a lack of up to date statistics, the number of informal sector workers by 2005 is likely to have been well above 4.5 million or three times those workers employed in the formal sector.

This picture of the labour market structure shows what the profound effects of economic decline have been on employment patterns. Conditions in the informal sector are precarious despite ease of entry. Incomes are low while social benefits such as health care are rare in the sector. The formal labour legislation is rarely applied in the sector to regulate employment and safety conditions, let alone minimum wages. But another effect of economic decline has been a significant out-migration in search of better employment opportunities. It has been estimated that about 3 million Zimbabweans (or about 25 per cent of the population) have migrated in the past five years mainly in search of economic opportunities.

Industrial relations: legal framework, stresses and strains

The key labour legislation introduced in post-independence Zimbabwe is the Labour Relations Act that was published in 1985. It has seen two major amendments, the first was in 1992 and the second in 2002. The objectives of the Act were spelt as:

- to define and declare the fundamental rights of workers,
- to regulate conditions of employment and related matters,
- to define and provide for the prevention of unfair labour practices and labour disputes,
- to provide for the formation and registration of trade unions and employment councils,
- to regulate and control employment agencies and
- to regulate the negotiation, scope and enforcement of collective bargaining agreements (Labour Relations Act, 1985).

The legislation also contains provisions on fair labour standards, equal pay for equal work, on occupational health and safety and against discrimination. A controversial section of the Act relates to strikes. The sectors in which strikes are prohibited constitute a vast proportion of the economy.

In the 1990s, collective bargaining became the main instrument of negotiating wages and other conditions of work unlike the situation in the 1980s when state-sanctioned minimum wages were the norm (Sachikonye and Dhlakama, 1991). National Employment Councils (NECs) were established in the various industries for this purpose and skills in wage bargaining were strengthened particularly in unions where skills and experience were initially weak. The institutionalisation of collective bargaining was accompanied by expansion of the scope of negotiations. Extra-wage benefits now featured more regularly in most negotiations as did job security and the new disciplinary regimes instituted under economic liberalisation. Amendments to the Labour Relations Act in 1992 allowed decentralised bargaining at works council level where there did not exist an NEC. In general, there were few reported instances of collective bargaining at works council level since most employers were more at ease with industry-level agreements which are sectorally binding than plant-level agreements that could be unfavourably compared with the former.

The period covered by this paper was one in which the onset and deepening of the economic crisis sparked an unparalleled degree of industrial conflict. In particular, the period between 1996 and 2002 witnessed numbers of industrial strikes as well as general strikes or 'national stay-aways'. The strikes took both economic and political dimensions. The economic dimension took the form of a collapse of real incomes for the majority of workers in a context of devaluation and escalating prices, and therefore of cost of living. For instance, public service experienced multiple factors that undermined their wages and other working conditions. These were low wages and benefits, declining spending and maintenance of critical public services such as health and education, authoritarian state labour practices and unfair labour laws (Saunders, 2001). These conditions generated the public service strike of 1996, the largest strike in post-independence Zimbabwe. A direct result of the growing crisis in public service industrial relations, the two-week strike underlined the improved organisational strength of most public sector workers' associations, and their determination to improve and 'normalise' industrial relations in the sector (ibid.). The strike also marked a turning point in the relationship between private sector unions on the one hand, and public workers associations on the other. Henceforth, there was closer co-ordination between the two sets of workers particularly on the campaign to have public and private sector laws harmonised (that was achieved in 2002). A general strike in December 1997 was organised on wage and tax issues and widely heeded in both the public and private sectors. More such strikes or stay-aways (as they were colloquially termed) followed in 1998 and 1999 as the economic crisis deepened and state ineptitude continued.

The number of industrial strikes in 1997 alone was 232, up from 2 in 1994 and 62 in 1996. The next five years witnessed an above average number of strikes as workers sought to stem the erosion of their wages and living standards. Employment security was adversely affected for thousands of workers in many sectors. At the same time, the instability in the macroeconomic environment made conditions more difficult and risky for companies. The combination of state hikes in taxes and price controls as well as shortages of key inputs such as fuel and equipment due to declining foreign exchange inflows made conditions uncompetitive for most companies. The last straw for them was the chaotic land reform from 2000 to 2003, a programme that disrupted the backward and forward linkages between agriculture and manufacturing and other sectors. After 2003, the frequency of strikes appeared to decline even though wage conditions did not improve. Although there were periodic strikes in the public sector (in the health service) and in the private sector (in the financial and mining sectors), they were significantly reduced in number.

The other dimension of industrial relations related to their explicit politicisation from about 1997. Not only were strikes viewed as 'political', but the national labour centre, the ZCTU, was increasingly viewed as harbouring political ambitions. The state response took several forms. First, it defined industrial action as 'politically motivated' strategy to bring pressure on it to change its policies. Strikes and stay-aways were banned under the Presidential Powers (Temporary Measures) Act. The government then threatened to de-register the ZCTU for its mobilising of the national stay-aways. Punitive action was taken against some of its leaders; this included the assault, indeed attempted murder, of the ZCTU Secretary General, Morgan Tsvangirai in 1997. Second, there emerged an implicit strategy on the part of the state to weaken the ZCTU by abetting the formation of a rival labour centre. To that end, the abovementioned rival Zimbabwe Federation of Trade Unions (ZFTU) was created with state support in 1998. It drew its support from a handful of unions mostly unregistered and consisting of negligible membership. Nevertheless, the state would ensure that ZFTU was aligned to the ruling Zanu PF party, and remain supportive of state policies. By 2000, there were thus two national labour centres aligned to the two major parties namely Zanu PF and the Movement for Democratic Change (MDC) respectively.

Finally, the state resorted to more explicitly authoritarian measures against labour unions and the ZCTU during the period 2000 and up to the present. Viewed as the backbone of the MDC, labour leaders have frequently been detained and tortured prompting condemnation from bodies such as the International Labour Organisation (ILO), International Confederation of Free Trade Unions (ICFTU) and the Congress of South African Trade Unions (COSATU). Repressive legislation has been introduced during this period. It includes the Public Order and Security Act (POSA), introduced in 2002, which denies unions freedoms of assembly and expression. In addition, the state media has mounted a 'hate campaign' at unions aligned to the ZCTU, as well as condemned its solidarity links with other national centres such as COSATU based in South Africa. Clearly, there is a stalemate in state-labour relations as repression continues to intensify. The overall atmosphere of industrial relations appears to have been poisoned in a context of repressive governance. However, this is not say that there were no attempts to forge some compromise in the form of a social contract between state, labour and business during the period under review. We turn to this theme in the next section.

An elusive social contract

Despite the deepening economic crisis and repressive framework, there have existed some hopes that it may still be possible to work out a compromise between organised business, labour and the state. Such a compromise was necessary in order to make improvements in the economy and political governance. Sometimes termed 'social contract', the idea or concept of a tripartite compromise began to be canvassed in the early 1990s as the anticipated gains of structural adjustment proved elusive. There was even a rare meeting of minds on the imperative of such a contract between the Reserve Bank and the ZCTU!

More flesh was put to the idea when a concrete suggestion was made by the ZCTU that there be set up a tripartite Zimbabwe Economic Development Council that would consult regularly on matters of economic and social policy.

Such a Council would build confidence amongst the three parties as well as provide a forum for a regular exchange of views and experiences (ZCTU, 1996). The Council was envisaged as providing equal institutional representation to the parties to ensure that decisions would be binding.

However, the state had a different conception of who should compose such an institution, and what its *modus operandi* should be. Rather than have a tripartite institution, the government preferred to set up what it termed a National Economic Consultative Forum (NECF) into which individuals from various sectors were selected on an individual basis. Although the agenda of the NECF was wide ranging – from economic to agrarian policies – its decisions and recommendations were non-binding. Thus the NECF had little, if any, power and influence in economic and social governance issues. The ZCTU boycotted its proceedings right from the beginning. It preferred to participate in the Tripartite Negotiating Forum (TNF) that engaged in tough negotiations over income and prices as from 1998. This was a more credible body but the government did undermine it whenever it was convenient for it to take unilateral decisions.

As the economic crisis deepened in 2003, another attempt at forging a social contract got under way between the three partners. The outcome of their attempt was the *Kadoma Declaration of Intent* of January 2003. The objectives of the *Declaration* were:

- to create a conducive and tolerant environment for the negotiation and conclusion of a social contract,
- to overcome stakeholder differences and work towards a common goal guided by a common vision of national development, and
- to promote confidence among social partners and generate commitment towards the sustainability of social dialogue in the spirit of smart partnership and tripartism (NECF, 2003).

The three parties broadly agreed to 'promote, observe and ensure good governance: transparency, openness and accountability; preventing and fighting corruption; and adhering to fair collective bargaining processes' (ibid.). On the face of it, the technocrats who drafted the principles of the Declaration were generally sincere in their motivations. However, it does not appear that the country's top political leadership was sold on the idea of a social contract. Its authoritarian style and manipulation of a patronage network sat uneasily with a Declaration that canvassed transparency and anti-corruption. The *Prices and Incomes Stabilisation Protocol* crafted by a team of technocrats from the three parties in 2003 met a similar fate from the political leadership. The aim of the *Protocol* was to manage the movement of prices and incomes in the context of an unstable macroeconomic environment; to ensure that any agreed formula of restraining price movements took into account 'legitimate' cost increases in a transparent and accountable manner; and to share the burden of economic stabilisation among all social partners. It also spelt out the specific obligations of each social partner. Unilateralism and arrogance on the part of government stymied the *Protocol*, and subsequently the ZCTU suspended its participation in the Tripartite Negotiating Forum which lay behind the *Protocol*. Draconian measures against the ZCTU in the form of raids on its offices, arrest of leadership and an orchestrated smear campaign by the government confirmed again that it had little faith in the concept of social contract.

Instead the state has preferred its strategy of economic recovery which has been steered by the Reserve Bank since the end of 2003. Thus undermining the social concept through unilateralism, this strategy found expression in a monetary policy crafted by the Bank's new governor, Gideon Gono. Appointed in December 2003, Gono's brief was to utilise monetary policy to address multiple problems: a viability crisis in many financial institutions, crippling shortages including those of production inputs and of foreign exchange and related constraints on the economy. A monetary policy statement issued in December 2003 argued that macroeconomic stability would be restored once the policy was fully implemented. Singling out inflation as 'enemy number one', Gideon Gono vowed to reduce it from about 600 per cent to less than 200 per cent by the end of 2004, and to double digits by the end of 2005. There were confident assertions that 'an economic turn-around' would be achieved in 2004 in a context of an expanded role of the Reserve Bank in economic affairs. The Bank's role ranged from 'cleaning up' the financial sector (more 10 banks and asset management firms were closed in 2004) to sending performance directives to parastatals and city and town councils. The Bank took a prominent role in a crack-down of what were termed 'economic crimes' that included a parallel foreign currency market that had continued to thrive. The monetary instrument was also utilised to extend low-interest credit to agrarian and manufacturing sectors on the assumption that they would be revived as a consequence.

However, by April 2005, the limitations of implementing monetary in isolation from complementary fiscal and deficit reduction measures had become clear. Foreign exchange and input shortages returned with a vengeance. Inflation could not maintain a downward trend. While it had provided 'a band aid support' of sorts, it was ultimately not sustainable. Arrears to external institutions such as the World Bank and IMF and other lenders continued to swell. The decline in GDP would continue into the fifth year in a row. It was in this broad context that Gideon Gono recommended the construction of more jails to incarcerate an increased number of citizens who were committing 'economic crimes'. Thus turning back on the social contract concept had not led to an improvement in macroeconomic stability and growth.

Conclusion

This Chapter has sought to assess industrial relations in a country experiencing economic decline. Some analysts have categorised such countries as 'failed states' on account of their economic and political fragility. While Zimbabwe retains a semblance of a functioning albeit authoritarian state, it is a state that is a steward of a very fragile economic base and of an increasing potential for a social explosion. In the long term, authoritarian repression will not ensure a permanent lid on rising discontent over unemployment, inflation and loss of livelihoods. A massive 'clean-up' of urban centres in mid-2005 was aimed at 'regulating' the sprawling informal sector but at enormous cost in terms of human displacement and loss of livelihoods by the urban unemployed. Industrial relations could not remain unscathed under this process of economic decline and state authoritarianism. Any improvement in the climate of industrial relations will be bound up with economic and political reform on a democratic path.

References

Bond, P. and Manyanya, M. (2002), *Zimbabwe's Plunge*. Harare: Weaver Press.
Davies, R. (2005), 'Memories of Underdevelopment', in Raftopoulos, B. and Savage, T. (eds), *Zimbabwe: Injustice and Political Reconciliation*. Cape Town: One World Books.
Fashoyin, T. (1998), *Industrial Relations in Southern Africa: the Challenge of Change*. Harare : ILO-SAMAT.
Games, D. (2005), *A Pre-Election Overview and Recovery Scenarios*. Johannesburg: SAIIA.
Grimsrud, B. (1998), 'Labour Markets in Zimbabwe', in Torres, L. (ed.), *Labour Markets in Southern Africa*. Oslo: FAFO.
Kanyenze, G. (2004), 'The Zimbabwe Economy 1980–2003: a ZCTU Perspective', in Harold-Barry, D. (ed.), *Zimbabwe: the Past Is the Future*. Harare: Weaver Press.
National Economic Consultative Forum (NECF) (2003), *Declaration of Intent Towards the Social Contract*. Harare.
Phimister, I. and Raftopoulos, B. (eds.) (1997), *Keep on Knocking*. Harare: Baobab.
Sachikonye, L. (1998), 'The State, Workers and Industrial Relations', in Agere, S. (ed.), *Zimbabwe Post-Independence Public Administration*. Dakar: Codesria.
Sachikonye, L. (1999), *Restructuring or De-Industrializing?: Textile and Metal Industries under Adjustment in Zimbabwe*. Uppsala: NAI.
Sachikonye, L. and Dhlakama, L. (1991), *Collective Bargaining: Problems and Prospects*. Geneva: ILO.
Saunders, R. (2001), 'Striking Ahead', in Raftpoulos, B. and Sachikonye, L. (eds) *Striking Back: the Labour Movement and the State in Zimbabwe*. Harare: Weaver Press.
Zimbabwe Congress of Trade Unions (ZCTU) (1996), *Beyond Esap*. Harare: ZCTU.

8
Trade Unions and Neo-Liberal Reforms in Mozambique: The 'Hollowing Out of Industrial Relations'?

Edward Webster and Geoffrey Wood

Introduction

This chapter provides an overview of the state of Mozambican trade unions. It seeks to shed further light on the effects of structural adjustment and political liberalisation on unions and the practice of employment relations. Whilst focusing on the case of organised labour in a newly democratised developing economy, the dilemmas posed by a shrinking of the employment base in traditional areas of union activity, reduced security of tenure and de facto legal deregulation, and the need to reach out to highly marginalised categories of labour, are also shared by unions throughout Africa.

Unions and democracy: issues and challenges

Within tropical Africa, unions face difficult choices. On the one hand, in an adverse global environment, good relations with ruling parties may help maintain – and expand – existing worker rights. Such relationships depend not only on trade-offs, but on the ability to marshal supporters in the event of elections; in turn, the rank and file are only likely to follow union leaders if they are seen as responsive to their needs. On the other hand, unions in tropical Africa have demonstrated little ability to restrain the imposition of structural adjustment policies: perceived acquiescence may undermine rank-and-file participation, whilst union membership has inevitably been cut through wholesale jobs losses that have been the inevitable consequences of such policies.

Given this, it would seem important to explore the extent of internal democracy within the Mozambican labour movement, representivity and coverage, and the proclivity to engage in collective action both in support of workplace and wider political goals. Internal democracy within trade unions concerns three key questions: the power of the rank-and-file to control vital decisions, the responsiveness of leadership to the desires of membership, and membership approval of leadership performance (Seidman, 2003: 35).

Morris and Fosh (2000: 100–1) argue that there are five elements of union democracy, as follows:

- Constitutional arrangements: regular election of officers; activist involvement (such as regular attendance at union meetings); decentralised and diffused decision making; active officer involvement.
- Political organisation: internal opposition factions; electoral competition.
- Representation: density and coverage of different sectors; representation of the disadvantaged.
- Involvement: high levels of participation in elections; high levels of membership involvement; lack of irregularities in elections.
- Outcomes: membership satisfaction with pay bargaining (decentralised bargaining is likely to extend managerial prerogatives and, hence, reduce the range of areas where workers may have a choice); choice regarding industrial action (see below); satisfaction with leadership; ability to advance the interests of members as a group not only within, but beyond the workplace.

(Morris and Fosh, 2000: 100–1; and see Flynn *et al.*, 2004; Traxler, 2003: 1)

The Mozambican political context

Many countries in tropical Africa and elsewhere in the developing world underwent a 'double transition' in the 1990s: simultaneously towards multi-party democracy and neo-liberalism. These developments have opened up new opportunities and challenges for organised labour. On the one hand, more open political climates have given unions more room to assert their independence both within and beyond the workplace. On the other hand, neo-liberal 'structural adjustment' policies imposed by international financial organisations such as the IMF, have, in many instances, resulted in a declining employment base in manufacturing and other areas of the formal sector (Stiglitz, 2002), and brought with it a reduced willingness by the authorities to uphold in any effective way the legal rights of employees (c.f. Manda *et al.*, 2001; Tangri, 2000; Hanlon, 1996).

Mozambique has suffered two major wars. First, an anti-colonial war of liberation, mostly confined to the far north that lasted from 1964 to 1974, ending in the accession to power of the liberation movement, Frelimo, which set about implementing a state socialist political programme. This was followed by civil war from 1976 to 1992, pitting Frelimo[1] against a rebel movement, Renamo. The latter was set up and supported as part and parcel of the systematic destabilisation strategies of, firstly, the then Rhodesian government, and, later, South Africa's apartheid government (Hanlon, 1991). The cessation of hostilities between Frelimo and the rebel movement, Renamo, in 1992, led to Mozambique's first democratic elections being held in 1994.

In the 1994 elections, Frelimo won 53 per cent of the vote in the presidential elections and 129 seats in parliament, compared to Renamo's 34 per cent and 112 seats. The tiny Democratic Union coalition won 9 seats. In 1999 Frelimo narrowly secured the presidency, with 52 per cent of the vote, and some 133 parliamentary seats. Renamo remained the main opposition, and performed relatively well in the 1999 elections, winning some 117 of 250 parliamentary seats and 48 per cent of the presidential vote. Its stronger performance in the presidential poll reflected both persistent rural discontent, and the fact that it had subsumed the Democratic Union coalition and a number of smaller parties into the Renamo Electoral Union. National elections were held again in 2004, in which Frelimo increased its share of parliamentary seats to 160, garnering 63.4 per cent of the presidential vote. Frelimo's successful presidential candidate was Armando Guebuza, a long-standing opponent of the preceding President Chissano, who retired from the presidency. Whilst there is little doubt that Frelimo remains the most sophisticated political actor with greater resources and expertise at its disposal, and many years of experience in government, it has been weakened by a lack of ideological direction, in-fighting and serious corruption amongst leading figures close to the office of the outgoing President (Fauvet and Mosse, 2003); Frelimo's woes in these areas were only exceeded by that of Renamo, which continued to face difficulties in voicing clear ideologies and policies, and cut-throat competition for the limited pool of resources at its disposal.

The economic context

The colonial legacy

In the colonial period, much of the Mozambican economy centred on the transport network and related services, with Maputo serving as a major outlet for South Africa's former Transvaal province, and Beira for the then Rhodesia (BIP, n.d.). The winning of independence, the hostility of white minority regimes in both South Africa and then Rhodesia – and the subsequent civil war, itself a product of destabilisation by the latter two states – brought Mozambique's transport network to it knees. The resultant economic problems were exacerbated by the flight of many of the white colonists who had dominated many of the skilled occupations in the colonial era, and poorly conceived attempts at centralised planning (Hanlon, 1991).

Structural adjustment

During the closing stages of the civil war, the end of Soviet financial aid forced Frelimo to abandon its socialist experiment, and turn to the IMF and the World Bank for financial support (Webster *et al.*, 2006). This, however, expectedly came with stringent conditions attached, centring on the reduction in state expenditure, the phasing out of protective tariffs and privatisation (ibid.). It soon became apparent that the projections of the development consequences were faulty (Metical, 1 August 1997); Mozambique's health and educational systems were severely damaged in the process. Further fine-tuning, and the reconstruction of the transport network facilitated rapid economic growth, albeit concentrated around the capital, Maputo. By 2000 Mozambique represented one of the world's fastest growing economies (*Africa Confidential*, 4 February 2000). What these figures masked were widening disparities in incomes between town and country, and between the mass of society and a tiny elite (c.f. Hanlon, 2000; Roper and Wood, 2003). The decline of formal sector employment has greatly exacerbated rising social inequality. By 1996, it has been estimated that a total number of 100,000 or about 40 per cent of workers were made redundant as a result of privatisation (Pitcher, 2002:189).

Mozambican unions

Colonial era unions in Mozambique represented branches of Portuguese unions, and concentrated their attentions on organising white colonists on craft lines; they collapsed following independence, and the wholesale flight of white settlers. On independence, two forms of workplace representation emerged. Firstly, there were the *Dynamising Groups*, clusters of activists who had emerged spontaneously or under the direction of Frelimo; whilst not confining their attentions to the workplace, the activities of the Groups posed a direct challenge to managers in many workplaces. Secondly, the flight of white colonialists had left many workplaces without owners or managers. Whilst these were generally replaced by Frelimo-appointed managers or Administrative Commissions, in some cases workers were accorded a formal say in the running of the company through *Production Councils*; again, these were either formally constituted by Frelimo, or emerged spontaneously as a result of the activities of grassroots activists (Pitcher, 2002: 37).

The emergence of an armed challenge to Frelimo's authority in the form of Renamo, the desire to co-ordinate production more effectively, and, a commitment by sections of the ruling party to emulating the Soviet model, led to increasing efforts to subordinate organisations representing workers at the shopfloor under the ruling party, and to relegate them to a transmission belt role (see Gumende, 1998: 31; Fauvet and Mosse, 2003). The Dynamising Groups were gradually transformed into party cells, whilst the Production Councils were united into industrial unions under the *Organicao dos Trabalhadores de Mozambique* ('OTM', the Organisation of Mozambican Workers) federation in 1983. On the one hand, for the first time in Mozambican history, unions became accessible to all industrial and service sector workers; indeed, membership became compulsory. On the other hand, they were firmly subject to 'direction' from Frelimo and no unions outside of the OTM umbrella were legally permitted. Multi-partyism resulted in the OTM gaining a greater degree of political independence, becoming an outspoken critic of some of the worst excesses of structural adjustment (Hanlon, 1996: 78; Nhaca, 1997) There remains a lack of a viable political alternative to Frelimo sympathetic to the needs of the urban working class (Webster and Mosoetsa, 2001). OTM's membership has dramatically declined, from 300,000 members in the early 1980s to 90,000 in 2003, largely due to widescale job losses in the manufacturing sector, in turn a result of the implementation of structural adjustment policies (OTM interview, 2003). The ending of OTM's legal monopoly in 1991 saw the establishment of a new union federation, the Confederation of Free and Independent Trade Unions of Mozambique (CONSILMO), during the following year. The new federation was formed by three former OTM unions, on the grounds that OTM remained too close to the ruling party and was 'a top-down federation' (Webster and Mosoetsa, 2001: 22; CONSILMO Interview, 2003). Whilst the 1998 Labour Law grants trade unions a range of organisational and bargaining rights, enforcement is weak; a large proportion of employers ignore its provisions with apparent impunity (Webster *et al.*, 2006). Since then, it appears that the government is intent on further diluting worker rights (AIM Reports 2 May 2006).

Mozambican unions in practice

The following sections of this article are based on a nationwide-survey of union members in Mozambique. It is evident that internal union democracy matters, not only in ensuring a responsive and dynamic labour movement, but as a means of enriching the wider political discourse that, in the absence of effective grassroots pressure, is likely to be even more firmly subordinate to elite interests (Moody, 1997; Friedman, 2003). Hence, we explore the relative strength of internal union democracy in Mozambique based upon Morris and Fosh's (2000) indicators.

Constitutional arrangements

The survey revealed that shop stewards were present in just over half (55 per cent) of the workplaces surveyed. Table 8.1 summarises how they gained office:

As can be seen, in just under half of all cases, shop stewards were democratically elected. In just over one third of workplaces, they were appointed

Table 8.1 Method of appointing shop stewards

Method of appointment	N	%
Did not answer	9	9
Elected	46	46
Appointed by union membership	7	7
Appointed by management	35	35
Other	3	3
Total	101	100

Source: Webster *et al.* (2006).

Table 8.2 When were shop steward elections last held?

When Last	N	%
Did not answer	16	16
Never	41	41
Less than 1 month ago	2	2
1–6 months ago	2	2
7–11 months ago	6	6
1–2 years ago	13	13
More than 2 years ago	20	20
Total	*101*	*100*

by management, most probably a legacy from the era when unions were firmly subordinated to management and the ruling party, and bound to maximise productivity in the intended interests of national development.

Table 8.2 indicates when shop stewards were last elected.

Again, this table would indicate the irregularity of democratic processes in many workplaces, reducing the possibilities for holding elected representatives to account. However, workers in situations where shop stewards were elected were more likely to demand higher standards of accountability; there was a statistically significant relationship between the manner in which shop stewards were elected and views on the need to report back (*chi-squared* = 7.005, *d.f.* = 2; *significance* = 0.030).

Internal political organisation and opposition

In addition to infrequent elections, the survey revealed relatively few instances when credible internal opposition to existing union representatives emerged at the workplace; few respondents had any recollection of a sitting shop steward being unseated from office: only 14 per cent of respondents had experienced a shop steward being dismissed for failing to respect the interests of workers or other failing in leadership. Whilst this could indicate that almost all shop stewards are in close contact with their constituents – and hence able to closely mirror their wishes – the irregularity of shop steward elections, and the undemocratic manner in which many are appointed, would suggest that this is not the case.

Representation

Figure 8.1 depicts the estimated level of union penetration in the workplaces covered by the survey:

As can be seen, approximately one quarter of workplaces had no union presence whatsoever. In contrast, in one third of workplaces, more than half of employees belonged to a union. On the one hand, as noted earlier, formal sector employment has dramatically decreased over the past few years; the bulk of Mozambican workers, in insecure and marginal occupations remain

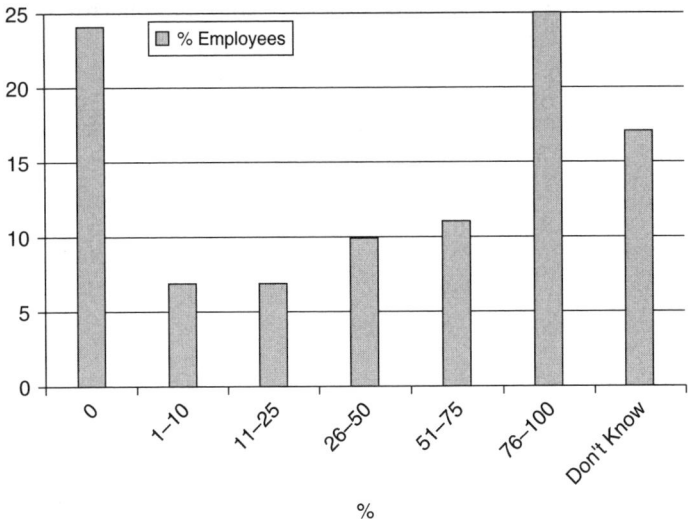

Source: Webster et al., 2006.

Figure 8.1 Estimated per cent of union penetration in respondents' workplaces

unrepresented. On the other hand, the union penetration rate in the formal sector remains relatively high. There is little doubt, however, that this largely represents a legacy of the era of compulsory union membership; 17 per cent of respondents were uncertain as to whether there was a union in their workplace or not.

Involvement

Sixty-three per cent of Mozambican respondents never attended union meetings, 15 per cent only doing so on an annual basis or less. In the absence of high levels of grassroots participation in their internal life, unions risk becoming irrelevant to the needs of their members (Moody, 1997). The survey would suggest there is limited capacity at the grassroots to transcend a tradition of centralism.

Outcomes

More than half of respondents (54 per cent) felt that the unions operating in their workplace had no influence on managerial decision-making whatsoever. Only 14 per cent felt that their union had increased its influence over the past 3 years, whilst 6 per cent said that it had decreased, the remainder believing that there had been no change in union influence. Again, this would underscore the difficulties which unions have experienced in making their influence felt in an age of downsizing, and of reduced state interest and support.

Some 44 per cent of respondents believed that some collective bargaining took place at their workplace; this would indicate that collective bargaining took place in some firms where the union penetration rate was less than 50 per cent. In the mode of cases, bargaining took place at firm level or on an even more decentralised basis. In 35 per cent of cases where collective bargaining took place, the latter did so at national level. Whilst unions retain a presence in many Mozambican workplaces, there is little evidence that unions have been successful in increasing their impact at firm level, despite the greater political independence they now enjoy. Echoing this finding, only 42 per cent of respondents felt that managers bothered to comply with the terms and conditions of union recognition agreements.

Fighting ability

Around 18 per cent of the companies surveyed reported having experienced work stoppages or strikes. Of these, 47 per cent reported that they had had a strike within the last 12 months; 55 per cent said that they had experienced a strike within the last two years. 41 per cent of strikes experienced were of less than one-day duration; only 27 per cent lasted more than 5 days. Only in 38 per cent of disputes did more than 70 per cent of workers participate; in 21 per cent participation rates were less than 30 per cent. On the one hand, the survey indicated that in a relatively large number of disputes workers could readily opt out of strikes: in short, the union lacked the power to coerce members into collectivism, maximising individual choice. On the other hand, many workers lacked the ability to choose shop stewards – even if they were present at their workplace – whilst the survey revealed patchy bargaining coverage and widespread managerial non-compliance with collective agreements. The inability of unions to mobilise sufficient numbers of workers in industrial disputes would further exacerbate shortfalls in representation and voice.

General issues

The inability of Mozambican unions to make much headway both in the wider social arena and the workplace, despite formal independence, reflects two critical weaknesses: in internal democracy, and in representation and coverage. Despite a more open political climate, the gaining of formal independence from state and management, and labour legislation that entrenches pluralism, internal union democracy remains weak. This would reflect not only adverse external circumstances, but the weakness of internal policy debates and the continued disengagement of the leadership from the rank-and-file. In many cases elections for workplace representatives are meaningless or simply absent; and, in most instances, workers seem to lack the means to recall representatives who fail to respect their wishes. There is little doubt that, at least in part, this reflects a tradition of centralisation and subordination. Whilst unions have begun to build links with other categories of labour – an example being OTM's formal relationship with ASSOTSI, an organisation recruiting street traders in the informal sector – progress has been slow, and the dividends slim.

Conclusion

Whilst 'double transitions' in many national contexts have resulted in unions winning organisational independence and other legal rights, they have proved both empowering and disempowering; any possible gains through new organisational and political rights have tended to be eroded by the weakening of the position of formal sector employees as a result of neo-liberal reforms and the painful industrial restructuring that tends to follow on their implementation. The ideological hegemony of neo-liberalism, and the enforcement of associated policies by international financial institutions such as the IMF, makes it difficult for unions to make headway in promoting alternative policy options; in turn, this may discourage grassroots activists from participation in national union structures. Finally, the problems associated with the lack of a tradition of internal democracy cannot be resolved simply through plurality in the wider political arena: union democracy is only likely to prove resilient when firmly rooted (Pateman, 1970). This requires both a degree of altruism by union leaders at key stages of organisational development and rank-and-file sentiments. Grassroots participation is likely to be encouraged if infused with a 'political vision' able to unite the different constituencies around a sense of common fate, and the possibility of bringing about meaningful alternatives (Jacoby, 2002: 732). Finally, internal democratic structures representing only a few are unlikely to make for effective unionism: democratic unionism is contingent on outreach. In many developing countries this necessitates an approach that goes beyond the strategies and methods associated with organising unionism to build bridges to the poorest: those in informal and marginalised categories of labor (c.f. Anonymous, 1999). However, the efficacy of any alliances forged is again contingent on the ability to reconcile sometimes competing immediate concerns under the umbrella of a meaningful political vision, revitalising the 'politics of the streets' to impact on workplace and community debates and at the level of formal governmental structures.

At the same time, union renewal is partially contingent on a change in objective circumstances that would strengthen the bargaining position of employers *vis-à-vis* employees. The present system – weak labour law enforcement and cut-throat competition between job seekers – might appear attractive to many more conservative employers. However, the maintenance of the current system is not without cost to employers: existing collective bargaining lacks legitimacy (especially, as the survey revealed that most managers did not keep to collective agreements) weakening managerial access to employee opinion and input, whilst an ability to hold wages down has failed to insulate firms from competition from ultra-low wage economies in Asia. At the same time, firms' over-reliance on low wages and high managerial autonomy as a basis for short term survival has precluded the large scale diffusion of higher value added production paradigms, that might have provided a more sustainable basis for competitive advantage. In this sense, the present trajectory of industrial relations in Mozambique has been costly not only to labour, but also capital.

Note

1. Frelimo used to be a Portuguese language acronym for the Revolutionary Front for the Liberation of Mozambique, but is now used as a proper noun. Renamo similarly was a Portuguese language acronym for the Mozambican National Resistance, but, again is now a proper noun.

References

Africa Confidential. London.
AIM Reports. Maputo.
Anonymous (1999), 'Gender and Informal Sector', *International Labor Review*, 138,3: 340.
BIP. (n.d.), 'Industry in Mozambique'. Maputo.
CONSILIMO Interview (2003), National Federation of the Liberated Trade Unions of Mozambique, Mr. Ibramo Ussense, 4 November 2003.
Fauvet, P. and Mosse, M. (2003), *Carlos Cardoso: Telling the Truth in Mozambique*. Cape Town: Double Storey.
Flynn, M., Brewster, C., Smith, R. and Rigby, M. (2004), 'Trade Union Democracy: The Dynamics of Different Forms', in Wood, G. and Harcourt, M. (eds), *Trade Unions and Democracy*. Manchester: Manchester University Press.
Friedman., S. (2003), 'Preface', in Gall, G. (ed.), *Union Organizing: Campaigning for Union Recognition*. London: Routledge.
Gumende, A. (1999), 'Industrial Relations in a Restructuring Economy: Implications for Corporate Strategy and Human Resource Management in Mozambique', unpublished MBA dissertation, Nottingham Trent University, Nottingham.
Hanlon, J. (1991), *Mozambique: Who Calls the Shots?* London: James Currey.
Hanlon, J. (1996), *Peace Without Profit: How the IMF Blocks Rebuilding* in *Mozambique*. Oxford: James Currey.
Hanlon, J. (2000), 'Mozambique: Will Growing Economic Divisions Provoke Violence in Mozambique?'. Geneva: Swiss Peace Foundation.
Jacoby, S. (2002), 'Mean and Variance', *Industrial and Labor Relations Review*, 54, 4: 729–30.
Manda, D.K., Bigsten, A. and Mwabu, G. (2001), 'Trade Union Membership and Earnings in Kenyan Manufacturing Firms', *Working Papers in Economics 50*. Goteborg: Goteborg University.
Metical. Maputo.
Moody, K. (1997), *Workers in a Lean World*. London: Verso.

Morris, H. and Fosh, P. (2000), 'Measuring Union Democracy: The Case of the UK Civil and Public Service Association', *British Journal of Industrial Relations*, 38, 1: 95–114.
Nhaca, S. (1997), 'A Candid Look at Economic Reform'. Maputo: OTM.
OTM Interview (2003), Organization of the Mozambican Workers: Mr Boaventura Mondlane, 4 November 2003, Maputo.
Pateman, C. (1970), *Participation and Democratic Theory*. Cambridge: Cambridge University Press.
Pitcher, A. (2002), *Transforming Mozambique: The Politics of Privatization*. Cambridge: Cambridge University Press.
Roper, I. and Wood, G. (2003), 'The Business of Politics in Mozambique', *Archiv Orientalni*, 71, 1: 65–78.
Seidman, J. (2003), *Democracy and Trade Unionism: Some Requirements for Union Democracy*. New York: American Economic Association.
Stiglitz, J. 2002. *Globalization and Its Discontents*. London: Allen Lane.
Tangri, R. (2000), *The Politics of Patronage in Africa: Parastatals, Privatization and Private Enterprise*. Oxford: James Currey.
Traxler, F. (2003), 'Bargaining (De)centralization, Macroeconomic Performance and Control Over the Employment Relationship', *British Journal of Industrial Relations*, 41, 1: 1–27.
Webster, E and Mosoetsa, S. (2001), *Connecting and Disconnecting: An Introductory Review of Labor in Selected SADC Countries in the Era of Globalisation*. Johannesburg: Friedrich Ebert Stiftung.
Webster, E., Wood, G., Mtyingizana, M. and Brookes, M. 2006. 'Residual Unionism and Renewal: Organized Labour in Mozambique', *Journal of Industrial Relations*, 48, 2: 257–78.

9
Labour Regulation in Namibia: From 'Colonial Despotism' to 'Flexible Taylorism'

Gilton Klerck

Introduction

The manner in which the colonial–apartheid labour market was consolidated and subsequently dismantled has had a profound impact on industrial relations in contemporary Namibia. By virtue of the fact that labour regulation is always embedded in a particular socio-economic and political environment, it is constrained and enabled by this wider context. Labour regulation is contingent on the interaction between the prevailing social structures and dynamics of production (structuring of labour demand) and the social structures and dynamics of reproduction (structuring of labour supply). Changes in industrial relations are therefore in large measure path-dependent. A central characteristic of colonial Namibia was the deep interpenetration of state and markets. The evolution of settler-colonialism in Namibia was premised on the exclusion of its black population from the rights and privileges accorded to the white community. With its monopoly on the legitimate use of violence, the colonial state played a pivotal role in social control by safeguarding the privileges of white people and securing the oppression of black people. As in many other countries on the sub-continent, apartheid policies created highly adversarial industrial relations and a labour market deeply segmented on race, gender and occupational lines. Industrial relations in colonial Namibia have been described as 'primitive in the extreme' (SALB, 1978: 31). At the risk of oversimplification, passive white trade unions were incorporated into an institutionalised system of labour regulation at a relatively early period of industrialisation. Black workers, by contrast, were denied collective bargaining rights and subjected to despotic forms of labour regulation until a relatively late stage in the process of industrialisation. Crucially, black Namibians experienced colonialism most directly through the efforts of the state and employers at regulating the conditions in which their labour was incorporated, allocated, controlled and reproduced in the labour market.

According to Burawoy (1985), it is not the labour process that distinguishes industrial production under colonialism, but rather the particular mechanisms through which production relations are regulated. He refers to this production regime as *colonial despotism:* 'despotic, because force prevails over consent; colonial, because one racial group dominates through political, legal and economic rights denied to the other' (1985: 226). Racism and physical violence were the organising principles on which this regime was founded. White supervisors had enormous power over the pay, bonuses, fines, employment conditions, job security and discipline of black workers. Given the absence of legitimate mechanisms of labour regulation such as trade unions, migrant workers invariably developed clandestine organisations, independent of the compound system and its network of functionaries, that were often much more difficult for managers to control (Van Onselen, 1980; Burawoy, 1985; Cohen, 1991). That is, the success of colonial despotism in suppressing the development of collective mediation by black workers precipitated a crisis of regulation. Despite significant differences in the pace, dynamics, and timing of its decline, the supremacy of the 'company state' was eroded by rising levels of discontent and conflict in the workplace; a decline in the arbitrary power of white supervisors; and a relaxation in the regulations governing the flow of workers into the urban centres. These developments clearly exposed the limitations of a reliance on the company state as a mechanism of industrial conciliation and social control. The decline of the company state and the subsequent rise of trade unions reshaped the mechanisms through which production relations were reproduced and conflict in the workplace was regulated.

In the post-colonial period, overt physical violence against black workers was largely eliminated; personnel departments were established to control black labour; the job colour-bar was shifted up the occupational hierarchy; and the power of white supervisors was drastically curtailed. While racial discrimination is still evident, the increasing bureaucratisation of labour regulation introduced a greater measure of administration by rules into the employment relationship and shifted managerial decision-making into the higher reaches of the enterprise. The dissolution of the production regime associated with colonial despotism facilitated a growing intervention of the state apparatuses in the processes of labour regulation. In particular, the post-colonial state endeavours to make the ex-colony attractive to foreign investment by investing in its physical and human infrastructure, and actively managing its labour market. With political independence and majority rule, surplus was 'transferred back to the metropolis via economic mechanisms, while external political constraints became internalised as class forces' (Burawoy, 1985:245). The rise of the post-colonial state was therefore accompanied by a greater interpenetration of production and state apparatuses. That is, since 'the company state was fragmented and the new production apparatuses were weaker, less extensive, and more autonomous from management, the state itself intervened to narrow the scope of purely industrial struggle ... [by introducing mechanisms] for the regulation and absorption of class struggle at the level of the firm' (1985: 245). As a result, colonial and post-colonial systems of labour regulation are characterised by distinct combinations of economic and extra-economic forms of compulsion.

Although there were significant continuities between the different historical phases demarcated below, each was characterised by the dominance of a particular set of regulatory mechanisms. These include the growing prominence of contractual regulation and racial segregation during the first period of South African colonial occupation; the processes of repression and reform, resistance and accommodation that moulded the institutionalisation and subsequent decline of the migrant labour system under apartheid-colonialism; and the increasing managerial preoccupation with employment 'flexibility' and Taylorist forms of work organisation in the post-independence era.

Namibia under South African rule: migrants, masters and the gendarmerie state

South Africa's colonial rule in Namibia revolved fundamentally around the consolidation of its economic dominance and the expansion of its political philosophy of racial segregation. As early as 1923, Gijsbert Hofmeyer, the first South African civilian Administrator, noted that 'native policy in South West Africa . . . is part and parcel of the native policy of . . . South Africa' (cited in Gottschalk, 1983: 71).

In the first period of South African rule (1915–50), the oppressive system of labour regulation introduced by the German colonial authority was consolidated, although there was now some attempt to legitimise it in terms of contractual principles and the virtues of hard work. Given the fact that a contractual regime depends largely on individual bargaining and market power, the authority of employers and the state over black workers was largely unbridled.

In 1943, the South West Africa Native Labour Association (SWANLA) was established to maximise the number of recruits at the lowest possible cost to itself and its industry clients. As a monopsonistic wage-fixing mechanism, SWANLA not only abolished free choice in the labour market, but also effectively eliminated wage competition for migrant labour. A key objective of the migrant labour system was to insulate farmers and small employers from wage competition with the mines and urban enterprises. Migrant workers recruited by SWANLA generally did not know for whom or where they would be working until they reached their destination. By regulating the incorporation and allocation of labour, the colonial state prevented a bidding up of wages despite recurring labour shortages.

The second period of South African rule (1950–77) witnessed the consolidation of an apartheid-style system of labour regulation geared primarily towards the control of labour migration. The balkanisation of Namibia and the associated system of labour migration assumed an increasingly pivotal role in mobilising, allocating, controlling and reproducing black labour.

Two-thirds of the labour force in Namibia were migrants in the 1970s – a higher proportion than almost anywhere else in the world, including South Africa itself (Cronje and Cronje, 1979: 6). By 1980, migrant workers dominated all three major economic sectors, comprising over 95 per cent of black workers in mining, 65 per cent in fishing and 50 per cent in agriculture (SWAPO, 1981: 68). In this system of retrogressive migration the demand for labour was decisively shaped by the structure of the colonial economy; while the supply of labour was strongly influenced by the cycles of planting and harvesting, annual rainfall and food security, degrees of dependence on wage labour, levels of cash trading in the sending areas, and established patterns of household resource distribution that consistently favoured older males.

As the struggle for national liberation gathered momentum, a range of draconian security laws passed by the South African government after 1948 were extended to Namibia. In the eyes of the National Party government, industrial action by black workers was an integral part of resistance to its policies and had to be suppressed along with the other activities of SWAPO (the main liberation movement). The banning of persons and publications; the harassment, detention and torture of political activists; the prohibition on public meetings; and the general suppression of oppositional activity authorised by these laws had deleterious consequences for the normal activities associated with trade unionism (Simons, 1967; Gottschalk, 1978; Konig, 1983).

Few employers took their contractual obligations towards their employees seriously and most continued to pursue the *ante bellum* methods of maintaining discipline in the workplace by meting out harsh punishment to their employees (Van Rooyen, 1996: 142). In their efforts to maintain order in the workplace, employers and the colonial authority sought to reinforce the idea of the 'happy native' by seeking to remove the 'contamination' by 'outside agitators' (Gordon, 1998: 71). Not surprisingly, therefore only nine strikes explicitly related to employment conditions have been identified in the period from 1916 to 1948 (Gottschalk, 1978: 90). More common and viable forms of worker opposition included individual defiance, go-slows, desertion, and the deliberate sabotage of production. Gordon (1977) argues that the totalitarian nature of authority in the workplace generated an occupationally-based code of 'brotherhood' as the key mechanism of solidarity among contract mine workers. This provided the primary organisational framework for the 'underground' or informal resistance network developed by migrant workers.

The occupational structure of most enterprises in Namibia reflected a systematic racial discrimination: a majority of unskilled, largely manual, jobs filled almost exclusively by black workers, and a predominantly white administrative, technical, supervisory and managerial hierarchy. By the late-1970s, whites held over 90 per cent of senior supervisory, professional and technical jobs while 85 per cent of black workers were employed as 'general labourers' (SWAPO, 1981: 66).

Working conditions were uniformly harsh and often dangerous, subject to crude forms of managerial control ranging from 'the regimented discipline of the big mines to the arbitrary violence of many small employers in the towns and on the ranches' (SWAPO, 1981: 78). Many employers were a law unto themselves and workers faced automatic reprisals if they aspired to any meaningful levels of collective influence on their conditions of employment.

As the largest and longest strike in Namibia's history, the mass action of 1971–72 played a profound role in eroding the credibility of South Africa's newly created tribal authorities; heightening the political consciousness and collective confidence of workers; and undermining the stability of the apartheid-based mode of labour regulation. The strike was coordinated through a strike committee whose members were elected on a regional basis, thereby incorporating clear democratic governing principles into the structure of the nascent labour movement. This wide-spread resistance to the migrant labour system provided the spark that re-ignited the struggle for national liberation as it broadened into a generalised opposition to South Africa's occupation of Namibia. SWAPO's national organisation and branch structures proved to be pivotal in the scale and efficacy of the general strike.

Under the combination of worker demands for employment reforms and pressure from prominent elements in the business sector to have the flow of labour 'normalised', the colonial authority finally relented and agreed to dissolve SWANLA and to ameliorate the harsher aspects of the migrant labour system. However, the proclamations of 1972 and 1973 that established tribal labour bureaux and repealed statutes such as the *Master and Servant Proclamation* of 1920, clearly highlighted the narrow parameters of the state's 'reform' process.

By the late-1970s, income distribution in Namibia was probably the most unequal in the world. Household income far below subsistence levels was a reality for black people in the rural areas – i.e. the bulk of the population. In addition to the whites, a small black urban elite benefited disproportionately from developmental efforts throughout the 1970s and 1980s. The 'Living Wage' campaign launched by the unions in 1986 graphically illustrated the inadequacy of minimum wage rates.

Trade union organisation among black workers was largely sporadic and limited to a narrow range of occupations, industries and regions until the late-1980s. The majority of trade unions were either formally or informally affiliated to a federation. The most significant of these was the National Union of Namibian Workers (NUNW) which was formally established as a trade union federation in 1989. In its formative years, the NUNW prioritised the struggle for national liberation over the improvement of employment conditions and the consolidation of shopfloor structures (Melber, 1983; Bauer, 1997). As a prominent trade union leader noted, it was impossible to separate the problems faced by workers from colonial oppression and therefore 'the workers' movement can only function as a part and parcel of the national liberation struggle' (cited in Wood, 1987: 68). This strategic orientation had a significant impact on the unions' role in both the workplace and the wider society. The efficacy of trade union organisation during this period was heavily circumscribed by security laws, the official encouragement of collaborationist unions, and rising levels of poverty, marginalisation and unemployment. By the late-1980s, an estimated 110 000 people were employed as migrant workers with effective trade unionism and rising wages confined to sectors with limited scope for further employment growth: the public (40 000 employees), manufacturing (28 500), and mining sectors (20 000). The bulk of the 240 000 people 'employed' in so-called subsistence farming, 148 000 as tertiary sector workers, and 56 000 in commercial agriculture remained beyond the reach of the trade unions (ILO, 1989: 76).

In the third period of South African rule (1977–89), the crisis in accumulation and regulation, rooted in structural contradictions which were already present in the earlier periods, become organic. The apartheid labour market that was consolidated in the previous period impeded the mobility and reduced the value of black labour power, fostered debilitating skill shortages, and generated extensive opposition from semi- and unskilled black workers. As the need for a more settled and skilled workforce increased, this rigid racial segmentation of the labour market became an obstacle to further economic growth and to the restructuring of the labour process. The apartheid regime's response to this crisis incorporated moments of repression and reform. Attempts at overcoming the barriers to profitability and stability included a strengthening of the repressive apparatuses, the incorporation of some black workers into the urban labour markets on a more permanent basis, the introduction of institutionalised collective bargaining and formal dispute-resolution mechanisms, and a greater reliance on market-induced movements of the reserve army of labour from the bantustans.

The low levels of industrial action in the first half of the period from 1977 to 1989 were followed by a complete cessation of strike activity from April 1983 to October 1986. This extraordinary period of 'industrial calm' was in large measure the product of the vigorous application of security measures by the Administrator-General in suppressing the liberation struggle. The sudden and dramatic increase in industrial action from 1986 onwards culminated, in 1989, in the second highest number of recorded strikes in a single year to date. A combination of factors that included the progressive liberalisation of the industrial relations regime and the growing inevitability of national liberation, contributed to this upsurge in worker militancy.

Rising international pressures coincided with intensified internal strains to place demands on the regulation of accumulation in South Africa, which its apartheid-based mode of regulation could not absorb. This confluence of national, regional and international pressures during the late-1980s compelled the apartheid regime to seek an internal negotiated settlement and to end its illegal occupation of Namibia. When it became clear to the South African government that any political solution which excluded SWAPO would lack legitimacy, the regime shifted its energies and resources towards a neo-colonial outcome that would ensure the continued protection of South African interests under a future SWAPO government. With the collapse of colonial despotism, the incorporation-marginalisation dialectic was shifted onto a new terrain, away from the local/settled versus migrant/transitory division towards an increasing segmentation of the labour market and rising urban unemployment. Consequently, changes in the regulation of the labour market have created opportunities for advancement by groups of more skilled and organised employees, while less skilled and unorganised groups have generally experienced a stagnation or deterioration in employment conditions.

Labour regulation in the first decade of independence: 'flexibility', globalisation and neo-colonialism

Existing forms of labour market segmentation, techniques of managerial control, levels of technological development and so on represent a distinct, prior set of possibilities and constraints for the establishment of new forms of labour regulation. At independence, Namibia presented a contradiction common in African decolonisation: 'the conditions that had allowed international capital to realise large, even vast profits, and were expected to do so again, were in contradiction with those for constructing an equitable and civilised society for its people' (Leys and Saul, 1995b:196). The Namibian government had to balance the heightened expectations among workers following the transition to democracy with the need to attract foreign investment and maintain stability in industrial relations. This balancing act has led to a contradictory fusion of neo-liberal and neo-corporatist forms of labour regulation: individual market solutions in the structuring of labour supplies, skills development and occupational mobility; and tripartite strategies geared towards the collective resolution of tensions between flexibility and security. The expanded social regulation of the labour market is increasingly at odds with the dictates of neo-liberal economic policies. This is reflected in, among others, the tensions between the promotion of 'quality jobs' by the Ministry of Labour and the idea of 'any job is better than none' that is implicit in the policies developed by the Ministry of Trade and Industry.

Namibia has all the hallmarks of a country that does not consume what it produces and does not produce what it consumes. At the time of independence, 90 per cent of physical goods produced in Namibia were exported to South Africa, while 90 per cent of imports were from South Africa. Approximately 85 per cent of all Namibia's imports are still sourced from South Africa (Ministry of Trade and Industry 1999: 21).

In an attempt to promote business confidence, minimise potential political instability, and prevent the flight of skills and capital, the SWAPO government adopted fairly conservative economic policies. There are already significant indications that the dualistic economic structure of the colonial era is being reproduced in a new form by the post-independence political order. The continued decline of the subsistence economies in the rural areas and the associated loss of employment opportunities contributed to a massive influx of people into the urban areas.

The labour market

The establishment of the Ministry of Labour, the Office of the Labour Commissioner, the Labour Inspectorate, the Labour Court and District Labour Courts, the Labour Advisory Council and other tripartite institutions such as the Social Security Commission reflect the growing institutionalisation of labour regulation after independence. However, the government's policies of economic liberalisation have inhibited the role of labour market institutions and patterned the distribution of economic rewards to the detriment of the poor and marginalised sectors of society. Despite rhetoric to the contrary, national policies for reconstruction and development have consolidated distinct sets of winners and losers in the labour market. There are significant tensions between the government's stated goal of creating 'good' jobs and the emphasis on developing an economic structure that is adaptable to rapid changes in highly competitive global markets.

The voluntarist nature of Namibia's post-independence labour dispensation means that there is little compelling employers to negotiate with workers. It has also left the negative perceptions of trade unionism unchallenged and reinforced the commitment to a *laissez-faire* philosophy among employers.

The institutionalised discrimination associated with apartheid-capitalism has created racial divisions that largely coincided with occupational and class boundaries. Whites are grossly over-represented in the technical, professional, administrative, and managerial occupations. Conversely, black Namibians are confined almost exclusively to unskilled and semi-skilled positions.

The statutory framework

The Constitution of the Republic of Namibia (1990), conventions of the International Labour Office (ILO), and an official declaration issued by the cabinet in 1990 entitled *National Policy on Labour and Manpower Development* constitute the primary sources of the new industrial relations regime. The principal piece of legislation which regulates employment conditions and labour market institutions in Namibia is the *Labour Act* of 1992. The Act is largely mandatory and allows for exemptions to very few provisions. It signalled the end of colonial-despotism in the workplace and attempted to regulate an increasing militant and assertive labour movement. The Act is universal in the sense that it applies to all economic sectors and all occupational categories. The agricultural, domestic service and public sectors were included in the statutory dispensation for the first time in Namibia's history. In contrast to the labour movements in many developed countries that have suffered major setbacks and are confronted with a hostile policy and legal framework, the role of the unions in Namibia is bolstered by the extensive legal protection of their organisational rights, the comprehensive safeguards against unfair dismissals and discrimination, and the statutory provisions on neo-corporatist forms of employee representation. The Labour Act is in large measure a product of SWAPO's historical emergence out of the labour movement and the pivotal role played by migrant workers in the struggle for national liberation.

The Labour Act deals with basic conditions of employment, dismissals and unfair disciplinary actions in considerable detail. On most substantive matters, the parties are encouraged to engage in voluntary collective regulation, albeit within the broad framework and spirit of the Act. State involvement is facilitating rather than dictating, leaving considerable room for the parties to conduct the employment relationship. While it retained the voluntarist principles of the previous dispensation, the Act provides for the creation of an institutional framework designed to regulate the individual and collective employment relationship. Within this framework there are administrative, regulatory and advisory functions designed largely to govern the employment conditions of 'regular' employees and to fortify the role of trade unions in workplace industrial relations. While collective bargaining is encouraged, basic conditions of employment are subject to statutory regulation and a Labour Court would adjudicate on industrial disputes. This blend of voluntarism and compulsion was strongly influenced by the ILO conventions implemented in Namibia.

Collective bargaining

The discriminatory statutory framework of the colonial era meant that the system of collective industrial relations was largely informal, subject to the balance of powers at a particular workplace, and prone to unpredictable outbursts of militancy. Labour legislation since independence has, however, curbed the autocratic discipline of the employer over permanent, full-time employees in the workplace. A balance of class forces decidedly in the employers' favour changed as new labour laws and the increasing power of organised labour limited management's discretion and room to manoeuvre.

The annual incidence of strikes during the first five years after independence was greater than the preceding twelve years of interim administrative rule. This was due in large measure to the high expectations of workers immediately after independence, widespread discontent with the pace of change, and continuing discrimination and inequality in the workplace (Jauch, 1996; Murray and Wood, 1997b). Workplace issues rather than overtly political demands increasingly emerged as the primary trigger for industrial action. The bulk of disputes in the workplace revolved around wages. The majority of strikes involved less than 500 employees and 70 per cent lasted only a day or less, with only 13.8 per cent lasting longer than three days (Van Rooyen, 1996: 255). The short duration of strikes reflects the fact that wildcat strikes continued to constitute the major type of industrial action in the country.

Due to lingering racial tensions in the workplace, strikes were often highly volatile with widespread accusations of intimidation, assault and obstructive picketing levelled against the workers. The government has actively intervened to prevent or terminate strikes in the larger enterprises, and senior officials repeatedly called for an end to unfair labour practices and stressed the need for labour discipline and improved productivity.

Following the widespread negotiation of recognition agreements under the new dispensation, annual wage negotiations soon became entrenched in the urban centres and in the larger enterprises. Typically, these agreements protect union officials and members from victimisation and provide for the deduction of union dues, the resolution of disputes, industrial action, grievance and disciplinary procedures, and training (Klerck and Murray, 1997). Workplace bargaining is the most prominent form of collective labour regulation. This narrow bargaining structure is a significant factor in the considerable variation that exists in the terms and conditions of employment within and between industries and occupations.

Virtually all NUNW-affiliates negotiate terms and conditions of employment on a decentralised basis, even in industries where they dominate in all companies. The highly decentralised nature of collective bargaining results in the unions spending the bulk of their time and meagre resources on a multitude of separate negotiations with predominantly small companies.

The Namibian trade union movement concentrated most of its energy and resources on the organisation of (predominantly male) black unskilled and semi-skilled workers. One unintended consequence of this organising strategy – despite its inherent logic and priority – was to cement the divisions between black and white, skilled and unskilled, and permanent and temporary workers. In sharp contrast to the successes of the industrial unions in organising semi-skilled employees in the manufacturing and mining sectors, union organisation in sectors (such as retail and construction) with a long-standing prevalence of female and casual labour has historically been inconsequential. It is precisely in the sectors where the need for collective regulation is the greatest that the unions have the least influence and where they experience the most difficulties in recruiting and retaining members. Jobs are fast disappearing in sectors (such as mining) with a history of high union density, while new jobs are created mainly in sectors (such as services) where the unions have traditionally been relatively weak. While collective bargaining has certainly improved the lot of organised workers in Namibia, it seems that these gains were made at the expense of other workers rather than profits.

Conclusion

The prevailing institutional and normative landscape has significantly constrained the ability of Namibian trade unions to develop an effective strategic vision to inform their interaction with employers and the state. As a result, the union movement has been 'unable to institutionalise the gains it has made at the shopfloor level, and has found itself marginalised from the national policy formulation arena' (Murray and Wood, 1997a: 159). In other words, the organisational framework and ideological orientation of the labour movement has decisively qualified the form of trade unionism that is possible or feasible in Namibia. In particular, the NUNW and its affiliates need to counter the threats posed by a narrow focus on job controls; a growing division between membership and leadership; a decline in worker control over decision-making processes; the marginalisation of local and regional structures; increasing bureaucracy and a corresponding decline in accountability; and a deteriorating organisational capacity. Perhaps the most pressing challenge facing organised labour is how to reconcile the calls for 'flexibility', the demands of globalisation, the encouragement of small businesses and so on with a flattening of the wage curve and an expanded social regulation of the labour market.

Collective bargaining in Namibia is, in many respects, at a cross-road. The choice confronting the state, employers and the trade union leadership is between a low-wage, low-skill, deregulated and fragmented framework which emphasises the need to attract foreign investment and reduce social spending; and a high-wage, high-skill, centralised and co-determinist framework in which employee participation and training are seen as vital for increasing the productivity of the economy.

Given the commitment of employers' organisations and the state to neoliberal economic policies, a critical issue for debate is whether the labour movement has the power, influence and resources necessary to (a) obstruct the cheap-labour route, and (b) constitute the driving force behind a high-wage and high-skill route to increased competitiveness. A new embeddedness of market forces in social relations is necessary to defend the most vulnerable and precarious employees in the lower echelons of the labour market. The balance of intra-class forces (e.g. large versus small employers, skilled versus unskilled, urban versus rural) has decisively influenced the pace, direction and dynamics of changes in bargaining structures and practices. A lack of centralised bargaining forums means that the current involvement of trade union leaders in policy-making is by and large divorced from active intervention by the membership. A labour movement consumed by disputes revolving around recognition, dismissals, wage increases, and the like would be hard pressed to sustain an informed and mandated presence in broader decision-making structures. The trade unions will have to consolidate and expand their presence in the workplace before they can engage successfully with broader decision-making forums. Strong, militant shop steward structures are the best insurance against both oligarchy in the union structure and subservience to the priorities of management or the state. If a balance cannot be found between seeking to influence the government and becoming the labour wing of SWAPO, the risk of demobilisation or aimless rank-and-file militancy will be considerable.

References

Bauer, G. (1997), 'Labour Relations in Occupied Namibia', in G. Klerck, A. Murray & M. Sycholt (eds), *Continuity and Change: Labour Relations in Independent Namibia.* Windhoek: Gamsberg Macmillan.

Burawoy, M. (1985), *The Politics o/Production. Factory Regimes Under Capitalism and Socialism.* London: Verso.

Cohen, R. (1991), *Contested Domains: Debates in International Labour Studies.* London: Zed Books.

Cooper, A.D. (1999), 'The Institutionalization of Contract Labour in Namibia', *Journal of Southern African Studies* 25 (1): 121–38.

Cronje, G. & Cronje, S. (1979), *The Workers of Namibia.* London: International Defence and Aid Fund.

Deakin, S. & Reed, H. (2000), *The Contested Meaning of Labour Market Flexibility: Economic Theory and the Discourse of European Integration.* Working Paper No. 162. Cambridge: ESRC Centre for Business Research, University of Cambridge.

Dekker, L.D. Hemson, D. Kane-Berman, J.S. Lever, J. & Schlemmer, L. (1975), 'Case Studies in African Labour Action in South Africa and Namibia (South West Africa)', in Sandbrook, R. and Cohen, R. (eds), *The Development of an African Working Class: Studies in Class Formation and Action.* London: Longman.

First, R. (1963), *South West Africa.* Harmondsworth: Penguin.

Gordon, R. (1977), *Mines, Masters and Migrants.* Johannesburg: Ravan.

Gordon, R. (1978), 'Some Organizational Aspects of Labour Protest Among Contract Workers', *South African Labour Bulletin,* 4, 1 &2: 116–23.

Gordon, R. (1982), 'Contract Workers in Namibian Mines', in Allen, C. and Williams, G. (eds), *Sociology of Developing Societies: Sub-Saharan Africa.* London: Macmillan.

Gordon, R.J. (1998), 'Vagrancy, Law and 'Shadow Knowledge': internal pacification, 1915–1939', in Hayes, P. Silvester, J., Wallace, M. and Hartmann, W. (eds), *Namibia Under South African Rule. Mobility and Containment:* 1915–46. Oxford: James Currey.

Gottschalk, K. (1978), 'South African Labour Policy in Namibia, 1915–1975' *South African Labour Bulletin* 4, 1&2: 75–106.

Gottschalk, K. (1983), 'South Africa in Namibia: 1915–1980s', in C. Saunders (ed.), *Perspectives on Namibia: Past and Present,* Occasional Paper No.4. Cape Town: Centre for African Studies, University of Cape Town.

Hayes, P. Silvester, J. Wallace, M. & Hartmann, W. (eds) (1998), *Namibia Under South African Rule. Mobility and Containment: 1915–46.* Oxford: James Currey.

Hishongwa, N. (1992), *The Contract Labour System and Its Effects on Family and Social Life in Namibia: A Historical Perspective.* Windhoek: Gamsberg Macmillan.

Jauch, H. (1996), 'Tension Grows: labour relations in Namibia', *South African Labour Bulletin* 20, 4: 90–3.

Jowell, K. (1983), 'Economic Priorities for an Independent Namibia', in R.I. Rotberg (ed.), *Namibia: Political and Economic Prospects.* Cape Town: David Philip.

Kane-Bennan, J.S. (1972), *Contract Labour in South West Africa.* Johannesburg: South African Institute of Race Relations.

Klerck, G. & Murray, A. (1997), 'Collective Bargaining: the joint regulation of terms and conditions of employment', Klerck, G., Murray, A. and Sycholt, M. (eds), *Continuity and Change: Labour Relations in Independent Namibia.* Windhoek: Gamsberg Macmillan.

Klerck, G. Murray, A. & Sycholt, M. (1997). 'The Environment of Labour Relations', in Klerck, G., Murray, A. and Sycholt, M. (eds), *Continuity and Change: Labour Relations in Independent Namibia.* Windhoek: Gamsberg Macmillan.

Konig, B. (1983), *Namibia: The Ravages of War*. London: International Defence and Aid Fund.
Leys, C. & Saul, J.S. (1995a), 'Introduction', in Leys, C. and Saul, J.S. (eds), *Namibia's Liberation Struggle: The Two-Edged Sword*. London: James Currey.
Leys, C. & Saul, J.S. (1995b), 'Conclusion' in C. Leys & J.S. Saul (eds), *Namibia's Liberation Struggle: The Two-Edged Sword*. London: James Currey.
Melber, H. (1983), 'National Union of Namibian Workers: Background and Information', *Journal of Modern African Studies*, 21, 1: 151-8.
Ministry of Trade and Industry (1999), *Review of the 1992 White Paper on Industrial Development*. Windhoek: Ministry of Trade and Industry.
Murray, A. & Wood, G. (1997a), 'The Namibian Trade Union Movement: Trends, Practices and Shopfloor Perceptions', in Klerck, G., Murray, A. and Sycholt, M. (eds), *Continuity and Change: Labour Relations in Independent Namibia*. Windhoek: Gamsberg Macmillan.
Murray, A. & Wood, G. (1997b), 'Industrial Action: Conflict and Accommodation', in Klerck, G., Murray, A. and Sycholt, M. (eds), *Continuity and Change: Labour Relations in Independent Namibia*. Windhoek: Gamsberg Macmillan.
National Union of Namibian Workers (NUNW) (1998), *Second National Congress: Namibian Workers Ready to Face the Challenges in the Next Millennium*. Windhoek: NUNW.
Ndadi, V. (1989), *Breaking Contract: The Story of Vinnia Ndadi*. London: International Defence and Aid Fund.
Simons, H. (1967), 'Techniques of Domination: South Africa's Colonialism', in Segal, C and First, R. (eds), *South West Africa: A Travesty of Trust*. London: Andre Deutsch.
South African Labour Bulletin (SALB), editorial board. (1979), 'The View from the Shop Floor', *South African Labouor Bulletin*, 4, 1&2: 4-74.
SWAPO. (1981), *To be Born a Nation*. London: Zed.
Van Onselen, C. (1980), *Chibaro: African Mine Labour in Southern Rhodesia, 1900-1933* Johannesburg: Ravan Press.
Van Rooyen, J. W.F. (1996), *Portfolio of Partnership. An Analysis of Labour Relations in a Transitional Society–Namibia*. Windhoek: Gamsberg Macmillan.
Voipio, R. (1981), 'Contract Work through Ovambo Eyes', in Green, R., Kiljunen, M.-L. and Kiljunen, K. (eds), *Namibia: The Last Colony*. London: Longman.
Wood, B. (1987), 'Ben Ulenga on Namibian Trade Unions', *South African Labour Bulletin* 12, 4: 62-70.

10
Industrial Relations and Employment Insecurity in South Africa: The Possibilities of Social Justice Unionism[1]

Pauline Dibben

Introduction

This chapter explores the implications for organised labour of changes in the South African labour market, and the regulation of the employment contract. In response, it is argued that South African trade unions should renew their focus on employment security, and in doing so embrace 'social justice unionism'. This is a term that has been applied more narrowly to an educational context (NCEA, 1994; Peterson, 1998), to the need to mobilise workers on a low income (Tait, 2005), and to broader social concerns (Gapasin and Yates, 2005; Scipes, 2005). As employed here, it encapsulates an underlying concern for distributive, interactional and procedural justice, and focuses on the advancement of job security through union advocacy, participatory democracy, mobilisation, strategic engagement, and links to community organisations.

The focus on job security is one that is strategically difficult, since it implies reduced attention on what has been generally regarded as the union's prime concern – the securing of higher wages – a tried and trusted focus for collective action (Burchell *et al.*, 2002). Instead, it requires the more difficult task of preventing redundancies and protecting the rights of vulnerable workers.[2] At the same time, it implies a reduced focus on broader societal concerns such as education and health, and infrastructure such as electricity, water and transport, albeit that these are relevant to job security.

The chapter proceeds as follows. The first section explores the dynamics of the South African labour market situation, the union response to such changes, and the key developments in employment legislation. Subsequently, 'social justice unionism' is defined through reference to five key propositions, and is distinguished from the established, although contestable, concept of 'social movement unionism'. Thirdly, through drawing on recent empirical research, the chapter seeks to determine whether the Confederation of South African Trade Unions (COSATU) – the main union federation in South Africa – appears to be a prime example of 'social justice unionism', and assesses the extent to which this is therefore a descriptive or normative concept. Based on the preceding analysis, the concluding section assesses potential challenges for the future.

The changing South African labour market, and the union response

The political and economic situation in South Africa was transformed in the landmark year of 1994, when the majority of South Africans welcomed full democratisation, and the previously banned African National Congress (ANC) gained political power. As a result, economic sanctions were ended, and new markets were opened up. South Africa sought global competitiveness, phasing out its protective barriers (Rogerson, 2001) and refocusing its macroeconomic policy through GEAR (Growth, Employment and Reconstruction). Competitiveness and efficiency were achieved through training and development, but also through industry restructuring and job cuts. By 2003, nearly 37 per cent of African workers were unemployed (*Labour Market Review*, 2003).

In addition to high levels of unemployment, the South African labour market is also characterised by a growing 'peripheral' workforce that holds part-time, temporary or 'casual' jobs that are often precarious, lack benefits, and offer low wages (Webster, 2004; Von Holdt and Webster, 2005). This trend is common to many developed countries in the Western world (Peetz and Ollett, 2004), but in the developing world, and more specifically in South Africa, there has also been a rise in informal sector work. By 2003, nearly 2 million people were employed in the informal economy compared to 7.5 million in the formal sector (excluding agriculture) (*Statistics South Africa*, 2004). The conditions experienced by these workers are generally worse than those who are formally employed, and as such, informal sector working tends to be a last resort. This is, at least partly, due to the largely unregulated nature of informal sector activity.

Trade unions have traditionally tended to organise those in unskilled or semi-skilled manual work and low grade service sector jobs, but these have declined during recent years. Although COSATU, the main trade union federation in South Africa, has adopted recommendations to organise what it terms as 'flexible' workers, little has been done in practice, arguably because it wishes to protect existing members, and only become involved in issues concerning highly marginal workers when the interests of existing members became threatened (Rees, 1997; Webster, 2006). Indeed, Webster and Buhlungu (2004) have argued that there are signs of both an internal and external crisis of representation: a misinterpretation of the needs of existing members, and a lack of engagement of the 'new working poor'.

The workers who most often suffer from insecure work include female, young and black workers. Female employment has risen in South Africa over the years, but most women tend to occupy low-paying jobs in wholesale or retail trade, or in clerical jobs which are often part-time and casual in nature, with low unionisation rates (Lalthapershad, 2001). They also face barriers in attending union meetings and becoming actively involved in union affairs (Tshoaedi and Hlela, 2006). Younger workers are also often on the margins of union life (Wood and Dibben, 2006), and black workers still appear to face prejudice in the workplace, irrespective of attempts by both unions and the Government to obtain 'Black Economic Empowerment'. Historically, under apartheid, higher level and skilled positions were reserved for the white population, and black workers were excluded from collective bargaining. Following the Wiehahn reforms in 1979, independent unions were included in collective bargaining and African workers gradually moved into semi-skilled and skilled jobs. However, divisions across racial lines still exist, albeit that they are now configured on informal rather than formal lines (Bezuidenhout, 2005). Unions have also struggled to reach out to informal sector workers, at least partly due to barriers such as the cultural background of these workers, difficulties in arranging meetings, and the lack of a clear employer to bargain with (Webster, 2004).

The role of COSATU and employment legislation in South Africa

COSATU was a principal opponent of the apartheid regime, and in the early 1990s became formally allied to the African National Congress and the South African Communist Party. By 1985, it had a membership of nearly 500,000, making it the biggest union federation in the country's history, rising to 1.26 million by 1991 (Maree, 1998). It has also been influential in the development of labour legislation. In 1995, following negotiations between political parties, business and trade unions, the Labour Relations Act was introduced. This provided for freedom of association rights, enabling employees and job seekers to participate freely in trade union activities, and also organisational rights, allowing union access to workplaces to arrange meetings, recruit workers and hold elections and ballots. It also reaffirmed the role of industry level bargaining, and introduced the idea of workplace forums. The provisions of this Act, together with its amendments in 2002, and other relevant pieces of legislation are outlined in Table 10.1.

The changes to legislation have impacted positively upon both individual and collective rights, but only cover the shrinking proportion of workers employed in the formal sector. In short, to be relevant to the needs of the bulk of South Africans, unions have to explore ways of meeting the concerns of both those outside of traditionally heavily unionised occupations, and long-standing members that remain concerned about the adverse consequences of neo-liberal reforms. Hence, in subsequent sections, I examine the extent to which the trade union movement in South Africa, and in particular, COSATU, can be characterised as a 'Social Justice Union' – one that is underpinned by social justice, and concerned about job security.

Table 10.1 Summary of South African labour legislation – 1995–2003

Legislation	Date	Details
Labour Relations Act	1995	Concerned with: • Fairness in promotion, demotion, probation; training or benefits; suspension or disciplinary action short of dismissal; refusal to re-instate or re-employ; occupational detriment (whistleblowing). • Dismissal for misconduct, incapability, or operational reasons. • Forming and joining of trade unions and employers organisations, collective organisation and bargaining • Closed shops and agency shops (employer contributions to a fund promoting worker's socio-economic interests) • Strikes and lock-outs (excluding essential services and maintenance services), secondary action and protected stay away protest action to defend the socio-economic interests of employees. • Workplace forums • Settling labour disputes through conciliation and negotiation, (Commission for Conciliation, Mediation and Arbitration – CCMA)
Labour Relations Act	Amended 2002	Provision for: • Right to strike and facilitation of disputes around retrenchments. • Increased powers to bargaining councils and officials; bargaining councils must report to the Registrar on the activities of small business. • Closing the loophole on "independent contractors" whereby employers did not contribute to the Unemployment Insurance Fund (UIF), and were not covered by the compensation fund or occupational health and safety legislation. • Classification as 'employees' if: under the direction or control of an employer, work hours subject to the control of the employer, form part of an organisation, worked an average of 40 hours for one person in the last three months, are economically dependent on the employer, are provided with tools of trade or equipment, or only work for one employer. • Domestic workers have almost equal rights except that a trade union may not enter a home unless the employer agrees, and an employer does not have to disclose information to a trade union. • Temporary employment services are responsible for complying with an employer's duties to the employee.

Act	Year	Description
Basic Conditions of Employment Act	1995, amended 2002	Applies to all employers and workers and regulates: • leave (incl. minimum 21 days paid annual leave, sickness, maternity leave of four months, and 3 days family responsibility leave) • working hours (45 hours a week and max 10 hours overtime, paid at 1.5 times usual rate) • employment contracts • deductions, pay slips and terminations. Also prohibits employment of children under 15 and forced labour.
Employment Equity Act	1998, amended 2002	• Promotes equal opportunity and fair treatment in employment through elimination of unfair discrimination • Affirmative action to address disadvantages in employment experienced by designated groups: Blacks (African, Coloured and Indian), women and those with disabilities. Commission for Employment Equity, set up in 1999, aims to eradicate unfair practices, implement and promote the Act, and advise Minister on codes of good practice.
Skills Development Act	1998, amended 2003	Provides an institutional framework to devise and implement national, sector and workplace strategies aiming to: • Improve and develop skills, quality of working life, prospects of work and mobility, productivity and employer competitiveness • Promote self-employment and the delivery of social services. • Increase investment in education and training and integrate those strategies within the National Qualifications Framework • Provide for learnerships that lead to recognised occupational qualifications • Provide for skills development through a levy-grant scheme and a National Skills Fund. • Provide for and regulate employment services, improve the prospects of those previously disadvantaged by unfair discrimination, and redress them through training and education.
Skills Development Levies Act	1999, amended 2003	• Financing mechanisms to incentivise the growth of skills among workers. • From 2002, all employers pay 1% of their workers' pay to the skills development levy, with money going to Sector Education and Training Authorities (SETAs) and the Skills Development Fund.
Unemployment Insurance Act	2001	• Assisting the unemployed and their beneficiaries through a fund to which employers and employees contribute. It prescribes unemployment, maternity, illness, adoption and dependents' benefits.

Source: Adapted from Dibben et al. (2005).

Defining 'social justice unionism': a distinct concept?

Social Justice Unionism assumes that 'social justice' underpins all aspects of a union's work; it is arguably the root of collective action (Kelly, 1998). More specifically, it requires that distributive, interactional and procedural justice underpins all aspects of a union's work. Thus, unions should try to ensure fair outcomes within the workplace (distributive justice), through fair decision-making processes (procedural justice), and convey outcomes to workers in a respectful way, or with dignity (interactional justice) (Johnson and Jarley, 2004).[3]

The term 'Social Movement Unionism' is one that has been applied in different ways, and in various contexts (see for example Moody, 1997; Munck, 2000; Dibben, 2004). The early analyses by Webster (1988) and Waterman (1993) neatly encapsulate its main features as: internal democracy, worker control and strategic engagement with the government. In addition, for Waterman, it is important for trade unions to proactively engage with a wide range of issues, and also to build international links with both trade unions and social movements.[4] However, as Waterman (ibid.) acknowledges, there has been a widening of the scope of the term 'social movement unionism', and it has arguably become 'too ambiguous through too broad an application' (von Holdt, 2002).

As a development, and also departure from 'Social Movement Unionism', 'Social Justice Unionism' can be understood through the following propositions for union purpose and action:

1. Advocacy – advocacy for those who risk losing jobs, applying distributive and interactional justice
2. Broad based participatory democracy – voice for those who might be at most risk of losing jobs, applying procedural justice
3. Mobilisation – engagement in collective action around job security
4. Strategic engagement – influence on government policy and legislation on job security issues
5. Coalition building – liaison with community organisations in seeking to address the needs of those who are in insecure work/unemployed.

The next section seeks to explore whether South African trade unions conform to this agenda, and in doing so draws on data from the recent Taking Democracy Seriously survey.[5]

COSATU: a 'Social Justice Union'?

In 2004, a nationwide survey was conducted of 655 COSATU members, exploring the nature of worker organisation and the attitudes and expectations of members toward workplace and parliamentary democracy. The workers interviewed included those who were in full-time permanent positions, and those in part-time and temporary employment.[6] In conducting the survey, area sampling was employed, and COSATU members were interviewed at their individual workplaces, replicating the methods used in the surveys conducted in 1994 and 1998. Each of the surveys was undertaken with the support of COSATU's national leadership and after consultation with regional offices; it was also facilitated by the support of the relevant employers from a broad range of sectors, including, in the 2004 survey, both private sector and public sector organisations.

In the sections below, the analysis of a selected number of questions from the 2004 survey helps to shed light on the extent to which COSATU conforms to the above propositions. In order to test statistical significance between key variables, and in particular, to identify the similarities and differences between the attitudes and perceptions of full-time permanent and less secure workers, chi-square analysis was employed.[7]

The concept of Social Justice Unionism, as used here, implies a primary concern for job security. This appears to accord with the views of COSATU members, since analysis of survey data found that more workers ranked jobs as the area where they most wanted to see improvement after the 2004 elections than any other workplace or broader concerns such as the level of wages, the degree of training, or health, education and skills development. This was the case for both full-time permanent and part-time or temporary workers, with no statistically significant differences.

In terms of the first proposition, *Advocacy*, the survey findings show that the majority of union members rely on trade unions to protect their interests – as shown in Table 10.2. This is arguably not surprising, since those questioned were all union members. At the same time, it can be noted that while over

Table 10.2 Reliance on unions to protect interests, by tenure

		Workers will always need trade unions to protect their interests				
		Strongly agree	*Agree*	*Neutral/ don't know*	*Disagree*	*Strongly disagree*
Security of tenure	Fixed term contract or part-time	26 (52%)	21 (42%)	2 (4%)	1 (2%)	0
	Permanent contract full-time	444 (74%)	129 (21%)	15 (3%)	11 (2%)	5 (1%)
Total		470 (72%)	150 (23%)	17 (3%)	12 (2%)	5 (1%)

Note: $p < 0.05$, $df = 4$, $n = 654$.

Table 10.3 Attendance at union meetings, by tenure

		How often do you attend union meetings?				
		Never	Once a week	Once a month	Once a year	Don't know/ can't remember
Security of tenure	Fixed term contract or part-time	11 (22%)	12 (25%)	15 (31%)	4 (8%)	7 (14%)
	Permanent contract fulltime	40 (7%)	162 (28%)	276 (48%)	48 (8%)	53 (9%)
Total		51 (8%)	174 (28%)	291 (46%)	52 (8%)	60 (10%)

Note: p < 0.01, df = 5, n = 629.

70 per cent of those in secure jobs strongly agreed with this, the figure of just over 50 per cent was somewhat lower for those in less secure jobs.

The second key proposition is the need for *participatory democracy* within the trade union, based on the premise of procedural justice. Attendance at union meetings is one possible indicator of participation in trade union affairs, and there was a statistically significant difference in the levels of attendance of those in more secure, and less secure jobs (p < 0.01, df = 5, n = 629). However, as Table 10.3 shows, while about 22 per cent of those in less secure jobs had never attended a meeting, this was the case for about 7 per cent of those in permanent full-time work. To a large extent, this might reflect the inability of part-time workers to attend meetings. However, the disparity is not a function of the difficulty for trade unions in recruiting temporary or part-time workers, since those workers responding were already union members. Again, it might, however, suggest a certain lack of commitment of less secure members to the trade union.

A further question that related to participation in union affairs was whether or not members were also shop stewards. Although there was some difference, so that 27 per cent of those in full-time permanent jobs answered in the affirmative, compared to 16 per cent of other workers, this was not statistically significant. On the other hand, there was such a difference between those who had participated in the elections of shop stewards (p < 0.01, df = 5, n = 621), again suggesting that insecure workers might be less engaged in union affairs.

A third test of 'social justice unionism', as propounded above, is the extent to which workers are *mobilised to take collective action*. In this case, the difference between the two groups of workers was statistically significant, as shown in Table 10.4.

While about 62 per cent of the more secure workers were in workplaces where workers had taken part in collective action, this was the case for 40 per cent

Table 10.4 Engaging in collective action, by tenure

		Participation in industrial action	
		No	Yes
Security of tenure	Fixed term contract or part-time	29 (59%)	20 (41%)
	Permanent contract fulltime	229 (38%)	369 (62%)
Total		258 (40%)	389 (60%)

Note: $p < 0.01$, df = 1, n = 647.

of other workers. Although the question asked whether those within respondents' workplaces took part in collective action, where this was the case it might be expected that a majority of union members would also have been involved.

In terms of *strategic engagement with government*, respondents were asked whether COSATU and its affiliates should send representatives to national parliament. There was not a statistically significant difference between responses to this question, but the vast majority (90 per cent of full-time permanent workers and 87.5 per cent of other workers) considered that this should happen. On the other hand, there was a divergence between groups when asked who the party should represent. Respondents were asked whether, if the majority of people voting for the party are workers, the party should represent: only the interests of workers; all of its supporters, including those who are not workers; or all South Africans, even if worker interests have to be sacrificed. As Table 10.5 illustrates, differences again appeared between those who were in more secure jobs and those who were not.

While almost 60 per cent of those in more secure work felt that the party should represent broader interests, this was the case for less than 50 per cent of those in less secure work. This is arguably surprising, since it might have been thought that those who were more at risk of losing jobs would be more concerned that there was adequate attention paid to those without work. Nevertheless, it seems to reflect the somewhat cynical idea that the more secure people are, the more they can afford to be altruistic.

Finally, the fifth proposition is based on union *liaison with community organisations* in order to advance the concerns of those who are at risk of losing their jobs, or seeking employment. The vast majority of workers considered that the trade union should have links with community organisations, civil society groupings and social movements. However, again, this was less the case for those in insecure work, 22 per cent of whom disagreed with the statement, compared to 6 per cent of full-time permanent workers ($p < 0.001$, df = 2,

Table 10.5 Party representation of workers, by tenure

		If the majority of people who vote for a party in an election are workers, then that party must represent		
		Only the interests of workers	All supporters, including those who are not workers	All South Africans, even if workers' interests are sacrificed
Security of tenure	Fixed term contract or part-time	8 (16%)	24 (48%)	18 (36%)
	Permanent contract full-time	32 (5%)	354 (59%)	215 (36%)
Total		40 (6%)	378 (58%)	233 (36%)

Note: p < 0.01, df = 2, n = 651.

n = 652). It might be expected that those who faced greater insecurity in the workplace would be better able to appreciate the need to link up with organisations that might address broader social problems. However, this is apparently not the case. Instead, it seems that they are focused primarily on workplace concerns.

'Social Justice Unionism' in South Africa: a descriptive or normative analysis?

From the above analysis, it is possible to gain some insight into whether or not 'Social Justice Unionism' is a descriptive model, insofar as COSATU members share behaviours and attitudes along the lines of the five propositions outlined earlier. If 'social justice unionism' is not fully apparent in South Africa, then perhaps it can be considered as a normative model – an ideal that has not yet been attained.

The survey results suggest that most workers prioritised 'jobs' as the area where most improvement was needed, and also that the majority of workers believed that they would always need trade unions to protect their interests. Of some concern, though, is the apparently lower reliance on trade unions of those in insecure work. Again, there is a generally high level of participatory democracy and collective action, albeit that those in insecure work appear to have been less engaged in both respects than full-time permanent members. Moreover, although most workers, irrespective of tenure, appear to have been in favour of the union sending representatives to Parliament, insecure workers appear to favour a narrow remit that does not address broader concerns.

Finally, although most respondents were in favour of links with other organisations, there were again apparent differences between those in secure and less secure jobs. In summary, it appears that although COSATAU goes some way toward fulfilling the remit of a 'social justice union', there are notable differences in attitudes between those in secure and insecure jobs.

Conclusions: moving toward 'Social Justice Unionism' in South Africa

If unions affiliated to COSTAU wish to embrace 'social justice unionism', they face many challenges. In South Africa – as in other developing countries – there has been a dramatic growth in the number of people employed in the informal sector, while those in secure employment are likely to have the most consistent voice in union affairs, but constitute a diminishing proportion of the overall labour market (see, for example, Kingdon and Knight, 2004; Webster and Buhlungu, 2004). At the same time, the number of those employed in formal workplaces but in contingent work appears to be growing. Unions find it difficult to organise these workers, but there are nevertheless some examples of success, as in the case of South African Clothing, Textile and Allied Workers' Union organising homeworkers in the clothing industry, and the National Union of Mineworkers successfully negotiating protection for the workers of sub-contractors (Von Holdt and Webster, 2005). Moreover, in other countries (such as Spain) insecure workers have had more positive attitudes toward trade unionism and mobilisation than stable employees (Macias, 2003) suggesting that it is possible to more effectively engage these workers.

A second challenge is that in focusing on 'job insecurity', it may be difficult to determine an appropriate balance for the use of resources in both strategic engagement and workplace democracy (COSATU, 1996; Naidoo, 2003); increased attention on one of these might imply reduced efforts on the other. A third area of concern is whether a focus on "Social Justice Unionism" is a risky strategy for unions to undertake: its focus on insecure work might lead to an alienation of core workers who seek improvements in pay, training and development or working conditions. Nevertheless, a counter argument is that if and when job security has largely been met, the union can then move on to embrace other concerns; the survey data, moreover, indicates that jobs are the prime concern for all members. Fourthly, such a strategy might result in the union distancing itself from the state, where the government wishes to focus on issues such as inward investment and capital accumulation. To prevent this happening, the union could maintain a stance of 'conditional participation' – engaging in state structures but also using a strategy of negotiation backed up by industrial action (Alder *et al.*, 1992:310). It could then continue to work in support of the government, but criticise government policies where these appear to emphasise competitiveness without adequate concern for long term employment protection and job creation (Makgetla, 2004, 2005).

'Social justice unionism' is not an easy solution, and there are still many tensions that need to be resolved. Nevertheless, it is argued here that a focus by South African trade unions on insecure work is necessary, given both the current crisis in the labour market situation and the need for trade unions to re-embrace their historical role of speaking out against injustice, and adequately representing the most vulnerable workers in society. Only through such a focus can the concerns of the bulk of South African workers be genuinely represented, and the rights of those workers that fall out of the present effective coverage of South African labour relations legislation be secured.

Acknowledgements

This chapter draws on data from the 'Taking Democracy Seriously' 2004 survey that was funded by SANPAD, and conducted by a team of scholars led by Sakhela Buhlungu, Witwatersrand University. Thanks are also due for comments on previous drafts by Anil Verma, Ian Roper, Geoffrey Wood and Michael Minch.

Notes

1. An earlier version of this paper was presented at the SASE conference, Budapest, 2005.
2. It could also embrace the linked concern of job creation, although this would mean diversifying union efforts further.
3. These terms have generally been applied to employer behaviour and also to the union role (Marsden, 2004).
4. More recently, Waterman has refocused and redefined the term as social unionism (see Waterman, 2001).
5. See Buhlungu (2006) for other detailed analyses of various aspects of the Taking Democracy Seriously survey
6. The nature of the survey means that although it is representative of a broad range of workers, those in informal employment, and therefore arguably in the most insecure areas of work, are not covered by the survey.
7. It is recognised that this test is somewhat limited, but it nevertheless enables the identification of key trends.

References

Adler, G., Maller, J. and Webster, E. (1992), 'Unions, Direct Action and Transition in South Africa', in Etherington, N. (ed.), *Peace, Politics and Violence in the New South Africa*. London: Hans Zell Publishers.
Bezuidenhout, A. (2005), 'Post-colonial Workplace Regimes in the Engineering Industry in South Africa', in Webster, E. and Von Holdt, K. (eds), *Beyond the Apartheid Workplace*. Durban: University of KwaZulu-Natal.

Burchell, F. Ladipo, D. and Wilkinson, F. (2002). *Job Insecurity and Work Intensification*. London: Routledge.
Buhlungu, S. (2006), *Trade Unions and Democracy: COSATU Workers' Political Attitudes in South Africa*. HSRC Press.
COSATU. (1996), *COSATU Submission on the Trade & Industry 1996/7 Budget Vote*, Presented to the Portfolio Committee on Trade & Industry, 19 June, 1996.
Dibben, P. (2004), 'Social Movement Unionism', in Wood, G. and Harcourt, M. (eds), *Trade Unions and Democracy*. Manchester: Manchester University Press, 280–302.
Dibben, P., Hinks, T. and Wood, G. (2005), 'Changing South African Industrial Relations and the Labour Movement: Sustaining Membership Levels and Internal Democracy in a Changing Economic and Political Context', unpublished working paper.
Gapasin, F. and Yates, M. (2005), 'Labor Movements: Is there Hope?', *Monthly Review*, 52, 2.
Ginsburg, D., Cherry, J. Klerck, G., Maree, J, Southall, R, Webster, E. and Wood, G. (1995), *Taking Democracy Seriously*. Durban: IPSA.
Johnson, N and Jarley, P. (2004), 'Justice and Union Participation: An Extension and Test of Mobilization Theory', *British Journal of Industrial Relations*, 42, 3: 543–62.
Kelly, J. (1998), *Rethinking Industrial Relations: Mobilization, Collectivism and Long Waves*. London: Routledge.
Kingdon, G. and Knight, J. (2004), 'Unemployment in South Africa: The Nature of the Beast', *World Development*, 32, 3: 391–408.
Kochan, T., Locke, R., Osterman, P. and Piore, M. (2004), 'Extended Networks: A Vision for the Next Generation Unions', in Verma, A. and Kochan, T. (eds), *Unions in the 21st Century: An International Perspective*. London: Palgrave.
Labour Market Review, September 2003.
Lalthapershad, P. (2001), 'Gender and Job Segregation: the South African Labour Market', *South African Labour Bulletin*, 25, 4, 12–15.
Macais, E. (2003), 'Job Instability and Political Attitudes Towards Work: Some Lessons from the Spanish Case', *European Journal of Industrial Relations*, 9, 2, 205–22.
Makgetla, N. Seidman (2004), 'Wages and Bargaining 10 Years On', *South African Labour Bulletin*, 28, 3, 12–14.
Makgetla, N. Seidman (2005), 'End Job Losses!: Fight Poverty and Unemployment', NALEDI Online, 25 June 2005, www.naledi.org.za/docs/cosatu_jobstrike.pdf.
Maree, J. (1998), 'The COSATU Participatory Democratic Tradition', *African Affairs*, 97, 29–51.
Marsden, D. (2004), 'Unions and Procedural Justice: An Alternative to the "Common Rule"', Verma, A. and Kochan, T. (eds), *Unions in the 21st Century: An International Perspective*. London: Palgrave.
Moody, K. (1997), *Workers in a Lean World*. London: Verso.
Mosoetsa, S. (2003), 'Are Unions and Political Parties facing a Crisis of Representation?', *South African Labour Bulletin*, 27, 4, 41–2.
Motlanthe, K. (2002), 'We are Restoring Democracy in the ANC . . .', *South African Labour Bulletin*, 26, 6, 15.
Munck, R. (2000), 'Labour and Globalization: Results and Prospects', Review Article, *Work, Employment and Society*, 14, 2: 385–93.
Naidoo, R. (2003), 'The Union Movement and South Africa's Transition', South African Labour Bulletin, 27,4: 15–20.
NCEA. (1994), 'Rethinking Our Unions Institute of the National Coalition of Education Activists, Social Justice Unionism: A Working Draft'. Washington, DC: NCEA.
Peetz, D. and Ollett, N. (2004), 'Union Growth and Reversal in Newly Industrialised Countries', in Harcourt, M. and Wood, G. (eds), *Trade Unions and Democracy: Strategies and Perspectives*. Manchester: Manchester University Press.

Peterson, B. (1998), 'What Will Be the Future of Teacher Unionism?', *Rethinking Schools*, 12,4.
Rees, R.(1997), 'Flexible Labour: Meeting the Challenge', *South African Labour Bulletin*, 21, 30–7.
Rogerson, C. 2001. 'Beyond Racial Fordism', in Jessop, B. (ed.), *Regulation Theory and the Crisis of Capitalism – Volume 4: Country Studies*. London: Edward Elgar.
Scipes, K. (2004), 'Organising for What? The Choice between Business Unionism and Social Justice Unionism in the Further Development of the US Labor Movement'. Public Lecture. University of Illinois. February 2004.
Statistics South Africa, (2004). Pretoria: Government Printer.
Tait, V. (2005), *Poor Workers' Unions: Lessons for Labor*. Cambridge (Ma.): South End Press.
Tshoaedi, M. and Hlela, H. (2006), 'The Marginalisation of Women Unionists during South Africa's Democratic Transition', in Buhlungu, S. (ed.), *Trade Unions and Democracy: COSATU Workers' Political Attitudes in South Africa*. Cape Town: HSRC Press.
Von Holdt, K. (2002), 'Social Movement Unionism: the Case of South Africa', *Work, Employment and Society*, 16, 2, 283–304.
Von Holdt, K. and Webster, E. (2005), 'Work Restructuring and the Crisis of Social Reproduction: A Southern Perspective', in Webster, E. and Von Holdt, K. (eds), *Beyond the Apartheid Workplace*. Durban: University of KwaZulu-Natal:3–40.
Waterman, P. (1993), 'Social Movement Unionism: A New Union Model for a New World Order', *Review* 6, 3: 245–78.
Waterman, P. (2001), 'Trade Union Internationalism in the Age of Seattle', *Antipode*, 29, 1: 312–36.
Webster, E. (1988), 'The Rise of Social-Movement Unionism: The Two Faces of the Black Trade Union Movement in South Africa', in Frankel, P., Pines, N., Swilling, M. (eds), *State, Resistance and Change in South Africa*. Kent: Croom Helm.
Webster, E. (2004), 'New Forms of Work and the Representational Gap: A Durban Case Study', Harcourt, M. and Wood, G. (eds), *Trade Unions and Democracy: Strategies and Perspectives*. Manchester: Manchester University Press.
Webster, E. (2006), 'Trade Unions and the Challenge of the Informalisation of Work', in Buhlungu, S. (ed.), *Trade Unions and Democracy: COSATU Workers' Political Attitudes in South Africa*. Cape Town: HSRC Press: 21–44.
Webster, E. and Buhlungu, S. (2004), 'Between Marginalisation and Revitalisation? The State of Trade Unionism in South Africa', *Review of African Political Economy*, 100, 229–45.
Wood, G. and Dibben, P. (2006), 'Broadening Internal Democracy with a Diverse Workforce: Challenges and Opportunities', in Buhlungu, S. (ed.), *Trade Unions and Democracy: COSATU Workers' Political Attitudes in South Africa. Cape Town*: HSRC Press.

11
The Emerging and Changing Industrial Relations Landscape in Botswana

Thabo Lucas Seleke

Introduction

The trade unionism movement in Botswana has undergone tremendous transformation from the colonial period to date, where we begin to see a new lease of life in the operations of these unions and changes in Botswana Labour Laws to recognise the fundamental right of employees to join organisations of their own, choosing to bargain collectively and to establish conditions where the free exercise of those rights are guaranteed. Historically, workers rights were routinely violated in Botswana: workers could not bargain collectively and they did not have the right to organise and had no freedom of association, up until 1997, when Botswana ratified ILO Convention Article 87 and 98.

Origins of trade unions in Botswana

The history of trade unions in Botswana can be traced as back to the colonial period, with the establishment of the Bechuanaland Protectorate Union in 1959, headed by Lenyeletse Seretse. In 1962, the Bechuanaland Trade Union Congress was formed under the leadership of Klass Motshidisi. All these collapsed and it was only in the 1970s when the country witnessed a properly established labour movement institution, Botswana Trade Union. It was replaced in 1977 by the Botswana Federation of Trade Unions and was subsequently followed by the establishment of:

- Botswana Mining Union
- Botswana Bank Employees Union
- Botswana Council and General Workers Union
- Botswana Construction Workers Union
- Botswana Railways Workers Union

Colonial trade unions were divided along political lines. Following on independence, Nengwenkulu (1980) argues that the development of trade unions in Botswana was accompanied by a process of depoliticisation, deradicalisation and stulfication. Obasi *et al.* (2006) further notes that, although the Southern African region is generally known for a culture of militant labour unionism deriving from its historical experience of armed struggle against colonialism and the apartheid system, the Republic of Botswana remained an exception: Botswana workers lacked revolutionary political consciousness unlike their counter parts within the region. This has primarily been due to the government's 'Corporate Nationalist Model' (Mogalakwe, 1994), which placed a lot of emphasis on the state, capital and labour working together to promote national development, even if at the expense of worker rights.

Botswana's political economy

From being one of the poorest countries in the world at independence in 1966, Botswana is widely cited as Africa's success story, an 'economic miracle' underpinned by peace and political stability. Taylor (2003) argues that it is not only the country's growth that is impressive; it has done well at the developmental level as well. Income poverty rates fell from 59 per cent in 1986 to 47 per cent in 1994; adult literacy rate improved from 41 per cent in 1970 to over 70 per cent in 1999 (ibid.). Botswana's GDP per head stood at US$3500 by 2005; it is now classified by the World Bank as a high middle income country (Maipose and Matsheka, 2004). The economy is driven by the mining sector in which diamonds are predominant. The latter are the major foreign exchange earner, which contributes 70 per cent to foreign exchange earnings and accounts for 50 per cent of government revenue. However, these positive figures mask a considerable disparity in income distribution, and as many as 40 per cent of households in rural areas are believed to be living in poverty.

All these have also been coupled with a stable political climate that has characterised the country since independence. Botswana is the continent's longest continuous multi-party democracy. This is evidenced by regular free and fair elections which have been held since independence from Britain in 1966, with the Bechuanaland Democratic Party[1] (BDP) government winning all the elections for the past forty years (Parsons, 1999). Sebudubudu and Osei-Hwedie (2006) argue that the BDP's successive electoral victories and the marginalisation of many of the opposition parties has meant that whilst Botswana operates a multi-party framework, it is in essence a de facto one party dominant system and, in reality, translating to a one party system.

Unlike many countries with rich natural resource endowments, Botswana has used positively revenue earned from diamonds for the development of its citizens, in a wide range of areas, including general education, school feeding, provision of health, manpower and human resource development Mogae (2005). However, the country has been faced with some challenges: most notably rates of employment growth have been not rapid enough to absorb the labour force. Statistics released by the government central statistics office shows that the overall unemployment rate is 24 per cent (21.4 per cent for males and males; 26.3 per cent for females (*Daily News*, 2004). Unemployment is highest among the young people, with those aged between 15 and 19 years recording 56 per cent while those between 20 and 24 recorded 49 per cent (Obasi *et al.*, 2006). Graduate unemployment is also gradually becoming a major problem.

Although Botswana has a small population, formal sector employment still is not enough: at March 2005, it stood at 299 000. The labour market has been characterised by a passive government policy that places emphasis on growth to deal with the problem of un- and under-employment. In addition there is no national social security scheme covering all workers. Level of unionisation remain low.

A second major challenge facing the country is the HIV/AIDS pandemic: indeed, this scourge has become a major threat to its economic and social development. Botswana is one of the most affected in the world with a level of infection exceeding 30 per cent of the 15–49 age group. This has compelled the country to divert funds towards programmes dealing with prevention, treatment, support, care and mitigation. Labour productivity is being adversely affected by the high level of mortality the country is experiencing, and the overall gains made over the last decades are being reversed.

The Botswanan labour movement

As noted earlier, the history of trade unions in Botswana can be traced as far back as the colonial period. During the latter period, unions were established in line with political divisions, and hence subscribed to different political ideologies. Mogalakwe, (1994) argues that these unions were concerned with issues such as wage restraint, industrial peace, political stability and national development: they were therefore, non militant and confrontational unlike their counterparts within the region. Because of the differences that existed in the political ideologies, unions continued to face bitter internal disputes in the years following independence, with only a few registered under the Trade Unions and Trade Disputes proclamation. Mogalakwe (1997) argued that these trade unions existed in names only in that they had degenerated into what he called 'personal fiefdoms'.

Mogalakwe's observation can be argued to hold true in that the post colonial union movement have not been active and vibrant. The culture of the trade union movement in Botswana has been one that reflects a weak civil society, and weaknesses in leadership, with the latter being required to be part-time only by law. Presently, there is only one labour federation in Botswana, the Botswana Federation of Trade Unions (BFTU); this was formed in 1972 with the assistance of the Botswana Government. At the time of its formation it had 25 Unions affiliating to it. Each of the affiliating unions are national unions with branches spread across the country where they have members. According to Obasi *et al.* (2006), the BFTU has remained a weak parent organisation as some affiliating unions have not been getting on well with it to the extent of stopping their financial contributions to it.

Unions are by and large politically neutral and have not formed an alliance with any political party in the country, including the ruling party. It has been argued that tensions over the federation's political affiliation to Botswana's ruling party led to a major split within the Botswana Federation of Trade Unions (BFTU) in 1988. The BFTU's two largest affiliates, the National Amalgamated Local and Central Government and Parastatal Manual Workers Union (NALCPM) and the Commercial and General Workers Union of Botswana (CGWU) broke away because they wanted the independence to decide which political party to support. In 2000, it was agreed that member unions can support a political party of their own (or none, for that matter). This concession restored unity within the labour movement, but also signaled a change in the relationship with the government. These developments reflected a victory for elements in the labour movement that have called for labour to play a more assertive, independent and proactive role in politics (Dlamini, 2002). At the same time, it can be argued that the issue has never been properly resolved, and still is at the root of serious political differences within the Botswana Federation of Trade Unions (BFTU).

Nonetheless, unions in Botswana are now taking union unity more seriously. Elias Mbonini, a past president of the Botswana Federation of Trade Unions (BFTU) and also a former Chairman of the Botswana Mine Workers Union (BMWU) has argued that unions need to speak with one voice and articulate issues bedeviling them: unions need to amalgamate and create a stronger voice, because currently they are not a threat to any employer and even the government. The Secretary for Labour Affairs for the Botswana National Front (BNF) has shared Mbonini's sentiments and has stated that 'we operate at the mercy of our employers and this is unfortunate'.

Labour laws and the changing industrial relations landscape in Botswana

In 2000, Botswana introduced major changes to its labour laws. The changes and reforms were effected not through the passage of a new law but by amendments of existing statutes. The legislative package also included the enactment of a new Trade Dispute Act and significant amendments to the Trade Unions and Employers Organisation Act (discussed below). These amendments were intended partially to bring labour laws in Botswana fully into compliance with relevant international standards, and ratified ILO Convention 87 and 98 respectively. These changes received wide support amongst the trade union movement as they represented a fundamental break with the past. The new labour laws marked the end of state intervention in labour relations. In particular, it was seen as bringing to an end legislative restriction on workers rights. The government has also initiated tripartite consultations involving it, the private sector and trade unions.

The reformed labour laws recognise the fundamental right of employers and employees to join organisation of their own choosing to bargain collectively and to establish conditions where the free exercise of those rights is guaranteed (ibid.). Nonetheless, it is not clear if the changes have had the desired effect: Makhale, Secretary General of the Botswana Teachers Union (BTU), stated in June 2005 that labour relations in Botswana are at a low ebb primarily due to government arrogance, the slow and complicated methods of labour dispute resolution process and the insensitivity of private sector employer; strikes remain endemic because of the absence of a credible platform of conflict resolution in Botswana. Indeed, the Botswana Federation of Trade Unions (BFTU) has delivered a petition to the President of Botswana's office demanding that a commission of enquiry be set up to discover the real reasons behind the labour unrest.

Although collective bargaining has become the main instrument for negotiating wages and other conditions of work in Botswana, this does not mean that negotiations have been uniformally smooth. For example, in 2004 the Debswana Mining Company dismissed 461 employees who had engaged in a strike to demand bonuses and wage increase from management. The strike was declared unlawful by the courts and ultimately led to the dismissal of the employees. Similarly, about 13 employees, five being union members, were dismissed by yet another mining company, Bamangwato Concession Limited (BCL), on allegations that they were actively involved in politics after being given an ultimatum to choose between active politics and their work. Recently the notorious Bamangwato Concession Limited dismissed about 178 employees in August 2006 from work on the grounds that they had engaged in an unlawful strike, after they had demanded wage increases from the company. Surprisingly their dismissal came even after they had gone back to work in compliance with the court order obtained by the management of BCL.

All these compelled the Botswana Mining Workers Union (BMWU), Botswana Federation of Trade Unions (BFTU) and even the Botswana National Front (BNF) to condemn the actions of Debswana and BCL Management respectively. They perceived their actions as unjustified. Botswana Federation of Trade Unions perceived these dismissals as unfortunate and portrayed Botswana labour laws as biased against workers. They feel that the relevant labour laws place still too many restrictions on workers rights; strikes are often declared illegal in the country.

It has also become accepted practice in Botswana that employees should not complain to their employers. This can also be illustrated by the recent sacking of the Botswana Teachers Union President in October 2006. The move came after threat of dismissal made by the Honourable Minister of Education. In his threat the Honourable Minister stated that '... teachers Union Leaders should focus on issues of their profession'.

The recent acceptance of a donation by the mining giant De Beers Company to the Botswana legal system (High Court) to the tune of P 100 000.00 has been perceived by many to compromise the independence of the judiciary, more so that the donation has been made at time when there is still a legal battle between the dismissal of 461 employees of Debswana (A partnership between De Beers and Botswana Government). In its defense, De Beers stated that the donations to the High Court of Botswana were made in good faith with no intension to influence judicial decision in its favour. De Beers's donation was also not received in good light by the trade union movement in Botswana which called for the Chief Justice to resign.

The 2004 Trade Dispute Act

This Act was promulgated to provide for settlement of Trade Disputes generally and for settlement of trade disputes in essential services and for the control and regulation of industrial action and related matters. It sets out a procedure to be followed once a trade dispute exists. The Act discourages strike action by failing to outline circumstances under which strike action will be deemed to be lawful. Indeed, it can be argued that current legislation provides a tight legal structure with too much government control. Despite amendments, the law still does not entrench the Right to Strike; it remains unclear as to what constitutes a lawful strike and or the circumstances under which strike action will be lawful, particularly in non-essential services. The Dispute resolution mechanism provided for under the Trade Dispute Act is also not very effective. The recommendations made by the labour departments do not have any legally binding effect and, as such have made labour office as the gate way to the Industrial Court. The Trade Dispute Act has been widely criticised and perceived as inadequate and exposes workers to abuse. This can also be illustrated by the Debswana Diamond mining case v/s Botswana Mine Workers Union (BMWU) where the latter dismissed 461 employees from work for having engaged in what they termed an unlawful strike. Similarly Morupule Colliery V/S BMWU (case number I C 4/95) underscored the weakness of employee protection in this area.

Trade Union and Employers' Organisation Act

Previously the provisions in the above Act restricted freedom of association and collective bargaining. The Act excluded public officers from joining trade unions; public officers now enjoy the right to join trade unions in accordance with ILO Convention 87 and 98 respectively. The new reforms also removed the threshold set previously at 30 for joining a union. This has been done so as to accommodate employees in small enterprises. This demonstrates government commitment to conform with its international obligations, even if employee protection remains weak in many areas.

This Act has been highly criticised by the Trade Union movement in that they can be de-registered easily at the discretion of the Registrar of the Industrial Court upon satisfying himself that there is a need to do so.

The introduction of the Industrial Court as the Court of equity under the Trade Dispute Amendment Act 1992 was seen by many as a first step to erode all the above; it was hoped that it would provide for labour autonomy in Botswana, hopes that have been dashed, especially with regard to protecting the right to strike: '. . . going on Strike, whether one works for government or the private sector means victimisation or dismissal'.

Challenges facing unions in Botswana

The dismissal of the 461 Debswana employees and the recent dismissal of 178 BCL employees, the latest dismissal of the President of the Botswana Teachers Union and the imprisonment of six BMWU union members fully illustrate that freedom of association remains under threat in Botswana, despite the government's initiative to ratify the ILO Convention 87 and 98. It is quite evident that the current legislation still provides a tight legal structure for intrusive government control. Workers in Botswana have been silenced from demanding improvements in wages and conditions of employment and hence remained a loyal recipient from employers and the state. The workers in Botswana, although formally accorded the right to collective bargaining, lack it in practice. There is little flexibility in terms of salary negotiations between employers and individual employees. Where that occurs, it is normally done within a particular range; more so if it involves a dispute of interest and not one of fact (see *Sunday Standard,* 14 October 2006).

Hence, trade unions still operate in a very hostile environment in Botswana even after 40 years of independence and formal multi-party democracy. They do not have an upper hand regarding when consultation and or negotiation may take place and which issues to be discussed in the employer's best interest, especially in terms of wage bargaining or wage bargaining process. Disputes often take a great deal of time to be settled from the date of inception, and may be even more protracted as there is no requirement on employers to resolve grievances expeditiously. If not settled, matters are referred to the Industrial Court which has a turn around time of not less than 20months. By comparison, the South African model has a turnaround time averaging 3 to 6 months.

Union are also limited on financial resources and do not have skilled full time trainers who can actually build competencies on a regular basis. They are also faced with loss of membership which has been made worse by waves of retrenchments across the country. Trade unions continue to be marginalised by employers: rather than being viewed as stakeholders they are normally seen as rivals and wage increase campaigners.

Conclusion

The study reveals that while the trade union movement in Botswana underwent tremendous transformation right from the colonial period to date, it has been characterised by non militancy and weak organisation. All these have been coupled by repressive labour laws that favour legislative authorities and employers as opposed to unions: recent reforms have had only limited impact in the field.

Although the ratification of ILO Convention 87 and 98 was met with great excitement by the trade union movement in Botswana, it is quite evident that such reforms were, in reality, cosmetic: the current legislature still provides a tight legal structure for intrusive government control and gives much discretion to employers. The continued sacking of union leaders and imprisonment of union members underscores the fragility of worker rights: again, recent court decisions highlight the weakness of employment protection.

Note

1. Now known as the Botswana Democratic Party, although the acronym has not changed.

Bibliography

BFTU (2005), 'National Solidarity Demonstration – 4th June 2005', *Monitor*, Monday, 30 May.
Dlhamini A., (2002), 'Botswana Unions Find Their Voice', *South African Labour Bulletin*, 26, 1.
Daily News (2004), *Survey Showing Income Disparities*, Monday, 20 December.
International Labour Organisation (ILO) (2005), *Freedom of Association*. Geneva.
Konopo, J. 2006. 'Untitled Mimeo'. Gaberone: BULGSA.
Madisha, W. (2005), 'Opening Address by the President of Congress of South African Unions (COSATU) delivered at the 31st Annual General Conference of the Botswana Unified Local Government Service Association (BULGSA) held at the Shoshong Senior Secondary on December 12–16', *Mmegi*, Friday, 23 December.
Maipose, G. and Matsheka, T.C. (2004), 'Explaining African Growth Performance: The Case of Botswana', AERC Growth Project.
Maudeni, Z. (2004a), 'Mutual Criticism and State/Society Interaction in Botswana', *Journal of Modern African Studies*, 42, 4.
Maudeni, Z. (2004b), *Civil Society, Politics and the State in Botswana*. Gaborone: Medi Publishing.

Mogalakwe, M. (1994), *State and Organized Labour in Botswana 1966–1990: Liberal Democracy in Emergent Capitalism*. London: Ashgate.

Mogalakwe, M. (1997), *State and Organized Labour in Botswana 1966–1990: Liberal Democracy in Emergent Capitalism*. London: Ashgate.

Mogae, F. (2005). 'Botswana Development Experience, Conference Opening Speech'. Francistown: BOCCIM.

Obasi, I., Motshegwa, B. and Mfundisi, A. (2005), 'The State, Globalization and the Survival of the Urban Informal Sector in Botswana'. Paper presented at the 15th Biennial Congress of African Association of Political Science (AAPS) held in Cairo, Egypt, 18–21 September.

Obasi, I., Mpabanga, D. and Seleke, T.L. (2006), 'Labour Organization and Transformation in an Era of Globalisation: The Case of Botswana in Southern African Region'. Paper presented at the 22nd European Group for Organisational Studies (EGOS) 2006 Colloquium The Organising Society held in Bergen, Norway 6–8 July 2006.

Republic of Botswana (1984), *Trade Unions and Employers Organisations Act*. Gaborone: Government Printer.

Republic of Botswana (2003), *Trade Dispute Act*. Gaborone: Government Printer *Sunday Standard* (Gaberone).

Sebudubudu, D. and Osei-Hwedie, B. (2006), 'Pitfalls of Parliamentary Democracy in Botswana' *Afrika Spectrum*, 41, 1: 35–53.

Taylor, I. (2003), 'As Good As It Gets? Botswana's Democratic Development', in Melber, H. (ed.), *Limits to Liberation in Southern Africa: The Unfinished Business of Democratic Consolidation*. Cape Town: Human Sciences Research Council.

Part III
Country Studies from West and North Africa

Part III

12
Industrial Relations in an Emerging Morocco
Mohamed Essaaidi

Introduction

This chapter reviews the Moroccan industrial relations context. After a broad country overview, it goes on to outline the legal context, and the present challenges facing work and employment relations. It is concluded that there is vital need for a greater social dialogue between the principle industrial relations actors, to promote employment, equity and productivity.

Morocco regained its sovereign independence in 1956 after having, for the previous 44 years, been administered as a Spanish Protectorate in the north and a French Protectorate in the south. Tangier's special status as an international zone also came to an end in 1956 and it became an integral part of Morocco. Following serious economic problems (Achy and Hamdouch, 2003) in the early 1980's, Morocco implemented a Structural Adjustment Programme with the help of the IMF and the World Bank. Economically, Morocco has until 2010 before all tariff barriers with the European Union come down. In that time, Moroccan business and wider society faced the enormous challenge of modernising to meet the full force of international competition. The government has forecast that one-third of businesses will prosper under the EU association agreement, one-third will carry on much as before but that another third will go under. There is also the prospect of a bilateral, no-holds barred, Free Trade Area with the USA in 2013 to contend with. In 2002, Morocco had a GDP of DH409 billion (US$40.9 billion). The economy is heavily dependent on agriculture and rainfall. Agriculture employs 50 per cent of the population and brings in 20 per cent of GDP. The 5 drought years of the 1990s reduced the average annual GDP growth for the decade to under 2.8 per cent. The outlook since is rather more promising.

Morocco has rolled out a privatisation programme (Achy and Seekkat, 2005): started by King Hassan II in 1992 it has included power, water and telecommunications. Forthcoming privatisations are to include the Moroccan state tobacco monopoly, *Regie des Tabacs*, as well as further segments of *Royal Air Maroc* – the state airline – and the national telecommunications company,

Maroc Telecom. The telecommunications sector was fully liberalised by the end of 2004. Nearly half of the country's electricity needs will be met by the privately run power plants at Jorf Lasfar.

Morocco's industrial sector is relatively strong – it is the world's first exporter and third largest producer of phosphates and produces enough lead, copper, coal and zinc for domestic consumption (US Department of State, 2003). Light industry consists of canned food, textile, metallurgy, wood, chemicals and vehicle assembly. Yet, modernisation is badly needed in a country suffering from high unemployment rates. The average rate of 25 per cent is far higher among university graduates, many of whom join the 2 million Moroccans in Europe, representing a severe loss in human capital. As prices decline for minerals, the country needs to diversify to other means of foreign currency earnings and move away from reliance on its precarious agricultural sector for employment, especially as the population continues to expand rapidly. In the short term, Morocco is benefiting from a strong euro and the devaluation of the Dirham by exporting textiles (40 per cent of exports) and high quality leather goods. Tourism, especially from Europe, is a major source of revenue as are cash remittances from Morocco's citizens working abroad.

The legal context

Labour law

The employment contract binding the employer to each of his employees is governed by the Royal Decree dated August 13, 1913, which lays down a code of obligations and contracts. Such contract may be written or oral (Touchent, 2002). A decree of October 23, 1948 sets out a specimen contract applicable to all industrial and commercial establishments. It defines the reciprocal rights and duties of employer and employees. Employers however, can make more favourable arrangements in their establishment, subject to agreement with the Minister of Labour.

Workers have the right to join together in unions for the protection of their rights and to strike in defence for their collective interests. Nevertheless, the Inspectorate of Labour endeavours to settle disputes by mediation. At the same time, if both parties agree, arbitration may avoid recourse to strike action or legal action before the Tribunal of First Instance.

There is no legal requirement for employees to be involved in the management of companies or to be represented on the board of directors. Although there is no legislation requiring participation by labour in the profits of a business, a number of companies have implemented profit sharing plans. The work week is limited to forty-eight hours, with no more than ten hours worked per day. Every employee is entitled to a weekly day of rest and a number of statutory paid holidays.

Salaries and wages

There are no legislated wage controls in Morocco other than the minimum wage. Therefore, wages and salaries can be freely contracted between employees and employers. Apart from agreed pay increases, an indexing system enables the government to raise by decree all wages and salaries effectively paid when the Central Commission for Prices and Wages records an increase of at least 5 per cent in the cost of living.

Wages, whatever the method of remuneration (time rates, piece rates or job rates) must be paid at least twice a month, at a maximum of sixteen days' interval. Salaries must be paid at least once a month.

Administration of labour law

The Ministry of Employment, Social Affairs, and Solidarity is the government agency responsible for employment and protection of workers' rights. It is divided into a Central Administration and External Services. The Ministry's Central Administration includes the Labour Department, the Department of Employment, the Department for the Social Protection of Workers, the Department of Social Affairs, the Department of Professional Training, and the Division of Cooperation.

The Labour Inspectorate operates within the External Services of the Ministry and comprises six prefectural delegations and 27 provincial delegations. Labour and social affairs inspectors conduct general labour inspections, while social law inspectors are responsible for labour inspections in the agricultural sector. Physicians and engineers also may be commissioned to conduct labour inspections within the scope of their specialties. Currently, Morocco has approximately 496 labour inspectors, including doctors, engineers, and hygienists. These labour inspectors are specifically tasked with supervising the application of legislative and regulatory labour provisions, providing employers and workers with technical advice on complying with the legal provisions, and attempting to reconcile labour disputes.

Training of labour inspectors has been identified as an area needing improvement, given that Moroccan labour inspectors have historically been provided little training. To address this issue, training was afforded as part of a technical cooperation program conducted by the Arab Safety and Health Institute in 1999 and 2000 on child labour in the agricultural sector. In addition, in October 2003, the US Department of Labour launched a two-year project, executed by the ILO, to provide necessary training to Moroccan labour inspectors on how to conduct general labour projects aimed at increasing compliance with labour standards in Morocco, which includes the training of labour inspectors in performing occupational safety and health inspections.

The Labour Inspectorate requires additional resources to properly monitor working conditions and investigate accidents, particularly in rural areas. In 2001, some 36,000 inspections were conducted in 8,000 companies (or 10 per cent of all enterprises). Very few workplace inspections occurred in rural areas. Labour inspectors spent the majority of their time (70 per cent) settling individual and collective labour disputes through conciliation. During the first nine months of 2003, the Labour Inspectorate intervened in 23,400 individual conflicts. It recouped 39 million dirhams (US$4.2 million) in back wages and reinstated some 3,000 workers. The majority of individual conflicts concerned dismissals of workers (27.5 per cent), non-payment of paid leave (24.2 per cent), and non-payment of salaries (22.7 per cent). Seventy-one percent of the disputes came from the industrial sector. The Labour Inspectorate settled roughly 70 per cent of the collective labour conflicts.

The Social Chamber of the Court of First Instance is the judicial body that hears labour cases. It is composed of three sections: industry, commerce and professionals, and agriculture. The court is presided over by a labour judge, who is assisted by four assessors appointed by the Minister of Labour and the Minister of Justice for a three-year period.

Labour rights and their application

Trade unions

The Constitution of Morocco guarantees freedom of association for the citizens of Morocco, including the freedom to belong to any union of their choice. The 2003 Labour Code provides workers with the right to freely join and to withdraw from trade unions. Civil servants also have the right to form unions (Touchent, 2002). Approximately 600,000 workers are unionised, representing about 5.8 per cent of Morocco's economically active population.

Workers may form one of two types of unions: (1) a trade union established by workers engaged in a single profession or occupation, or (2) a union established by workers in professions or occupations that are similar or connected to each other. The judiciary may order the dissolution of a union if its members do not fall into the above categories. Trade unions have the right to form federations and to affiliate with international organisations of workers. Labour federations are allowed to receive in-kind or financial aid from the state for rental expenses, staff salaries, or labour education activities for their members. Morocco currently has 19 labour federations (US Department of State, 2003), of which five play major roles:

- The Moroccan Labour Union (UMT) dominates the private sector and has negotiated the most collective labour agreements. The UMT claims to have no political affiliation, although commentators assert that it has close ties with the monarchy. It is affiliated with the International Confederation of Free Trade Unions (ICFTU).
- The Democratic Confederation of Labour (CDT) represents public sector workers and was aligned with the Socialist Union of Popular Forces (USFP)

until the 2002 parliamentary elections, when its Secretary General created his own political party.
- The General Union of Moroccan Workers (UGTM) is closely affiliated with the *Istiqlal* party.
- The National Labour Union of Morocco (UNTM) represents workers in the public education, public health, building trades, textiles, and agricultural sectors. Founded in 1973, it is the labour affiliate of the Justice and Development Party (PJD), the country's only legal Islamist political party.
- In April 2003, disaffected members of the CDT broke away to form the Democratic Federation of Labour (FDT), citing the CDT's lack of internal democracy as the reason for the split. The FDT's first Secretary-General is a member of Parliament from the Socialist Union of Popular Forces (USFP).

To form a union, workers must provide the local administrative authority and the provincial labour commissioner with the trade union's articles of association and a complete list of union officials. Any changes made to the union's statutes or its management structure must also be reported. Failure to submit these documents to the appropriate authorities may result in a fine of 10,000–20,000 dirhams (US$1,082–2,165) against the founders, heads, directors, or managers of the union. Repeated violations are punishable with a doubling of the fine. The above requirements are also applicable to labour federations.

All establishments with a minimum of 10 permanent workers must hold elections for labour representatives, whose duty it is to submit individual complaints about working conditions to the employer and to refer unresolved complaints to the labour inspector. Candidates must be Moroccan citizens, who are at least 20 years of age, and must have worked at the establishment for one year continuously. Workers may vote in the election if they are at least 16 years old, have been on the job for at least six months, and have not been sentenced or imprisoned for a crime. Before the election, the workers and their employer must agree on the distribution of the worker members among the electing organisations (i.e., trade unions in unionised companies) and the distribution of seats among these organisations. If no agreement is reached, the labour inspector must arbitrate the matter. Failure by the employer to hold the election for the labour representatives may result in a fine between 25,000–30,000 dirhams (US$2,706–3,247), and any infringements on the freedom to elect the labour representatives or on the discharge of their duties are punishable with a fine between 10,000–20,000 dirhams (US$1,082–2,165).

Only the 'most representative' union may conduct collective bargaining. To attain this status at the enterprise level, a trade union must have at least 35 per cent of the total number of labour representatives elected in the enterprise and must have the ability to negotiate. The most representative labour organisation at the national level is decided by the following factors: obtaining a minimum of six percent of the total number of labour representatives elected in the public and private sectors, the union's actual independence, and its capacity to negotiate.

The Government of Morocco ratified ILO Convention No. 11 on the Right of Association in Agriculture in May 1957, and, in April 2003, the social partners pledged that Morocco would ratify ILO Convention No. 87 on Freedom of Association and Protection of the Right to organise. Subsequent 2004 reforms accorded unions legal rights, and obliged employers to engage in collective bargaining with representative union(s).

Right to strike

The Constitution guarantees the right to strike and mandates that the implementation of this right is to be determined by organic law (Touchent, 2002). Workers regularly exercise this right. Several articles in the new Labour Code strengthen the right to strike by prohibiting attempts by employers to undermine a strike by hiring substitute workers and by prohibiting employers from discriminating against any worker or union who engage in strike activities. The Labour Code requires that any labour dispute that could become a collective dispute must go to reconciliation.

Some restrictions exist on the right to strike. Civil servants may be punished, without regard to disciplinary guarantees, for participating in coordinated work stoppages or collective acts of indiscipline. In addition, the Penal Code establishes a sanction of one month to two years imprisonment for any individual using force, threat, or fraudulent activities to cause a coordinated stoppage of work in order to force a change in wages, or that jeopardises the free exercise of work. The Penal Code also prescribes compulsory labour for persons sentenced to imprisonment.

The ILO's Committee of Experts on the Application of Conventions and Recommendations (International Labour Conference, 2001) has remarked on the high number of prison sentences given to striking workers in Morocco's private sector and has indicated the possibility of abuse of Article 288 of the Penal Code. The Government has acknowledged that an abundance of court decisions have been rendered pursuant to Article 288 but has observed that, when exercising the right to strike, workers must also respect the constitutional guarantee of freedom to work. The Government contends that Article 288 constitutes an assurance of this freedom. The ILO's Committee on Freedom of Association (ILO CFA) and the ILO CEACR (International Labour Conference, 2003) have stressed to the Government that workers should not be deprived of their freedom or be subject to penal sanctions for organising or participating in peaceful strikes. The ILO CEACR has further urged the Government to ensure that sanctions, including compulsory labour, are not imposed for strike participation. The United Nations Committee on Economic, Social and Cultural Rights also has recommended that Morocco abolish some of the provisions criminalising strikes found in Article 288.

Right to organise and bargain collectively

The new Labour Code (Alaoui, 2000) bans employer and worker organisations from interfering in each other's affairs with regard to their formation, management, and administration. Acts of interference include the establishment of employer-controlled unions or the provision of financial or other support to unions by employers to assert control. The Labour Code also prohibits employers from taking disciplinary action against workers or firing them for belonging to a union, participating in union activities during non-work hours or during work hours with the employer's consent, being nominated as a labour representative, performing the duties of a labour representative, or filing a complaint against an employer. The courts have the authority to reinstate unfairly dismissed workers and are able to enforce rulings that compel employers to pay damages and back pay (US Department of Labour, 2004).

Two cases concerning alleged anti-union discrimination are before the ILO CFA. In a case filed by the CDT in December 2002, the Committee has commented that it cannot rule out the possibility of a connection between the creation of the trade union executive committee and the transfers and dismissals of those who participated in its establishment. With regard to a case submitted by the UMT and ICFTU in December 2000, the UMT reported that workers who participated in the establishment of the trade union executive committee at a multinational company had been harassed by militia hired by management and that the trade union officers had been dismissed and then physically assaulted and arrested briefly. The Government of Morocco does not dispute the facts of the case, observing that the Labour Inspectorate determined that there had been a violation of freedom of association and an unauthorised collective dismissal at the factory and had requested that the company reinstate the dismissed workers. The trade unionists ultimately were reinstated and were able to establish the union. The ILO CFA suggested to the Government that steps needed to be taken to ensure that the relevant authorities receive appropriate instructions to prevent acts of intimidation and other measures aimed at depriving trade unionists of their freedom.

The Labour Code (Touchent, 2002) grants the right to bargain collectively with employers or employer associations to the 'most representative' labour organisations. Collective bargaining must be for the purpose of establishing conditions of employment and work and/or to regulate relations between workers and employers. Collective labour agreements must include the types and conditions of employment, the elements for determining professional qualification levels, work conditions, wage components to be applied to each occupational class, occupational safety and health protections, provisions for the dismissal of workers, procedures to settle collective labour disputes, training for workers, compensations, and union facilities. Collective bargaining may be conducted at the enterprise, sectoral, or national levels, with negotiations being required at the enterprise and sectoral levels annually unless otherwise specified in the collective labour agreements. Labour inspectors are authorised to monitor compliance with the requirements of collective labour agreements.

Currently there are 30 collective labour agreements in force in Morocco that cover overall labour–management relations and are for an indefinite period. An average of 100 accords are concluded annually in response to specific disputes and have a limited duration. Collective bargaining is a long-standing tradition within the industrial sector and is becoming more prevalent in the public sector, as well as in banking and health services. In general, the wages and conditions of employment for unionised workers in Morocco are determined by collective bargaining. Labour disputes have arisen when employers failed to implement collective bargaining agreements or withheld wages. The new Labour Code provides for conciliation and voluntary arbitration in resolving such disputes.

Morocco ratified ILO Convention No. 98 on the Right to Organise and Collective Bargaining in May 1957 (ILO, 2003).

Prohibition of forced or compulsory labour

The new Labour Code (Alaoui, 2000) prohibits employers from coercively or forcibly subjugating workers to perform work, and those who violate this provision may be sanctioned with a fine of 25,000–30,000 dirhams (US$2,706–3,247). However, the Government lacks the resources to inspect all workplaces to ensure that compulsory labour is not being used, forced labour is not viewed as an issue in the commercial and agricultural sectors. Morocco ratified ILO Convention No. 29 on Forced Labour in May 1957 and Convention No. 105 on the Abolition of Forced Labour in December 1966.

A widespread form of involuntary labour is 'adoptive servitude'. Children, predominantly girls from rural areas, are contracted by their parents or sold by orphanages as maids to wealthy urban families and work for little or no payment. A law was enacted in 1993 for the protection of abandoned children in Morocco. According to this law, persons younger than 18 and unable to support themselves economically are identified as abandoned if their parents are unknown, unable to be located, or incompetent of assuming a parental role. These children are then considered eligible for adoption, and adoptive parents are entitled to a stipend from the Government. However, there has been some concern that girls are being adopted at higher rates than boys, and that some of these girls find themselves in situations equivalent to forced domestic servitude.

Child maids usually receive little or no payment or their wages are given directly to their families, and many report being forced to work long hours and in abusive conditions. The practice of adoptive servitude is socially accepted and unregulated by the Government because domestic workers are not specifically covered by the new Labour Code. However, the new Labour Code does empower inspectors to bring charges for employing children under age 15. The US Department of Labour is supporting a US$3 million project, being executed by Management Systems International (MSI), which aims to eliminate the practice of selling and hiring child domestic workers. Various decrees authorise the calling up of individuals to satisfy national needs. The Government claims that these provisions may only be invoked during emergencies as allowed by ILO Convention No. 29, e.g. during war or natural disasters. The ILO CEACR has requested that the Government amend or repeal its law in order to bring the legislation into conformity with practice.

The ILO CEACR (International Labour Conference, 2001) has determined that the Decree of February 24, 1958, establishing the General Conditions of Employment of the Public Service, is not compatible with ILO Convention No. 29, because it denies public servants the right to resign freely from employment.

As noted in the right to strike section of this chapter, strikers may face imprisonment with compulsory labour under the Penal Code if they are found guilty of committing acts of violence, force, threats, or fraudulent activities during work stoppages. The ILO CEACR has asked the Government to ensure that compulsory labour not be imposed on workers who participate in peaceful strikes. Additionally, the ILO CEACR has indicated that the employment of prisoners by private individuals in general is not compatible with ILO Convention No. 29, unless it is similar to a free labour relationship. Act No. 23-98 allows for convicts to be employed by a private individual or organisation under an administrative agreement setting the terms of employment and remuneration.

Conclusions

Making its industries and enterprises more competitive is an urgent priority for Morocco both to generate the jobs it desperately needs, and to help it carve out a place in the global economy. However, unemployment is high and precarious with informal sector work becoming more common. There are several obstacles in the way of Morocco's pursuit of competitiveness including low skill levels among its workers, and rising levels of industrial conflict. In many cases, enterprises bring in changes they believe will boost productivity without consultation with the workforce. And while there has been some progress, including a shift away from state ownership of industries that has seen dialogue between employers and workers increase, much remains to be done.

One of the key areas of concern to both employers' and workers' representatives is the lack of negotiation skills needed to reach productive agreements and avert disputes. The government also needs to strengthen its capacity for dispute prevention, including monitoring the application of labour laws and encouraging dialogue. Stronger social dialogue will help Morocco address the wider challenges linked with competitiveness, including finding ways to establish workplace cooperation and communication to boost productivity.

References

Achy, L. and Hamdouch, B. (2003), *Economic Growth in Morocco: Review of the Last Two Decades and Future Prospects.* n.p.: Forthcoming Economic Research Forum.

Achy, L. and Seekkat, K. (2005), *Trade Liberalization and Employment in the Moroccan Manufacturing Sector*, International Trade 0512011, EconWPA.

Alaoui M., (2000), *Labor Legislation in Morocco: A Practical Guide.* Casablanca.

Currie, J. and Harrison, A. E. (1997), 'Sharing the Costs: The Impact of Trade Reform on Capital and Labor in Morocco', *Journal of Labour Economics*, 15, 3: 44–71.

ILO, (2003), *Committee on Freedom of Association*, Report, LXXXVI. Geneva.

International Labour Conference (2001), *Report of the CEACR*. Geneva.

International Labour Conference (2003), *Report of the CEACR*. Geneva.

Salman, M., Salman, A. and Bradlow, D. D. (2006), *Regulatory Frameworks for Water Resources Management.* Washington: World Bank Publications.

Touchent, D. (2002), *Guide to the Morocco Legal System*, Legal and Technology Articles and Resources for Librarians, Layers and law firms, (available at http://www.llrx.com/features/morocco.htm).

US Department of Labour, (2004), *International Labour Affairs, Morocco Labour Rights Report.* Washington.

US Department of State, (2003), *Country Reports*, Section 6b.

World Intellectual Property Organization (2003), *Performance of Copyright Industries in Selected Arab Countries.*

13
The Development of Industrial Relations in Nigeria: 1900–2006

Sola Fajana

Introduction

Nigeria's system of industrial relations evolved in a unique way. Unlike countries of the West where significant industrialisation and meaningful economic growth preceded the emergence of trade unions, Nigeria's unions emerged through the period of colonialism as politically conscious institutions even before the nation had achieved any meaningful industrialisation. The objective of this chapter is to highlight the dynamic historical processes that led to this situation and to assess the response of each of the industrial relations stakeholders (organised labour, employers and the state) as well as the future modes of their interaction.

Nigeria is one of the most strategically important countries in Africa. However, the country is also one of Africa's poorest, with a long legacy of corruption, weak institutions, as well as poor and inconsistent economic management. To fight these problems, President Olusegun Obasanjo started, in 1999, an all-inclusive course of reforms to boost growth and reduce poverty.

In 2003 Nigeria introduced and implemented its National Economic Empowerment and Development Strategy (NEEDS). NEEDS is a wide-ranging set of reforms covering all aspects of the economy, including macroeconomic policy, government institutions, the private sector, and social policy (National Planning Commission, 2005). However, NEEDS has been criticised for being too ambitious given Nigeria's difficult circumstances (Fajana, 2005a). Some of the challenges that are being experienced are:

- The changeover to civilian rule has not ended outbreaks of ethnic and religious violence. Sectarian unrest remains widespread, affecting almost every region of the country and killing thousands of Nigerians during 2000 to 2005. In May 2004, violent clashes in central Nigeria's Plateau State led the country to declare a state of emergency. Meanwhile, the northern states are time and again vulnerable with outbreaks of violence.

- A culture of corruption is embedded in the political and economic system in Nigeria. This is the biggest obstacle to growth. While the ruling People's Democratic Party (PDP) has consolidated its power since the 2003 elections, powerful economic forces from within and outside the ruling party remain, notably the trade unions, and have attempted to oppose reforms that are not people-friendly.
- Nigeria recently removed the domestic petrol subsidy, resulting in a price increase of nearly 25 per cent. Oil sector deregulation is central to the government reform programme, but public reaction has been swift and harsh. Because many impoverished Nigerians view the subsidy as one of their only social benefits, trade unions reacted with general strikes to disrupt the nation's oil production.

Developments in the oil sector feature prominently in contemporary industrial relations in Nigeria. Oil companies have been struggling with continuous community unrests and vandalisation of oil insfrastructure. This is because Nigerians see that the extraction of crude oil has adversely affected the social, economic and cultural lives of the people. For example, oil exploration activities in the Niger Delta have been associated with the destruction of indigenous forest reserves, houses, and symbols of religious worship, leading communities to seek recompense from the oil companies (Fajana, 2005a). But what roles are being played by the stakeholders in Nigeria's model of industrial relations? First, we start with the origins and evolution of the trade unions.

Origin and development of trade unions

The origin of labour unions in Nigeria is vague. A school of thought (e.g. Seibel, 1973) considered guilds, mutual aid societies, and other bodies of craftsmen as trade unions. These were pre-colonial organisations regulating entry into their professions, imposing levies and prescribing codes of entry and conduct in their trades. However, these embryonic organisations were largely not in wage employment. They cannot be regarded therefore as modern trade unions even though they exhibited traits similar to those of professional associations. Besides, their organisations were comprehensively destroyed by the disorganisation of various Nigerian societies during the trading in slaves and the inundation of the economies with cheap European hardware and other metals (Otobo, 1987: 12).

Another view is that trade unions might be an import of colonialism, the first set of unions having been modelled after the British unions. Again, this view cannot be accepted wholly without question. In contrast to the developments in the colonising country (Britain), trade unions preceded industrialisation in Nigeria. The employers, perhaps having been exposed to trade unions in Britain, were aware of the power of trade unions as potential agents of sociopolitical change. Consequently, employers and the colonial administration both opposed the formation of labour unions on flimsy excuses such as that 'trade unions would rival the authority already accorded the natural rulers'. Chiefs and natural rulers were appointed labour contractors in Sierra Leone and Nigeria. For many years, mine labour was procured through the chiefs and natural rulers around Enugu (Akpala, 1965). Hence it was considered illogical to allow trade unions to operate in colonial enterprises. In the account of the mines rendered by Akpala (1965) and Freund (1981), when trade unions were eventually allowed, the worst offence to report was that the workers had joined a trade union.

However, the very first union (the Civil Service Union, CSU) was formally organised in the public sector in 1912. In 1931, two other unions were formed: the Nigerian Union of Teachers (NUT) and the Railway Workers Union (RWU). The RWU was part of the CSU until it broke off because of dissatisfaction with the tempo with which the latter was pursuing industrial relations activities. But the position of the CSU could be better understood if we consider the cultural environment at the time.

The colonial employer (largely government) operated a form of arbitrary paternalism. This partly explains the slow tempo of industrial relations activities by the union of government workers, aside from the consideration that civil servants were indoctrinated to feel they were part of the State apparatus, just like the judiciary, police or army, and were therefore not expected to be active or militant union members. At any rate, the RWU broke off from the CSU on account of the latter's slow approach to unionism.

Similarly, the NUT wanted a better forum where they could maintain good professionalism and forge a good standard of education in Nigeria. The NUT was also dissatisfied with the wide differential that existed between the wages of government teachers and their mission school counterparts. Formal organisation of workers into unions dates back, therefore, to 1912. Yet, no significant development in the labour movement took place until the late 1930s.

The absence of legal backing for Nigerian unions was removed when the colonial administration passed the Trade Union Ordinance into law in 1938. Earlier, the Secretary for the colonies had sent general directives to all colonies, beginning in the 1930s, that trade unions were desirable institutions for industrial democracy and as such were to be encouraged in the colonies. What is more, trade unions were operating in Britain, and it was thought to be a good thing. The colonial administration resisted this directive, claiming that trade unions would not be appropriate for a country on the verge of industrialisation. Furthermore, given the emerging movements for political independence, trades union organisations, it was feared, might fall into the hands of unscrupulous politicians.

However, the colonial administration succumbed in 1938 and the ordinance, put into force only in 1939 and even then reluctantly, provided legal backing for the existing unions and facilitated the formation of new ones. Specifically, the law allowed any group of five or more workers to form a trade union.

Most of the unions that emerged were centred on one employer or one branch of an enterprise and comprised of few members indeed.

Other factors perhaps played equally important parts in the course of developments in Nigerian labour movement. These factors are the 1939–45 World Wars and the emerging nationalist movement. The role of the nationalist movement is a very significant one in the development of trade unionism in Nigeria. Formal political parties were banned during this period but, as things were, the same set of people led the unions and the clandestine or illegal political parties. Naturally, they must have used competencies gained from trade unionism to political advantage. At any rate, one could note the infiltration of conflicting externally based ideologies in the labour movement.

Evolution of industrial unionism in Nigeria

As at 1971, the number of registered trade unions had risen to 751 with a membership of a little more than 700,000. Average membership was only 957 (Fashoyin, 1980). The consequence of this development was that the unions lacked proper organisational structures and dependable financial resources, with inevitable consequences for their security.

These undesirable developments were responsible for the decision of the military administration of Obasanjo and Murtala to introduce a national labour policy. The highlights of the National Labour Policy which was unveiled in 1975 include: the need to give a new sense of direction and a new image to the trade union movement in Nigeria; and the need to rationalise the structure and organisation of trade unions and to make certain that they are financially self sufficient in the future.

The policy facilitated the transformation of the labour movement. For example, international organisations such as International Confederation of Free Trade Unions (ICFTU) and World Federation of Trade Unions (WFTU), which were known to propagate ideological conflicts, were proscribed. Only the Organisation of African Trades Union Unity (OATUU) was retained.

Furthermore, an Administrator of Trade Unions worked on the structure of trade unions and reduced the number of Nigerian unions from more than 1000 in 1975 to 70 unions, all organised along industrial lines. The industrial unions were by law affiliated to the Nigeria Labour Congress. Under this structure, each union has its exclusive jurisdiction or territory, in which it claims the right to organise workers and to control labour relations.

Under this arrangement, emergent unions were automatically registered. Their employers were obliged to recognise them for the purpose of collective bargaining. Hitherto, the process of recognition of a union involved the acceptance of the employers, even after necessary papers had been filed with and approved by the Minister of Labour. The process of registration of a new union is guided by the enabling labour laws. A rival union cannot emerge to organise workers where duplication of unions would result and so that the attendant inter-union conflicts which characterised the industrial scene in the days of the 'mushroom' unions may not be repeated.

The restructuring exercise led to a number of positive outcomes: lessening of damaging ideological conflicts among Nigerian unions; removal of moribund unions and the substitution of large and effective industrial unions; assurance of dependable internally generated financial resources through automatic checkoffs; dependable resources. These changes have encouraged the employment of well disciplined and experienced trade union leaders performing full-time duties; and the creation of one central labour organisation (NLC).

However, the restructuring exercise led to some negative effects: the State-authorship of the constitutions and structure of the trade unions that were created, thereby tying them securely to the dictates of the State; the increased opportunity for the State to intervene in the affairs of voluntary associations such as trade unions and employers associations; the confusion brought about by the restructure which left workers in certain industries without unions and created two or more unions in some other industries; and the reduced capacity of the branch unions to handle industrial relations matters as negotiation became national and industry-wide. After a decade of experimenting with this structure, the actors realised these negative effects, and took steps to correct them. Hence, the incidence of trade union reforms in the 1990s.

The trade unions: further reforms

The State found it necessary to grant requests engineering further reforms to the 1978 structure. There were occasions for registration of new unions and also the de-registration of a few of the existing ones during the 1990s. Most union types were somewhat affected by state socio-political reforms as reflected in Table 13.1.

Industrial unions

The number of industrial unions remained stable between 1978 and 1990. The Customs, Excise, and Immigration Staff Union (CEISU), was disbanded in 1988 because its existence necessarily contradicts the State's policy that

Table 13.1 Structure of Unions – 1978–2006

Type of union	1978	1986	1988	1990	1996–2006
Industrial unions	42	42	41	41	29
Senior staff associations	15	18	21	20	20
Employers associations	9	22	22	22	22
Professional unions	4	4	4	4	4
All	70	86	88	87	75

Source: Fajana (2006).

arms-carrying employees should be precluded from unionisation. This was the only 1978 union permanently deregistered by the Nigerian state. The State equally deployed its labour policy of limited intervention and guided democracy in 1988 to apprehend the problem within the Nigeria Labour Congress when it could not hold its delegate conference and elections successfully. An administrator was appointed for running the Congress on behalf of the unions and to assist them to reach a compromise at the end of which a new President, Comrade Paschal Bafyau, emerged.

In 1996, the State, assiduously working with the unions, finally facilitated the process of amalgamation of overlapping industrial unions, reducing the number from 41 to 29. The mergers became necessary to redress overlaps in the jurisdiction of the unions, and the incidence of job interests not properly recognised, which had existed since 1978 in the aftermath of the restructuring exercise. Solutions to these problems were attempted by the State during the late 1990s by forming a committee with the labour movement for the purpose of minimising these problems.

Senior staff unions

There has been an upward trend in the unionisation of managerial employees since 1978. For instance, from 19 (professional unions inclusive) in 1978, it increased to 22 by 1986 and 25 by 1988. The increase in the unionisation rate of these white-collar staffers was possibly due to economic vulnerability during the recession of the early 1980s. However the ability of the senior staff associations (SSAs) to increase their membership was no doubt negatively affected by the wave of retrenchments since the 1980s. Consequently, whilst the number of evolved senior staff associations maintained an increase, membership numbers suffered under the heavy weight of staff retrenchments. Further developments in 1986 pertained to the withdrawal of automatic membership of senior staff by the State; this merely served to increase the resolve of the SSAs, who responded by forming a consultative body; the Senior Staff Consultative Association of Nigeria (SESCAN).

Employers' associations

The incidence of trade unions of employers in Nigeria is supported by the Trade Union Act, which prescribes and recognises the existence of trade unions of employers. Employers Associations, which are found in every industrial sector of Nigeria, serve both labour market and infrastructural roles nationwide. It is only in the oil and gas sector where the absence of an employers association continues to linger. Attempts were made to form the Petroleum and Natural Gas Employers Association, as well as the Oil Producers Trade Sectors (OPTS). But none of these attempts were realised. However, there is a coordinating body of oil employers among the members of the Nigerian Employers Consultative Association (NECA). However, it does not have the capacity to negotiate a collective agreement with oil workers.

Foreign employers played significant roles in Nigeria's industrial relations system. Part of a report by a multinational in the food and beverage sector reads as follows: 'As one of the leading companies in Nigeria and an active member of the Organised Private Sector (OPS), we enjoy excellent relations with government agencies and are a point of reference for policy formulation.' Unionised foreign employers dominate the state lobby as they sought to influence the access to public infrastructure, and influenced smaller employers as they determine pay ranges (minimum and maximum) in the course of bargaining with trade unions. Even foreign employers who are not themselves members of an employer association may also seek to nominate and sponsor preferred employees for leadership positions in the workers' union, thereby effectively planting their loyalists in national trade union executives. The ineffectiveness of labour actions in some of Nigeria's key industrial sectors would seem to be at least partly explained by this backdrop.

Developments within labour centres

What is significant about the evolution of labour centres in Nigeria is the oscillation that characterised their growths and decline as reflected in the classic accounts by Ananaba (1969) and Fashoyin (1980), the basis of this section. The Trade Union Ordinance of 1938 also provided for the formation of trade union centres. The technical workers in the civil service initiated a move to form the African Civil Servants Technical Workers Union (ACSTWU) for the purpose of coordinating the 42 unions which had registered by 1941. By 1942, the ACSTWU had had 12 affiliate members from the list of registered unions.

Simultaneously, during the post-war period, a movement called the Trade Union Congress (TUC), probably fashioned after the British TUC, arose among workers. The purpose was to improve wages. It was particularly spearheaded by the RWU. One of its major activities was the strike called in 1942 on cost of living difficulties unleashed by the Second World War. The strike led to the banning of Michael Imoudu, Nigeria's foremost trade unionist and leader of the striking workers.

In 1943, the Trade Union Congress and the ACSTWU came together to form the Trades Union Congress (TUC). By the end of 1949, there were factions in the TUC arising from arguments over the role trade unions should play in the nationalist movement. One group believed that trade unions should be neutral while the other wanted a political trade union centre. Thus, the TUC split into the Nigerian National Federation of Labour (NNFL) and the TUC proper. The NNFL affiliated with the National Congress of Nigerian Citizens (NCNC) –a political party.

The TUC became the Trade Union Congress of Nigeria (TUCN) in the same year. Simultaneously, the Enugu shooting of striking coal workers rekindled the need for solidarity to fight colonialism. It was thought that division among the labour movement might jeopardise the nationalist struggle. But factionalism continued until 1950 when the first Nigeria Labour Congress (NLC) was born. In 1951, the NLC chose to affiliate with the World Federation of Trade Unions (WFTU) and sponsored political candidates. Thus, the international trade union centre, i.e. the WFTU, became a feature of industrial relations in Nigeria.

In 1953, the All Nigeria Trade Union Federation (ANTUF) was fashioned and lasted up to 1956. The NLC was nominally integrated into ANTUF. It pretended to be neutral and favoured no affiliation with political parties or international federations. In 1957, the National Council of Trade Unions of Nigeria (NCTUN) was formed to compete with the ANTUF on the grounds of non-affiliation to the WFTU. This perhaps strengthened the voice of those who were anti-affiliation. Between 1957 and 1959, both NCTUN and ANTUF co-existed. In 1959, however, the second TUC of Nigeria was created with the NCTUN and ANTUF collaborating. This situation continued into the nation's independence celebrations in 1960.

The factionalisation which characterised the labour movement during the colonial period continued unabated after independence. For instance, a faction broke off in 1961 to form the Nigeria Trade Union Congress (NTUC). This was led by Imoudu, and another group, the Trade Union Congress of Nigeria (TUCN) emerged and was led by H A Adebola. These confusions marked the post-independence period affecting trade unions and their economic and organisational activities. In 1962, a conference was held at Ibadan at the instance of government to get the trade unions to unite and play an important role in the development process. That conference led to the formation of the Adebola-led United Labour Congress in 1962. The following day, the organisation broke into two, the ULC and the new IULC. The Imoudu-led IULC changed its name to NTUC.

In the same year, a third union centre was born, the Nigerian Workers Council (NWC). It came into being after a conference organised jointly by the Pan-African Workers Congress and the ICFTU, to serve as the umbrella for all trade unions. In 1963, the labour movement was further balkanised along political and ideological lines. Two of the best-run unions, the NUT and the NCSU, tried to serve as peace-makers, by forming a peace committee to resolve the conflicts and bring about unity. The committee failed to unite the labour movement but itself became a centre, the Labour Unity Front (LUF).

During the civil war years, the unions were by and large sober, and less turbulent, ostensibly to support government effort in bringing the war to a satisfactory end. Up to 1973, there were thus four labour centres, the LUF, NWC, NTUC, and ULC.

In 1974, factions of the four groups came together to have another attempt at unity. Thus, the Nigerian Trade Union Federation was formed. This was however not recognised by government. In the same year at the burial ceremony of a veteran trade unionist, the labour leaders considered the issue of unity. They resolved to form the Nigeria Labour Congress in 1975. But this was again not recognised by government, who had already instituted an inquiry into the affairs of the trade unions. Thus, recognition of the labour-formed NLC (1975) might contradict or pre-empt the findings of the (Adebiyi) tribunal. The tribunal thereafter recommended a restructure of the entire labour movement. Thus in 1976, a government-appointed administrator of trade unions implemented the recommendations and created a single central labour organisation, i.e., the current NLC which was inaugurated at Ibadan in 1978.

At the turn of the new millennium, the issue of factions became less prevalent in Nigerian labour centres. Rather, the labour movement was confronted with a common foe arising from the economic reforms which affected workers significantly. Consequently, at this time, the role of the labour centres became primarily political. Even the senior staff associations which had expressed the wish for a federation and which had been denied by the State, conveniently closed ranks with the NLC to vanquish the unpopular reform policies of the State, especially that of petroleum pricing.

In 2004, Nigeria abrogated its Central Labour Organisation law, which hitherto gave a monopoly to the NLC, with a view to democratising the labour movement. The 2004 Trade Union Act was therefore passed to allow the registration of multiple labour centres. The TUC as well as the CFTU took advantage of this reform to register as federations of trade unions, while the NLC is still processing its registration. Commentators have attempted a motive for these series of trade union reforms; they were said to be targeted at a few 'troublemakers' in the trade union movement who have disallowed the State from imposing higher fuel prices on the Nigerian people.

Union–state relations

In pre-industrial societies of the now developed countries, the State was, in most parts, a constituent of the economic system as merchants. But as a distinct industrial class emerged, the State's role shifted to legal regulation of hours and conditions of work. Subsequently, as governments assumed overall responsibility for the economy, the role of the State had expanded to include co-ordination of the activities of employers, employees, political parties etc.

The character of the Nigerian state is incontrovertible. The country is structurally divided into 36 states and local governments with a presidential system of political administration. Currently, labour matters are on the exclusive list, thus strengthening the stature of the centre in industrial relations. Resource distribution between the federal and state units is also centre-biased. The process of labour legislation, like most law-making processes, is largely non-inclusive as public debates of bills at the national assembly are very uncommon. This undemocratic tendency had been with the country since colonial times.

The philosophy of government in industrial relations instituted in 1975 is the principle of 'limited intervention and guided democracy'. This policy stipulates the right of the State to intervene in union, management and labour–management relations. The policy itself became necessary due principally to the chaotic industrial relations situation in the country before 1975. However, Otobo (1987) has argued that the intention of the military regime that engineered the restructure is in fact not just to discipline the unionists but rather to achieve some objectives which are, at least in part, connected with controlling the labour movement by incorporating it as a State apparatus. For instance, the real motive could have been to re-orient the labour movement so as to achieve one of the political ambitions of the government. Be that as it may, there is no doubt that the restructure had profound effects on the labour movement and the patterning of industrial relations in the years that followed. The new policy had effects on union affairs, labour–management relations and on the resolution of industrial conflicts.

In the area of union-management relations, the principle of 'limited intervention and guided democracy' was again adopted in the settlement of trade disputes, union recognition and enforcement of collective agreements. For example, although the parties must inform the Minister of Employment, Labour and Productivity of all disputes, the Minister may apprehend any dispute, especially in essential services, and prescribe appropriate steps in settling it. This is considered necessary especially if the economic activities rendered are deemed as essential to the economy (Trade Disputes Essential Services Decree, 1977). As for union recognition, the State has made this compulsory for any registered union. Moreover, the Minister under the enabling law is empowered to enforce any provisions of a bilateral collective agreement on the parties. This provision in the law may be used to confer legitimacy and legality to that particular portion of the collective agreement. It is noteworthy that without this provision, a collective agreement in Nigeria is not automatically a legal contract but a 'gentleman's agreement'.

Petroleum pricing and further reforms of trade unions

From 1999, aside from the minor adjustment to the number of registered industrial unions, the controversy surrounding the pricing of petroleum products by the state was the major incident which pre-occupied the stakeholders up to 2004 and beyond. During these periods, the labour movement carried several protests to the federal government on the issue of continued and sustained increases in the prices of petroleum products. Against the backdrop of the criticality of this source of energy for industrial and human development, the Nigeria Labour Congress under the leadership of Comrade Adams Oshiomhole led the civil societies to resist the actions of government. These attempts were somewhat successful as government had to reduce advertised prices at least marginally on each occasion.

The Nigerian government has consistently hedged the right of Nigerian workers to strike. Some of the relevant legislation is in the Trade Disputes Acts 1969, 1976, 1996 and 2005. The Trade Unions (Amendment) Decree of 1996, makes check-off payments conditional on a 'no strike' clause during the lifetime of a collective agreement. This clause stipulates that employers will not remit union checkoff dues to the union office unless a union agrees to a 'no strike' clause in the collective agreements. Trade unions must also give 15 days' notice for a planned strike.

Strikes in essential services are forbidden in Nigeria, as confirmed again in the 2005 law. First, the law clearly bans industrial actions in the oil sector, and Section 9 of the Trade Dispute (Essential Services) Act, 1976 lists the economic sectors which fall within 'essential service'. Subsection (b) states that 'any service established, provided or maintained by the Government of the Federation or of a State, by a Local Government Council or any municipal or statutory authority, or by private enterprise (i) for, or in connection with, the supply of electricity, power or water, or of fuel of any kind'. The preface in the Act also states that the Act was to 'empower the President to proscribe any trade union or association the members of which are employed in any essential service if such Union or Association has been engaged in industrial unrest or acts calculated to disrupt the smooth running of any essential service, or has, where applicable, wilfully failed to comply with the procedure specified in the Trade Disputes Act in relation to the reporting of the settlement of trade disputes'.

Second, the Government of Nigeria declares any trade union activities illegal in the name of wrongful politically motivated activities. For example, (1) a strike at Shell-BP and Allied Workers Union in October 1977 (Proscription Order No. 2) and (2) a strike at the Pan Ocean Branch of the Consolidated Petroleum, Chemical and General Workers Union of Nigeria in November 1977 (Proscription Order No. 3). Between 1993 and 1994, many strikes staged by NUPENG and PENGASSAN were claimed as illegal because they were politically instigated in the aftermath of the Nigerian national election.

In October 2003, a new law was proposed to the National Assembly to amend the Trade Union (Amendment) Act. After some revisions, the law came into effect in March 2005. The law ends automatic trade union membership for both industrial unions and senior staff associations and introduces a general strike ban. Chapter 432 of the Trade Disputes Act, 1990, compels trade unions to follow strict procedures on arbitration, before embarking upon a strike, and a simple majority of registered members vote in favour of strike action before it is legal.

In addition, legislation also makes it difficult for workers to go on strike by demanding that they meet certain procedural requirements. For example, Section 17 (a & b), Paragraph 14 of the Trade Union Act states that union rules must include a provision which forbids trade union members from taking part in any strike unless there was a majority vote in favour of the action.

Provisions of the 2005 law included: the prohibition of strikes in services that were regarded as essential; in non-essential services, strikes are now subjected to the taking of a strike ballot among the members of such unions; strikes can only occur after the due process has been exhausted and for *disputes of rights* (violation, non-implementation of collective agreements). Where the issues are over *disputes of interest* (fresh issues that are being processed for negotiation), strikes are prohibited.

According to the International Confederation of Free Trade Unions (ICFTU), many strikes took place in 2003 and 2004, over increasing oil prices and the proposed amendment to the Trade Union (Amendment) Act. In June 2003, the government announced yet another plan to increase oil prices by 50 per cent. During the ensuing general strike 19 trade unionists were killed by police violence and shooting. Six trade unionists that were arrested in October 2003 were severely beaten up in prison. During 2004, several strikes were planned by the NLC against the hike in oil prices, but the High Court issued injunctions against these strikes and, in September, ruled such strikes illegal on the grounds that they did not concern an industrial dispute. In June 2004, armed police descended on NLC headquarters during a general strike against an increase in oil prices. One trade unionist was shot dead, another was injured, and several arrests took place. A peaceful strike in September 2004, protesting against 18 months wage and pension arrears, was responded to with teargas and police attacks. The NLC president was arrested at gunpoint after the announcement of a four-day general strike with the aim of reversing hikes in petrol prices. Five other trade unionists were arrested that day as well. During the 11 October 2004 general strike a 12-year-old boy and a man were killed by police firing on protesters, and mass arrests took place.

There was a strategy shift in the reactions of organised labour during the September 2005 price hike. As the legal existence of the NLC as a federation was still a controversial, and the general societal acceptability of strikes waning, a new strategy was called for. Thus, rather than the characteristic shunning of work actions which often end within four days without definite agreements, the civil society opted for programmed mass rallies held on various dates in different locations of the country – Lagos, Kano, Maiduguri, etc. This proved somewhat effective. Whether this pragmatic strategy would enjoy continued adoption in the future is to be seen as the unavoidable struggle between organised labour and a government avowedly committed to globalisation and deregulation is expected to persist.

Industrial conflict

In Nigeria, postcolonial governments are ostensibly aggressive about development, as professed routinely in official declarations. There is emphasis on the harmony of interests and adopted strategies have focussed on effective containment of strike and other overt forms of industrial actions, which had characteristically been violent. Even at the verge of independence, it is evident that colonial strikes were partly economic and partly politically motivated (see Otobo, 1987 for details), hence the interest evidently shown by the Nigerian State.

In a developing country like Nigeria, one of the elements of the sustained system of industrial relations is that it is difficult to separate labour from political matters. For instance, as reported by the Nigeria Police: 'the Chief Commissioners (police) have given it as their opinion that there can be no comfortable line of demarcation between labour affairs and politics . . . and that in consequence, labour policy becomes mainly the concern of the Provincial Administration itself . . .' (Fajana, 1992, 184). Expectedly therefore, there has been no relationship between strike proneness and the political situation in Nigeria. All Administrations since colonialism have continued to use the police to stop industrial protests. As found in a study of 'Conflict regulation and the Role of the Nigerian Police', it is an interesting irony that the Police seek to get recognition not only for preventing industrial crises by keeping the peace through regular police work, but also secondarily assisting workers and employers to sit down and resolve their differences through negotiations (Fajana, 1992, 2005b). This development calls into question the role of the Ministry of Labour and other agencies whose primary duty it is to facilitate collective negotiations and effectively resolve conflicts at work.

In spite of State coercion, Nigerian workers have been resilient as participants in industrial conflict. They have continued to respond more to economic conditions than political systems. For instance, Agbon (1986) has shown that the pattern of industrial disputes is strongly and positively associated with the trends in the petroleum sector.

In the 1980s and 1990s, strikes became less frequent than the preceding decade, reflecting State coercive strategies putting industrial actions in safer channels through the use of the police (Fajana, 1992). By this time, it had become imperative to embark upon economic restructuring to bail out the economy, which decelerated during the beginning of the period. Strikes have also become longer in duration and tend to involve more workers, a reflection of the industry-wide nature of bargaining units sequel to the 1978 restructure of labour unions.

In the 2000s, the oil-flavoured strikes became national in scope because Nigeria adopted a kind of federalism in which the centre is over-strong, and the periphery (states, local governments administrations) were relatively weak on account of resources mobilised and controlled. The conflicts therefore became amenable to central organisation through the NLC, who inevitably carried its struggle to the federal governments where the decisions for control of resources are taken and where the bulk of state resources are controlled. Other dimensions of the conflicts include hostage taking at the oil rich Niger Delta in which several foreigners and some Nigerian nationals have become victims as well as political assassinations. These developments threaten national security and international credit ratings, throwing more challenges to the future of industrial relations in Africa's most populous country.

Future prospects and concluding remarks

The outcomes of the 1975 restructure exercise, which was inherited by the Babangida administration in the 1980s, have had to be operated amidst serious economic hardships. Thus, coping strategies of the unions, amidst public policies that are severally constraining of the goals and objects of organised labour, had been largely sacrificial. Industrial relations in Nigeria since the turn of the century has been characterised by the politics of petroleum pricing which in turn had been remotely controlled by the forces of globalisation, and promoted unrepentantly by the Obasanjo democratic rule.

From the foregoing analysis, it is evident that a unique system of industrial relations has emerged in Nigeria. Restated, some of the features of this model are as follows:

- the emergence of trade unions before the country embarked on industrialisation;
- the inability of the trade union leaders for a long time to conduct industrial relations matters with deserved effectiveness, against the highly constraining environment created by colonial and post-colonial governments;
- the domination of the employers' lobby by multinationals, and other foreign interests, thus determining, with States' support and power, the direction and amount of pay, perquisites and employment conditions;
- the undue interventionist role of the various States (colonial and post colonial) as explained by the need to control labour for development efforts;
- the inconsistencies of the State as socio-economic policies are jettisoned midstream and others are adopted in their stead;
- the tendency for State policies to be targeted at individuals, and for such policies to become irrelevant as soon as the targeted persons are no longer in office;
- the difficulty of separating pure labour from political disturbances;
- the tendency for labour disputes to become destructive, and the State to deploy coercive measures in its control; and
- the currently dysfunctional character of Nigeria's federalism which is centre-strong and periphery-weak, thus encouraging the unions to carry their struggles to the federal government.

These features are expected to continue because industrialisation is yet to be carried to a satisfactory level. Some of the trade unions and employers still continue their seeming misunderstanding of their roles in the development process. The structure of ownership of industry has not changed. The political system has not matured to the extent that instability and thence inconsistencies of government policies can be forestalled. The State has much motivation to continue to increase its focus on the IR system.

References

Agbon I.S. (1986), 'Industrial Conflict and the Nigerian Petroleum Economy, 1976–84', *Proceedings of the 4th Annual Conference of the Department of Industrial Relations*, University of Lagos, October.

Akpala, A. (1965), 'The Background of the Enugu Colliery Shooting Incident in 1949'. *Journal of the Historical Society of Nigeria*, 3, 2: 335–63.

Ananaba, W. (1969), *The Trade Union Movement in Nigeria*. Benin: Fourth Dimension Press.

Fajana, S. (1987), 'Collective Bargaining and Affiliation with the NLC: A Survey of the Attitude of Senior Staff in Nigeria', *Research for Development*, 5, 2: 222–44.

Fajana, S. (1992), 'The Police and Conflict Regulation in Industry', in Otobo, D. (ed.), *Further Readings in Industrial Relations in Nigeria*. Lagos: Malthouse.

Fajana, S. (2005a), 'Industrial Relations in the Oil Sector in Nigeria', Working Paper Series, International Labour Organisation, Geneva.

Fajana, S. (2005b), 'Enforcement Mechanisms And Conflict Resolution In Industry: The Role Of The Nigerian Police', Nigeria Industrial Relations Association and Friedrich Ebert Foundation Conference on the State, Democratisation and Industrial Relations in Nigeria. Jos, 19–21 September 2005.

Fajana, S. (2006), *Industrial Relations in Nigeria: Theory and Features*. Lagos: Labofin and co.

Fashoyin, T. (1980), *Industrial Relations in Nigeria*. London: Longman.

Freund, W. (1981). *Capital and Labour in Nigerian Tin Mines*, University of Ibadan Press, Ibadan.

ICFTU (2006), 'Nigeria: Annual Survey of Violations of Trade Union Rights', www.icftu.org/pdf

Kilby, P. (1975), 'Manufacturing in Colonial Africa', in Digman, P. and Gann, L. (eds), *Colonialism in Africa, Vol IV: The Economics of Colonialism*. Cambridge: Cambridge University Press.

National Planning Commission (2005). *National Economic Empowerment and Development Strategy*. Abuja: Central Bank of Nigeria.

Otobo, D. (1987), *Readings in Industrial Relations in Nigeria*. Lagos: Malthouse.

Otobo, D. (1988), *State and Industrial Relations in Nigeria*. Lagos: Malthouse.

Poole, M (1986), *Industrial Relations: The Origin of National Diversity*. London: Routledge and Kegan Paul.

Seibel, H.D. (1973), 'Systems of Allocation and Receptivity to Modernisaton', in Damachi, U.G. and Seibel, H.D. (eds), *Social Change and Economic Development in Nigeria*. New York: Praeger.

14
Contemporary Industrial Relations in Nigeria

Dafe Otobo

Introduction – the Nigerian context

The 1951 census put the Nigerian population as 30.3 million; subsequent attempts at national body count have controversially been marred by gross inaccuracies, so much so that the last one ended with a bit less than 100 million when the United Nations estimates put it closer to 120 million mark. As a result today official working figures, we are told, are extrapolated from the 1973 figures, which were themselves officially dubbed 'tentative figures' at the time. According to the Federal Office of Statistics, the labour force was 29.2 million in 1975, 32.2 million in 1981, 36.08 million in 1985 and 45.6 million in 1993. The current figure of nearly 49 million as the 'labour force' is thus suspect, as well as figures of the population distribution according to sex, age, etc. The labour force is distributed among the following major economic and industrial sectors of agriculture; automobile, boatyards, transport equipment; chemical and non-metallic; construction industry; food, beverage and tobacco; hotel and personal services; metal products, iron and steel; paper, paper board and paper products; petroleum and natural gas; precision, electrical and related equipment; shipping, clearing and forwarding; shop and distributive trade; solid minerals; textile, garment and tailoring; and training and consultancy. Less than 35 per cent of these are found in the formal sector, the rest in the ever-expanding informal sector.

In Nigeria, the public sector is much larger than the private sector in most respects, especially quantum of investment, employment opportunities, and size of work force. These are part spin-offs from the politico-administrative structure of a federation of thirty-six states,[1] excluding the federal capital territory of Abuja, each state boasting a complement of capital city, main civil service, public utilities and/or parastatals, and local governments. Competition among the states, political parties and elite have over the decades led to investing public funds in all manner of businesses, many of which are currently being privatised.

The private sector is often classified into two, organised and unorganised. Within each category are small, medium and large scale enterprises or companies but the unorganised private sector is also christened the 'informal sector', has more of small and medium scale businesses but a much larger work force and firms therein are usually outlets for manufactured products and services of multinational companies. The 'organised private sector' (OPS), is dominated by subsidiaries of European, North American, British, Japanese, Asian and Levantine multinational companies. Some would argue that, aside from consultancy and the provision of a variety of professional services by indigenous firms, the private sector is coterminous with multinational companies' operations in all sectors of the economy, where even the few large indigenous firms have multinational partners. This also means the existence of a variety of management styles and practices.

The *legal framework* is the web of rules and regulations that guide and govern the conduct of the parties. Most often, state authorities lay down such rules or laws, and those directly pertaining to industrial and labour relations matters are collectively known as 'labour law'. Labour law regulates most aspects of collective relations in industry or at work: for example, terms of employment, health and safety standards, determination of wages and salaries, conflict, formation and functioning of workers' and employers' organisations, and types and future of jobs. The sources of these laws in Nigeria include the Common Law of England, statutes enacted/decreed at various times by the Colonial Parliament, the pre-Military Parliament, Military Decrees, and post-Military Elected/Civilian National Assembly. The 1979 Constitution of the Federal Republic of Nigeria provides that only the National Assembly can legislate on 'labour, including trade unionism; industrial relations; conditions, safety and welfare of labour; industrial dispute; prescribing a national minimum wage for the federation or any part thereof; and industrial arbitration'. This is what is meant by 'labour' being 'exclusive jurisdiction' of the federal government.

Labour law has five main legislative pieces which comprise part of the industrial relations legal framework. These are the Labour or Employment Act, Trade Union Act, Trade Disputes Act, Factory Act, and Workmen's Compensation Act. The Labour or Employment Act concerns itself with the contract of employment, and protection of job, and wages: written terms of employment within three months; withdrawal/termination of service at various notices to be given by both employers and employees, status of collective agreements, mode of payment of wages/salaries, etc. The Trade Union Act deals with the formation, functioning and administration of trade unions, and spells out the powers of the Minister for Labour and Productivity and of the Registrar of Trade Unions and labour officers regarding these. The Trade Disputes Act contains provisions for internal and external disputes settlement mechanisms: mediation, conciliation and arbitration procedures and processes which revolve around the Minister for Labour and Productivity, and the Industrial Arbitration Panel and the National Industrial Court warehoused by the Federal Ministry of Labour and Productivity. A subsidiary legislation deals with dispute resolution in essential services. The Factory Acts attempts to establish health and safety standards in places of work, to be monitored and enforced by Factory Inspectors. While the Workmen's Compensation Act deals with diseases and injuries at work, containing remedies and reliefs entitled to by victims.

The IMF-imposed structural adjustment programme (SAP) from the mid-1980s formed the context within which state authorities, private employers, workers and their organisations and respective Nigerian communities grappled with serious social, economic and political upheavals, similar to those experienced to other tropical African countries.

Lastly, the advent of military regimes, which began on 15 January 1966 and continued till May 1999 when President Obasanjo's elected government was sworn in, with a short interregnum of civilian government from 1979 October to 31 December 1983. From the practical dictates of a three-year long civil war (1967–70) and inherent authoritarianism of dictatorships emerged decrees to regulate all aspects of the citizen's life, much of the labour law and industrial relations institutions being products of this period. The symbiotic relationship between military regimes and the IMF/World Bank arguably affected the character of industrial relations practices, processes and institutions.

The industrial relations system

The industrial relations system is thus based on a model tripartite structure or tripod: state/government, private (organised) employers and their organisations, and workers and their organisations. These interests are often found and represented at (a) national level; (b) industrial level; and (c) plant or company level. At the national level for state authorities, the Presidency, Ministry of Establishment and the Ministry of Labour and Productivity play a prominent part, while the Nigeria Employers' Consultative Association (NECA) – complemented by the lobbying activities of the Manufacturers' Association of Nigeria (MAN) and National Association of Chambers of Commerce, Industrial, Mines and Agriculture (NACCIMA) – represents private employers, and the Nigeria Labour Congress (NLC), the Trade Union Congress (TUC) and other federations of trade unions represent workers.

The consequent tripartite relations are both formal and informal but with a tendency toward their institutionalisation. In terms of institutional tripartism, the membership of the National Labour Advisory Board (now, Council), the Industrial Arbitration Panel (IAP), the National Industrial Court (NIC) and appointments to the boards of many parastatals or public utilities, *ad hoc* committees on privatisation, deregulation, minimum wage, have tended to be tripartite in nature.

At the industry level, in the Organised Private Sector (OPS), there are employers' organisations for respective industries that are involved in bipartite relations with both senior staff associations and industrial unions which represent the two classes of workers, senior and junior as defined by law. Aside from resolving challenges facing their respective industries, every two years both parties embark upon formal negotiations to produce a new collective agreement, modified terms of employment that are meant to be implemented by all employers in the industry concerned.

At the plant or company level, respective managements are engaged in continuous relations with workers and branches of industrial unions and senior staff associations where they exist. A good many of such managements also engaged themselves in 'domestic negotiations' with officials of branch unions and whose outcomes tend to supplement the rates and other conditions agreed at the industry level. More often than not, therefore, collective agreements tend to contain minimum rather than maximum rates and conditions.

Out of 29 million wage earners, less than 3 million are organised into trade unions – industrial unions and senior staff associations. Except for the public sector, union coverage in the private sector is less than 50 per cent in each industry because of the prevalence of small and medium scale enterprises where paternalism is the philosophy of management and as such characterised by rabid anti-unionism. Until the 1976–77 reform of the trade union structure, both the formation and recognition of trade unions were voluntary – although trade unions were compulsorily registered since the 1939 Trade Union Ordinance.

The Trade Union Act 1973 concerns itself with the formation and functioning of workers' and employers' organisations, especially union federations. Decree 27 of 1977 specifically recognised separate unions for so-called junior workers (industrial unions) and senior staff (senior staff associations), and the Nigerian Labour Congress (NLC) as the only central labour organisation and to which all industrial unions must affiliate. It also imposed constitutions on all the unions and the NLC. The definition of a trade union also includes organisations of employers, as in Britain.

The political climate that prevailed during military rule encouraged anti-union policies in both private and public sectors of the economy. As a result, a good many disputes and strikes were directed against anti-union actions and anti-labour legislation between 1996 and 1998. The state took advantage of moves by unionists to merge some industrial unions to engage in formal restructuring of union structures, a process that was drawn out and deadlock as union leaders opposed the preferences of government officials. In the end and in 1996, Decree No 4 reduced the 41 trade unions to 29, a union structure that is still bedevilled by jurisdictional issues. The regime increased its intervention in the internal affairs of union in the form of Decree No 26 which made a dubious distinction between 'card-carrying' members and 'non-card carrying' members, allowing only the former to contest union positions. It was a ploy to prevent professional union leaders and bureaucrats from holding critical positions within the industrial unions. This decree was quickly followed by Decree No 29 that prohibited affiliation by Nigerian Trade Unions with International Labour Organisations, and by the banning of the Academic

Staff Union of Universities (ASUU) which was on strike (and later de-proscribed in 1998). The Trade Union Act (as amended after subsequent restructuring exercises, the last being in 1996) specifically mentions the unions by name, no new union can really be formed; it, hence, renders intra-union disputes more intractable as none of the factions can legally constitute itself into a union even where potential and actual members run into thousands.

Compulsory registration has remained contentious because (a) an unregistered trade union is an illegal body, while (b) it has the effect of workers having to obtain the consent of public authorities, through the office of the Registrar of Trade Unions, for a union to function. All these would seem to go against ILO Convention 87 which recognises the right of workers to form or belong to any union of their choosing and Section 40 of the Constitution that guarantees the right to form or belong to any trade union.

The powers of the Registrar of Trade Unions are overwhelming, including accepting/rejecting audited annual accounts of the trade unions,[2] de-registration of a union, and approving ground rules for mergers. The conditions to be met are so many and demanding to have the net effect of discouraging, if not rendering impossible, voluntary mergers and federations.

De-unionisation has been on the increase, especially in the banking and manufacturing sectors. In addition, growing unemployment due to restructuring, downsizing and bankruptcies is thinning the ranks and membership of trade unions. In the oil and gas sector, outsourcing and subcontracting of 'non-core' jobs could easily lead to the demise of NUPENG in not to distant future, and for the past three years over 100 textile mills have closed down due to the premature opening up of the local market to international competition.

Collective bargaining and wage bargaining in the public sector

The public sector as at today may be divided into the following sub-sectors, and each sub-sector has its own peculiar characteristics:

- the main civil service;
- public utilities (monopolies and near-monopolies);
- public sector companies operating in near-private sector environment;
- the primary and secondary teaching service;
- higher education and research institutions; and
- local governments.

Main civil service

Originally created upon the recommendation of the 1963/4 Morgan Commission, the current National Public Service Negotiating Councils were revamped by the 1974 Udoji Commission and which remain the main bipartite collective bargaining institution for the main civil service till date. The Negotiating

Councils which were created for federal, state and local government levels had identical constitutions and procedures and:

(i) have a general responsibility for negotiating all matters affecting the conditions of service of civil servants;
(ii) advise the government where necessary of the best means of utilising the ideas and experience of civil servants with a view to improving productivity;
(iii) review the general conditions of civil servants, e.g. recruitment, hours of work, promotion, discipline, salary, fringe benefits and superannuation, provided that in matters relating to recruitment, discipline and promotion, the Council shall restrict itself to general principles; and
(iv) refer all disputes or differences whatsoever to the Federal Ministry of Employment, Labour & Productivity for settlement in accordance with the Trade Disputes Act No. 7 of 1976 or any statutory modification or re-enactment thereof for the time being in force.

Although all the governments of the federation are represented at the negotiating table, officials and staff representatives have little or no power to bind their governments regarding the decisions and agreements reached at the negotiating table. These are referred to such higher bodies as the National Council on Establishments (NCE), the Presidency, for ratification before they can be finalised. By 1998 the Committee on Harmonisation of Public Service Remuneration reorganised the thirty-five different salary structures in the public service into five broad salary structures for all ministries, extra-ministerial departments, agencies, military, police and para-military services and parastatals whose personnel costs are fully funded by the federal government.

Public utilities

According to Ezeife (1987: 99–104) most public utilities/monopolies operate like the Civil Service. The competence of the management to negotiate with the unions suffers about the same weakness as in the Civil Service, since, for major decisions, the management would refer to the board which refers to the supervising ministry for possible transmission to the government. Successive military regimes to attempted to regulate collective relations in this subsector by increasing the number of parastatals in the 'essential services' category, legal constraint that includes the prohibition of strikes while imposing compulsory conciliation and arbitration. By the time the Abacha regime included educational institutions just to combat ASUU, nearly the whole of the public sector had become essential services, including a huge chunk of the private sector (e.g. telecommunications): Nigeria must have the widest definition of essential services in the world.

The main bipartite collective relations institution is the Joint Industrial Committees (JICs) or Joint Consultative Committees (JCCs) which, as has been well documented, have not been negotiating bodies. A good deal of management highhandedness and arbitrariness have been evidenced, strikes leading to summary dismissal of many employees, the most notorious being the security printing corporation, alias the Mint.

Public sector companies operating in near-private sector environment

In this sector, apart from the weakness associated with the management, party to the bargain (i.e. they do not have keenly interested shareholders looking over their shoulders), the bargaining situation approaches the situation in the private sector. Examples of this sub-sector include the National Insurance Corporation of Nigeria, the Nigerian National Petroleum Corporation, many banks till only recently, etc. These companies have conditions of service which should be more related to the private sector business environment in which they operate than with the public sector. For example, an engineer or driller in an NNPC oil-producing subsidiary (NPDC) sees little justification for differentials between his pay and that of his counterpart in Shell or Total and, as such, his benchmark will always be prevailing rates in the private sector in the oil and gas industry.

The teaching service, higher education, and others

Industrial relations and collective bargaining in these subsectors have also been driven by the desire of teachers at the primary, secondary and, especially tertiary levels, to opt out of the unified salary structure, get employers to pay salaries regularly, and improve upon inadequate and decaying infrastructure. Issues dominating negotiations in this sector are (i) there is lack of formal structural negotiating bodies; (ii) irregular payment of salaries; (iii) low basic salaries; (iv) stagnation due to lack of promotion; (v) differentials between academic and non-academic in the case of tertiary institutions (in some cases, even among the non-academic, there is a distinction between 'admin' and 'technical' staff); and (vi) decay of and inadequate facilities due to insufficient funding.

Essential services

Under the Trade Disputes (Essential Services) Act 1976, a majority of public servants at the federal, state and local government levels are not only legally denied the right to strike, the right to organise and collective bargain is also severely circumscribed. All parastatals (transport, the civil services, law enforcement agencies, the armed forces, etc.) as well as certain private sector establishments (financial institutions, telecommunications), educational institutions are affected by the no-strike law.

Second, there was no provision for either individual or group bargaining in the parastatals, and the structure of the main civil service did not appear to recognise the possibility of individual and group grievances. The Joint

Industrial Councils (JICs), bipartite structures, are weakened by the fact that they are not negotiating bodies; rather, avenues for examining specific government's circulars regarding a variety of fringe benefits and on awards. The issues on such occasions dealt with relativities, timing of implementation and payment of arrears where applicable.

Emerging issues in the public sector

The challenges and issues that have surfaced in public sector collective bargaining and wage determination include the following:

1. Collective bargaining involves the employer and its representatives on the one hand, and employees and their representatives on the other. In the public sector, the employer is not immediately visible. The Public Service Commission (and the equivalent for the Police, Judiciary, etc.), the Ministry of Establishments, among others, have a hand in the recruitment and disciplining of public servants and yet have nothing to do with day-to-day management of the main civil service and parastatals. The contract of employment is thus not with each ministry, although developments within can lead to the eventual termination of such contract over disciplinary issues.
2. Second, what constitutes 'management' in the public sector is also problematic. There seems to exist an amorphous group of public servants seen as 'projection of management', usually across ministries and parastatals, and this has several consequences: (i) in the main civil service, even if one can identify the civil servants who fall under this category, no management of a ministry is empowered to negotiate terms and conditions of employment; (ii) indeed, staff of the ministry may be transferred to other ministries without any reference to the management of ministry or ministries affected; (iii) there is little evidence to suggest that management of each ministry defines its responsibilities to include looking after the welfare and advancement of each civil servant or employee; (iv) no management of a ministry thinks its own fortunes might depend on how well it manages its staff, and as such productivity and morale of staff would not loom large in their considerations; (v) conversely, each civil servant has no reason to believe the management of his/her ministry has serious regard for his/her progress on the job, thereby encouraging feelings of dissatisfaction, lack of commitment and low productivity.
3. The Udoji Commission eliminated multiple salary and wages systems, which prevailed right up to the civil war period, by re-arranging basic pay rates and fringe benefits in the whole public sector in a seventeen grade unified salary structure, with no civil servant earning more than the permanent secretary which hitherto was not the case. Even federal permanent

secretaries did not earn the same salaries before Adebo and Udoji Commissions' recommendations of 1970–71 and 1974 respectively.
4. The issue of mandate for and during negotiations, when they do take place, brings out more clearly the consequences for collective bargaining in the public sector of the questions of who the employer and management are in day-to-day relations at work. The hierarchy of a chain of decision-makers and approving authorities tends to limit the mandate and empowerment of the negotiator representing the employer and subsequently result in lack of respect for the outcome of the negotiation process by the ultimate employer (or decision-maker). This could undermine goodwill and encourage the growth of distrust and adversarial relations.
5. Related to this is the refusal and/or unwillingness of public sector employers at all levels to negotiate, and when forced by circumstances or out of rational choice to do so, they not only resent the counter-offers and demands of the other parties, but also maintain the right to have a final say as the state/government. This is the so-called *sovereignty doctrine*, and the Morgan Commission (1964, Report, para 103) put it so well: '. . . it appears that in dealing with their employees, the governments are unduly conscious of their prerogative to determine the levels of remuneration and conditions of service, irrespective of their acceptability to the workers . . .'.
6. For these same reasons, it is much easier for government to renege or go back on agreements without feeling any great sense of responsibility for subsequent conflict situations, or that a breach of agreement is sanctionable. Integrity is a critical element in sustaining collective relations, and appears not to be taken into sufficient cognisance here. This likely explains why the sanctity of wages are not respected.
7. Following from this is the legal status of collective agreements. Perhaps, like the Australian experience, it is about time we had legally justiciable collective agreements, and all parties might then inculcate the habit of taking their respective contractual obligations seriously. Public sector industrial relations that are characterised by blatant disregard for agreements and procedures are dominated by conflicts and low trust relations among and between the parties. If the proposed Financial/Fiscal Responsibility Act that is currently in the National Assembly is passed, this might address the situation somewhat for sums owed to workers and others may be deducted at source and paid directly to those affected.
8. The wage/salary systems are rigid, and there appears to be no real trigger mechanism, except for threats of and actual strikes by public servants and in spite of the existence of the National Public Service Negotiating Councils and other similar mechanisms, for initiating a general review or to respond to devaluation of take home pay by inflation.
9. There was/is the practice of promoting civil servants in sets or groups, such largely determined by date of commencement of employment (also

in the military and para-military establishments) without reference to differences in performance levels of individuals.
10. Except a civil servant is skipped in the promotion exercise, it did/does not seem that the possibility of a civil servant disagreeing with quantum of increment or range of fringe benefits available would be regarded as legitimate or expected. This also partly explains the demand for monetary palliatives pending a comprehensive review of salaries and wages as alluded to above.
11. The bases for wages and salaries in the whole public sector remain unclear, of particular concern being pay relativities. Tied to the above issue of wages and salaries determination basis is the issue of ability to pay. The disparity at the Top (especially Director) level between the state and federal levels could be explained by the scope of responsibilities and span of control; despite that, there might still be some exceptions. Furthermore, in the budgeting process recurrent expenditure is budgeted for, the public servants live in the same towns and cities and barring a dramatic drop in the price of crude oil, there is limited justifiable reason to reduce budgetary allocations to such a level as to affect the salaries of public servants.
12. Deregulation of collective bargaining in the public sector needs to be thought through than has been the case. In fact, there has been no deregulation. As it is, no parastatal and or ministry has the autonomy to negotiate binding terms of employment with employees. For example, the pretence of academic staff negotiating with individual university councils was gravely undermined by circular to the universities' authorities imposing an upper ceiling on increases and basic salaries; it was still a centralised system, and so ASUU opted to negotiate directly with the approving authority! And for another, the NNPC hands over all proceeds from sale of crude oil to the federal government and thus has no independent finances to operate in the manner of Shell or Total or ChevronTexaco.
13. The periodic and arbitrary mass sack of public servants do not appear to be subjected to collective bargaining processes, aside from being an indication of some form of disregard for civil and human rights, contractual obligations, due process and rule of law. There is not much point in moaning declining morale and productivity, and corruption in the public service when job insecurity is institutionalised.

Collective bargaining and wage bargaining in the private sector

The very rapid growth of both private and public sectors necessarily threw up problems associated with pay relativities. Such problems were necessarily in the private sector which had finally caught up with and overtaken public sector rates since the early 1970s, and the emergence of vocal and strategically located groups of workers who would rather look after their own interests.

In addition, the abrupt rise in the general level of prices that accompanied the 1970–71 Adebo awards, and subsequently pushed along by the 1974 Udoji Commission awards themselves and the high volume of currency in circulation, gave room for more workers' protests and a seemingly anarchic wage bargain situation, with the State's or government's labour costs escalating proportionately. To address this situation, the Wages Boards and Industrial Councils Decree No. 1 of 1973 was enacted to give a measure of structure and coherence.

A section of the Wages Boards and Industrial Councils Decree No. 1 of 1973 repealed the Wages Boards Ordinance of 1957 and established the Industrial Wages Board and National Wages Board for the private and public sectors respectively, and the Area Minimum Wages Committees for the states. State governors could also establish equivalents for local government workers after due consultation with the Commissioner.

The 1971 Labour Act, aside from defining a worker as any person who has entered into or works under a contract of service or a contract to execute any work or labour in person, concerns itself with written particulars of terms and conditions of employment, protection of wages, recruitment and related miscellaneous matters. In the Organised Private Sector, most employees do have an idea of their terms of employment: an idea, because not all receive personal letters/contract of employment, depending on their level and nature of job.

As for workers in unorganised establishments, banking and finance, manufacturing and oil and gas sectors, evidence indicates that most managements therein meticulously draft contracts of employment, some so ingeniously so that they often have little regard for human and other rights (e.g. no pregnancy allowed for a number of years; spouses may not work in the same establishment; working hours exceeding 48 hours a week by a wide margin; confirmation of appointment depending on deposits brought in irrespective of job function and performance on that job). Although Section 7 of the Labour Act requires an employer to give a written statement specifying terms of employment within 3 months of such a worker commencing work, in these days of 'casualisation' many employers avoid complying with this provision by dismissing workers within three months – in effect creating a constant stream of workers whose careers in that establishment are just a bit short of three months. Why should an employer be given a whole three months to issue a simple letter?

The government is also heavily involved in regulating collective bargaining despite its official position of being fully in support of *free collective bargaining*, a policy it declared publicly in 1954 as noted earlier. The government as an employer has been determining public sector terms through the establishment and functioning of wages and salaries commissions (there is now a permanent salaries, incomes and wages commission), and was later to strive to isolate the demonstration effect of private sector terms of employment in order to keep its own wage bill down. It also sought to influence the size of wage settlements and fringe benefits in the private sector in its fight against inflation.

Since the 1980s the dramatically deteriorating standard of living in the face of stagflation and decreasing capacity utilisation in many industries has presented problems of sorts for all parties in industry. Not all the problems in the economy and industry have been caused by the bogey of world-wide economic depression. The rate of inflation, monetary and fiscal policy, autonomy and effectiveness of monetary institutions and authorities, extra-budgetary expenditures and budget deficits, official housing, health and educational policies, elite-generated political crises and tensions, sourcing of raw materials, pricing policies of trading and manufacturing industries, activities of middlemen and of market-women and men, just to mention a few, all impact upon the situation. The variety of levies imposed by state and local governments has increased the impoverishment of the general population and of wage earners in particular.

Collective agreements are industry-based, though supplemented by in-plant or domestic negotiations. Domestic negotiations are particularly important in the oil and gas sector, where Shell–BP's rates remain the pace setter to be matched by other companies. Although, employers in this industry do compare notes on terms and conditions of employment, there is some secrecy over certain fringe benefits in order to maintain a competitive edge on this score. This appears to be one of the reasons why employers have seen little need to form a formal association that would make certain conditions binding on all members. There has always been tension and grievances over disparity in private and public sector rates, especially in the oil and gas industry.

Collective agreements are generally not enforceable in a regular court of law. It has been suggested by many that given the increasing incidence of abandonment of agreements by employers, especially in the public sector, collective agreements should be legally binding.

Emerging issues in the private sector

(a) Collective agreements are industry-based, though supplemented by in-plant or domestic negotiations. Domestic negotiations are particularly important in the oil and gas sector, where Shell–BP's rates remain the pacesetter to be matched by other companies. Although, employers in this industry do compare notes on terms and conditions of employment, there is some secrecy over certain fringe benefits in order to maintain a competitive edge on this score. This appears to be one of the reasons why employers have seen little need to form a formal association that would make certain conditions binding on all members. In the Food, Beverage and Tobacco sector, the attempt is directed more at achieving uniform rates, narrowing of differences in rates and thus taking labour cost out of competition.
(b) There has always been tension and grievances over disparity in private and public sector rates, especially in the oil and gas industry.
(c) Collective agreements are generally not enforceable in a court of law. Given the increasing incidence of abandonment of agreements by employers,

especially in the public sector, one wonders whether the Australian and American-type agreements that are fully justiciable may not be more appropriate.
(d) Following from (ii) bargaining in good faith has become a problem, and trust is proving to be very elusive. Entering into agreements with the intention not to respect them undermines any system of collective relations.
(e) The monitoring of safety and health standards in industry by the regulatory authorities has been very slack, while compensation rates contained in the Workmen's Compensation Act for injury sustained at work are laughable and provoking.[3]
(f) Management, bearing the cost of venue, accommodation, board and allowances, mostly funds negotiations themselves. The process is often triggered by workers' side sending a 'shopping list' in a booklet or pamphlet dubbed 'charter of demand', followed by informal exchanges of views before formal negotiating sessions.
(g) Only a minority of wage earners are covered by institutionalised collective bargaining, the majority fending as best can for itself.
(h) The management of pension in the public sector seems to have collapsed, state authorities unable to pay pensioners arrears of their entitlements, and this in spite of the tripartite structure of the Nigeria Social Insurance Trust Fund (NSITF). Pensions and their management are likely to prove intractable and conflict-inducing for the near future.

Institutionalised conflict regulation: disputes, strikes and lockouts

In practice and in the Nigerian labour law, there appears to be no recognition of, nor explicit definition of actions and decisions to be regarded as 'unfair labour practices'. Thus, aside from a few stipulations contained in the procedural[4] agreement (i.e. conflict of interest; fraud; stealing; fighting, insubordination) that may attract such sanctions as 'warning', 'suspension' and 'dismissal', management would seem to have the freedom to define and redefine punishable actions. A contentious problem in labour-management relations in Nigeria is what constitutes 'insubordination'.[5] Sexual harassment and unfair dismissals are hardly covered, except for dismissal on account of union membership that Section 9(6)(b) of the Labour Act expressly prohibits. Indeed, an employer does not have to state why 'the service of an employee is no longer required'.

The Trade Disputes Act makes provision for the settlement of trade disputes and other related matters. The procedure outlined includes (a) an internal dispute settlement mechanism of the establishment in question must first be exhausted where there is an existing agreement between employer and workers on how to settle trade disputes; (b) followed by mediation/conciliation, and then (c) arbitration by the Industrial Arbitration Panel (IAP) and the National Industrial Court (NIC).

Section 17 of the Trade Disputes Act prohibits strikes and lock-outs where there is a trade dispute and a mediator has not been appointed or the Minister of Labour and Productivity has referred the dispute to conciliation, or to the IAP or the NIC. While the Trade Disputes (Essential Services) Act,[6] spells out procedure to be followed in sorting out disputes in essential services which revolves around the Minister.

The enormous powers of, and the central role played by the Minister in the dispute settlement mechanism, from 'apprehending' (which means unilateral action), provision of conciliators, referral to the IAP and NIC, to confirmation of awards/decisions of the arbitration bodies are certainly overwhelming. Section 12(1)(b) requires that the IAP can only communicate its awards to the Minister and not to the parties to the dispute; all stages of the procedure are compulsory, leaving no room for voluntary options without involvement of public authorities (except for the internal dispute settlement machinery); the procedure is cumbersome, taking some 50 days from apprehension to the NIC should the Minister decides to exhaust each stage – and this not including the 30 days within which the NIC is required to make its award/decision.

Section 17 of the Act has the effect of prohibiting or banning strikes contrary to ILO Convention 87 on the right to strike. Indeed, workers in the so-called essential services are denied the right to strike. Although, this follows the convention in many countries, it is pertinent to point out that the definition of essential services in Nigeria is unusual, as we see below, embracing most of the public sector, including all educational institutions and sections of the private sector where the government has invested.

The Trade Disputes Act No. 7 of 1976, section 37 defines a dispute as any conflict between the employers and workers or between workers which is connected with the employment or physical conditions of work of any person. It does not seem to recognise or does not concern itself with conflict between and among employers. It identifies two broad types of interests, (a) *disputes of interest* (disputes over interests) and (b) *disputes of rights* (disputes over rights).

In Nigeria, the following factors are important in explaining the nature and types of disputes:

(a) sector of the economy – i.e. whether public or private sector;
(b) the sub-sector of each sector – i.e. for the public sector, whether main civil service or parastatal, while for the private sector whether industrial, service or commercial subsectors;
(c) presence or absence of unions; and
(d) the type of workers involved (white collar, junior worker, essential service, etc.)

The first caveat to be entered is that statistics are unlikely to be accurate for several reasons: not all disputes and strikes are reported despite legal provisions enjoining managements and workers to report them officially; a great many disputes are resolved quietly; most disputes are short-lived and thus not even documented; in non-unionised establishments conflict situations are hardly overt.

Explanations of disputes and strikes

By 1982 when President Shagari embarked on his Economic Stabilisation Programme, most sectors of the economy had been buffeted by strikes, sabotage and absenteeism. Given a more democratic political environment and a multi-party situation with all the dissent and mutual criticism and rivalry, it seemed much easier for the government to reach some accommodation with labour and employers over many issues – the notable exception being the vexed question of arrears of salaries which those parastatals and state governments affected claimed they could do nothing about because of huge deficits they had already accumulated. The pattern of strikes in the public sector, which had been established since the 1940s, was re-enacted faithfully: a spate of strikes before the establishment of, and during the sitting of wage tribunal, and more strikes after the publication of its findings and awards. The private sector was inevitably affected by the spill-over or demonstration effect of industrial protests in the public sector, especially over such issues as national monthly minimum wage, rent and transport allowances which applied nationally to all workers.

The period 1990–2000 was not substantially different in respect of the public sector in particular. It was a period characterised by crisis in public sector compensation, partly as a result of the indifference of military dictators and partly as policy fall-out of SAP which required a cut back on public expenditure, holding down of wages and reducing the size of the work force.

Industrial actions by employees engaged in the provision of essential services to the community are declared illegal by the Trade Disputes (Essential Services) Act, nor does it permit workers therein to belong to trade unions. These notwithstanding, most essential services have been plagued by disputes and strikes. Part of the problem here, since mid-1970s, is that successive Nigerian governments, civil or military, have tended to politicise what may be regarded 'essential services'.

Unfortunately, the dearth of data and statistics makes the presentation of the full range of dispute-inducing issues in essential services difficult, but many managements of parastatals were autocratic and some others downright incompetent and corrupt. As such, internal developments, obviously also constrained by budget shortfalls and erratic statutory allocations of funds from the presidency, also account for an increasing number of disputes and strikes.

Those parastatals in the gas and oil sector, such as the NNPC and many of its subsidiaries and joint projects, seemed also afflicted by prevailing rates of pay and other terms of employment among workers in the private sector of the industry. It was difficult to explain away the yawning pay gap between workers with the same skills, and performing similar jobs in the same industry but in different sectors of the economy. Even the Central Bank confirms that 'the phenomenal surge in industrial strikes during the year was largely due to the protracted disputes between most state governments and civil servants over the implementation of the new minimum wage in the public sector'.[7]

The other class of disputes are intra-union and inter-union in nature, the intra-union disputes caused by factional in-fighting while the latter arise from jurisdictional problems associated with untidy trade union structure. Though occurring infrequently, reliable statistics do not exist as, in any case, most go unreported save where members get drawn in and themselves embark upon sympathy strikes in favour one or other set of union leaders. The two most prominent cases have been those factions among dockworkers and maritime workers were antagonistic and rival union executives coexisted for years. The intricacies of these situations are better understood in the context of the trade union structure and management anti-union and divide and rule strategy.

Institutionalised disputes settlement mechanisms

The mechanisms for the resolution of labour disputes in Nigeria come under two categories: *internal*, and *external*.

Internal disputes settlement mechanism

The *internal* grievance and dispute procedure has a dual nature, internal to the organisation or company and externally imposed by law. It is logical to expect parties in industry to fashion out a voluntary disputes procedure, and a good many have done so and where collective agreements exist they usual contain one such procedure. In Nigeria, however, the Trade Disputes Act 1976 (as amended in 1977 and subsequent amendments since then) makes it compulsory for managements and unions to stipulate in their collective agreements the various stages involved in processing grievances and settling disputes.

The internal disputes procedure is thus expected to be voluntarily pre-agreed and self-imposed undertaking by the parties to resolve grievances through specified machinery without resort to industrial action in the first instance. It is when the parties have exhausted the internal machinery to no avail that the external machinery is resorted to.

External dispute settlement mechanism: the Trades Disputes Act 1976

An external dispute procedure is often provided by a body external to both parties in industry, quite often in most countries is the government or state agency. The statutory procedure comprises the following: mediation; conciliation; board of inquiry, arbitration; and the Industrial Court. The Trade Disputes Decree (1976) as amended by the Trade Disputes (Amendment) Act of 1977 provided for the use of external machinery in the settlement of grievances and disputes; parties can make use of external mediation, and, should the dispute still not be settled within a demarcated period of time, the matter is referred to the Ministry, who after due process, may appoint a conciliator, refer a dispute to the Industrial Arbitration Panel (IAP), refer certain types of disputes directly to the National Industrial Court (NIC) and to appoint a board of inquiry.

The NIC is conferred with jurisdiction 'to the exclusion of any other court' to (a) make awards for the purpose of settling trade disputes and (b) determine questions as to the interpretation of (i) any collective agreement (ii) any award by the court or an arbitration tribunal and (iii) the terms of settlement of any trade dispute as recorded in the memorandum of settlement signed by the parties.

The main purpose of all the foregoing is a mere presentation of the formal and institutional mechanisms for the resolution of disputes and regulation of conflict in Nigeria. There is no suggestion here that these mechanisms work perfectly or that they were and are absolute neutral third party forms of intervention. If they were, some of the disputes might not have occurred and when they did, might have been resolved to the satisfaction of all parties. Under all the military regimes, therefore, the resolution of major disputes was also a political process that involved all the intelligence organisations and police.

For the more widespread work stoppages and protests, the failure of both clandestine and open operations of the police and intelligence agencies have often culminated in the orchestrated involvement or 'intervention' of traditional elders, or traditional rulers, or parents' associations of various types (i.e. in the case of the primary, secondary and tertiary educational subsectors) or some amorphous 'leaders of thought'. This indicates that the tripod model of industrial relations requires modification to bring it in tune with reality.

Concluding remarks: the state, globalisation and industrial relations

The militarisation of civil society and politics has tended to increase unilateralism, to the detriment of tripartism or social dialogue, in policy-making. This, in turn, has served to increase tensions, conflict situations, and adversarial relations at work places. There is notable increase in anti-unionism and deliberate de-unionisation of the work force. Should workers on their own decide not to formally organise themselves into trade unions or associations, that should be their prerogative. Fundamental human rights are often not respected, along with the relevant ILO Conventions on freedom of association, right to collective bargain, etc. which successive Nigerian governments have ratified.

The impacts of globalisation on the economy and politics are multi-faceted, ranging from the impoverishment of a majority of wage-earners, continuing loss of members by way of down-sizing (restructuring, retirements, dismissals, etc.), abandonment of indigenisation schemes, and difficulties facing many companies (especially in the manufacturing sector faced by rising costs and competition from smuggled substitute products and administrative bottlenecks), declining capacity among union leadership due to wastages, attrition, and prevalence of younger and relatively inexperienced hands, the rapid growth in the number of rival non-governmental organisations (NGOs) many of which concentrate on some traditional concerns of the labour movement (civil liberties, human rights, child abuse, gender discrimination, occupational hazards, inequity and corruption, etc.) to deliberate anti-unionism tactics of both private and public employers, especially sub-contracting of operations and labour.

However, whereas the freedom to organise remains important for trade unionism, neo-liberalism as manifested in globalisation of capital may portend graver consequences for those conditions that account for trade unionism itself, especially (a) there must be wage employment, and (b) workers must depend solely on their wages/salaries for survival. The increasing cases of 'rationalisations', 'down-sizing', mergers/take-overs, bankruptcies, technological changes, privatisation, commercialisation, removal of subsidies, and drastic cut-backs in 'public expenditure' have not only led to massive loss of jobs that can be 'organised', surviving on wages/salaries has become very difficult – in spite of those attractive remuneration packages for a class of employees in certain industries. Many workers in Nigeria have become part-time workers in orientation, pre-occupied with how to supplement the pay-packet (de-proletarianisation, de-industrialisation and pauperisation). Although there has been a corresponding growth in the development of certain skills and jobs accompanying rapid changes in technology, they are yet to be organised by unions. There thus has been a notable accretion of power to the state in the Nigerian industrial relations system, the ensuing unilateralism many a private employer have taken advantage of by reneging on agreements and imposing all manner of work practices.

Notes

1. The smallest state has some 3 million people and the largest 15 million.
2. Aside from having powers to call for the accounts of the union at any time, the Registrar may also institute civil or criminal proceedings against the union if not satisfied with the audited accounts!
3. Details are set out in the Second Schedule, especially Sections 7, 8 and 41.
4. See above.
5. In the oil and gas sector, for example, where workers have refused to go near a furnace or enter a room because managements have not provided stipulated safety overalls and boots, gloves and goggles, disciplinary action had been taken on grounds of 'insubordination'.
6. Cap 433, Laws of the Federation of Nigeria, 1990.
7. CBN Annual Report and Statement of Account year ended 31 December 1999, p. 38.

Bibliography

Adesina, J. (1994), *Labour in the Explanation of an African Crisis*. Dakar: Codesria.
Ananaba, W. (1969), *The Trade Union Movement in Nigeria*. Benin City: Ethiope.
Aremu, I. (2001), *The Crises of Pricing Petroleum Products in Nigeria*. Lagos: Malthouse.
Arrighi, G. and Saul, J.S. (1973), *Essays on the Political Economy of Africa*. New York: Monthly Review Press.
Bates, R. (1981), *Markets and States in Tropical Africa: The Political Basis of Agricultural Politics*. Berkeley: University of California Press.
Berg, E.G. (1969), 'Urban Real Wages and the Nigerian Trade Union Movement, 1939-1960: a Comment', *EDCC*, 17, 4.
CBN (1999), *Annual Report and Statement of Account*, year ended 31 December 1999. Lagos: Central Bank of Nigeria.
Central Bank of Nigeria (1999), *Nigeria Development Prospects: Poverty Assessment and Alleviation Study*. Lagos.
Clegg, H.A. (1969), *A New Approach to Industrial Democracy*. Oxford: Blackwell.
Coleman, J.S. (1964), *Nigeria: Background to Nationalism*. Berkeley: University of California Press.
Crowder, M. (1966), *The Story of Nigeria*. London: Faber.
Department of Labour (1955), *Annual Report of the Department of Labour, 1954–55*. Lagos.
Department of Labour (1971), *Annual Report of the Department of Labour, 1969–71*. Lagos.
Ezeife, T. (1987), 'National Incomes Policy and Bargaining in the Public Sector', in Fashoyin, T. (ed.), *Collective Bargaining in the Public Sector in Nigeria*. Lagos: Macmillan.
Ezera, K. (1960), *Constitutional Developments in Nigeria*. Cambridge: Cambridge University Press.
Fashoyin, T. (ed.) (1987), *Collective Bargaining in the Public Sector in Nigeria*. Lagos: Macmillan.
Freund, B. (1981), *Capital and Labour in the Nigerian Tin Mines*. London: Longman, London1.
Galenson, W. (1959), *Labour and Economic Development*. New York: Wiley.
Kilby, P. (1968), 'Industrial Relations and Wage Determination: Failure of the Anglo-Saxon0 Model', *Journal of Developing Areas*, 3, 1.
Kilby, P. (1969), *Industrialization in an Open Economy, Nigeria 1946–1966*. Cambridge: Cambridge University Press.
Lee, J.M. (1967), *Colonial Development and Good Government*. Oxford: Oxford University Press.
Mars, J. (1948), 'Extra-Territorial Enterprises', in Perham, M. (ed.), *Mining, Commerce and Finance in Nigeria*. London: Faber & Faber.
Otobo, D. (ed.) (1992), *Further Readings in Nigerian Industrial Relations*. Lagos: Malthouse.
Otobo, D. (ed.) (1993), *Labour relations in Nigeria Vol I*. Lagos: Malthouse.
Otobo, D. (1982), 'The Nigerian General Strike of 1981', *Review of African Political Economy*, 24.
Otobo, D. (1986), *Foreign Interests and Nigerian Trade Unions*. Ibadan: Heinemann.
Otobo, D. (1988), *State and Industrial Relations in Nigeria*. Lagos: Malthouse.
Otobo, D. and Omole, M. (eds) (1987), *Readings in Industrial Relations in Nigeria*. Lagos: Malthouse.
Roberts, B.C. (1964), *Labour in the Tropical Territories of the Commonwealth*. London.

Roper, J. (1958), *Labour Problems in West Africa*. Harmondsworth: Penguin.
Sokunbi, O. (1975), 'The Role of the State in Industrial Relations', 11the Advanced Course on Industrial Relations, NECA, 1975 May Day address by the Federal Commissioner for Labour.
Sklar, R. (1963), *Nigerian Political Parties*. Princeton: Princeton University Press.
Suffrin, S.C. (1964), *Unions in Emerging Societies*. Syracus, NY: Syracuse University Press.
Warren, B. (1966), 'Urban Real Wages and the Nigerian Trade Union Movement, 1939–1960', *Economic Development and Cultural Change*, 15, 1.
Weeks, J. (1968), 'A Comment on the P. Kilby Industrial Relations and Wage Determination', *Journal of Developing Areas*, 3, 1.
World Bank (1981), *Accelerated Development in Sub-Saharan Africa*. Washington.
Yesufu, T.M. (1962), *An Introduction to Industrial Relations in Nigeria*. Lagos: OUP/NISER.

15
Industrial Relations in Ghana
Garth Frazer

Introduction

Unions have a long history in Ghana. In fact, unions played an important role in the birth of Ghana as a nation, and were influential in Ghana's first independent government. A significant part of that strength is related to the historic strength of the Trades Union Congress, which was the monopoly umbrella organisation for trade unions from shortly after independence until 1993. As a result, unions in Ghana have a stronger voice in Ghanaian political life than their sister unions do in some other African nations. While that influence has certainly fluctuated over time, and Ghanaian unions today are no longer an active participant in the Ghanaian government as they were at independence, the unions remain significant institutions throughout the formal sector in Ghana, in both the public and private sectors.

The purpose of this chapter is to describe union activities, as well as the changing nature of industrial relations in Ghana. The relative importance of unions in Ghana is best understood within a historical context, and that, therefore, is where the survey begins. Then, the current and former mechanics of industrial relations in the Ghanaian legal context is described; and we explore the structure and membership of Ghanaian unions, and how this has changed over time. Finally, the chapter explores the recent context of Ghana, including the changes to Ghanaian labour legislation, their origins and significance, and concludes by exploring some current trends in industrial relations.

A brief history of industrial relations in Ghana

The history of the collective action of workers, as well as government intervention to facilitate such collective action, goes back many decades in Ghana. Historically, the largest set of formal sector workers in Ghana have been in the public sector and in the mines, and so it was in these sectors that the initial actions took place. At least as early as 1919, Public Works Department (PWD) employees, as well as mine workers, were collectively protesting the delay in payment of their wages (Roper, 1958: 52), whilst Accra artisans came out on strike in April, 1921. Later that year, in December 1921, PWD workers went on strike, as did railway employees, both protesting against reductions in their wages that were demanded by the administration. During this part of the colonial period, unions were actively discouraged by European managers and administrators, as well as at times by native administrations (Roper, 1958: 54).

However, things changed, both in terms of the workers actions and in terms of the colonial administration's labour policy, with the onset of world depression from 1930 to 1933. During this period, falling wages and unemployment mobilised many groups of workers into efforts to form trade unions, and planted the seeds for later trade union formation. Still, these seeds did not come to immediate fruition after 1933, as civil service salaries were raised in 1934, and most wage-earners outside the mining industry continued to be public employees.

This increase in wages was part of a larger shift in the colonial administration's labour policy, not just in the Ghana, but also in other African colonies as well. The British government now began encouraging the formation of trade unions in colonial territories (Roper, 1958: 57). This led to the creation of Labour Departments, and the appointment of Labour Officers in the West African colonies over the period 1938 to 1942 and, specifically in the Ghanaian case, to the passing of the Trade Union Ordinance in 1941 (as well as the Compensation Ordinance in 1940, the Arbitration Ordinance in 1941, and the Labour Code (consolidating statutes) in 1948). At the end of the war, the protections offered in this new legal framework, combined with rising prices (and falling real wages) were elements in a period of labour unrest. Twenty-seven unions were registered in Ghana within two years of the end of the war. The Trades Union Congress, a federation of trade unions, was formed in 1945.

These newly-formed unions were very active from the outset, spurred on by the cost-of-living increases that they were facing (Kraus, 1988: 181). Over the period from 1946 through 1950, there were frequent strikes in Ghana. For example, in 1949–50, there were 54 strikes in Ghana, involving nearly 40,000 workers. In addition, arbitration for the settlement of disputes stems from this period. The Mines' Employees Union came into existence in 1944, and was registered in September, 1945. The union engaged in a six-day strike at the Konongo mine in 1945, involving 750 underground workers. They pushed their case with the Chamber of Mines, and Mr. Justice Gorman was appointed as arbitrator to settle their dispute, in what was the first industrial arbitration case in Ghana (Roper, 1958: 64–5).

The aforementioned cost-of-living increases, as well as the growing movement for self-government over the period led to political unrest, concomitant with the industrial unrest, as the formation of new political parties accompanied the formation of unions. The UGCC (United Gold Coast Convention) was founded in 1947, followed by the more militant CPP (Convention People's Party) led by Kwame Nkrumah in 1949, with the struggle for self-government the dominating issue. A climax to this activism occurred in the general strike of 1950, which was a strongly-supported, country-wide strike that lasted two weeks, but was unsuccessful, and was followed by massive dismissals, which damaged union organisation and membership growth for some years (Kraus, 1988: 181). The nature of the relationship between CPP and organised labour, particularly the TUC, was a central issue for the TUC throughout the 1950s, but by the end of the 1950s the TUC and the CPP were clear allies.

In 1958, shortly after independence, with the CPP still at the helm of the government, John Tettegah, the TUC's Secretary-General pushed the CPP to enact the Industrial Relations Act, 1958, which, with a couple of interregnums, and a couple of major amendments, formed the foundation of industrial relations law until the Labour Act of 2003 (Act 651).

Several major changes were ushered in by the Industrial Relations Act (Jeffries, 1978: 67–8; Kraus, 1988: 185). First, the law initially reduced the number of unions from roughly 85–95 relatively small unions to 24 unions in 1959. The number of unions fluctuated in subsequent years, but the smaller number of larger unions generally produced stronger unions. Secondly, the Act established a check-off system for union dues. This, along with the union shop provision introduced in 1960, greatly increased union membership and, concomitantly, union financial resources, which enabled unions to hire independent staff. These union staff members could independently engage in the organisation of branches, collective bargaining, and attending to worker grievances. Previously, such work frequently relied on the volunteer labour of employees who remained subject to employer discipline. Thirdly, the law required that employers bargain collectively with unions, which many of them had previously refused to do. This advance in collective bargaining eventually resulted in the private sector becoming the wage leaders instead of government, which had been the case previously. Fourthly, strikes became virtually illegal, with a compulsory conciliation and arbitration system established. While the ban on strikes certainly had the goal of limiting union behaviour, the compulsory arbitration system was actually generally regarded positively by unions, given their previous experience. Fifth, the TUC retained certain powers over the member unions and, at least initially, the government retained strong control over the TUC, giving the CPP government considerable control over union actions. Overall, the Act gave a number of new powers to unions compared to the previous regime. At the same time, the monopoly position of the TUC, coupled with compulsory check-off, and anti-strike pressures, significantly reduced the degree of democratic control of union members over their leaders.

In the subsequent years, the tensions between the TUC and the CPP government eventually grew (Damachi, 1974: 42–56). In general, the union movement was weakened over the subsequent years until 1966, with Nkrumah's overthrow in a military coup led by the National Liberation Council. At this point, 'the union movement was revitalised, union elections held regularly, leadership accountability forced on the leaders by the rank and file strikes and protest, and important degrees of autonomy regained' (Kraus, 1988: 186–7). The National Liberation Council period was accompanied by increased labour unrest. This was partly a result of the increased level of freedom and independence granted to the TUC by the National Liberation Council, and partly a result of problems related to working conditions (Damachi, 1974: 79–84). With the return of democracy and the election of the Busia Progress Party (PP) in 1969, an increased level of tension developed between the government and labour. Over this period, the government was generally unsupportive of workers' goals and tactics and in particular of the TUC. The PP ushered in a number of anti-union changes to the Industrial Relations Act, including the abolition of the TUC as a legally-mandated institution, allowance of the free formation of unions, the ending of check-off dues, and the freezing of union funds. At the same time, strikes remained illegal, and strong anti-strike powers were given to the Minister of Labour.

As a result, workers were generally supportive of the military coup in January 1972 that brought Colonel Acheampong and the Supreme Military Council to power. While the government initially mounted strong pressure on the unions to stop strikes, which did drop sharply over the period 1972–73, it also implemented a number of pro-union legislative changes (Kraus, 1988: 189–91). It forced firms to deal more quickly with worker/union grievances. It restored the TUC's formal legal status, as well as the check-off provision. It also forbade dismissals of over five employees without permission of the Department of Labour, which was difficult to obtain. These changes brought a degree of union allegiance that meant that unions were slow to join the growing protests about the SMC's poor management of the economy over the subsequent years. The period of military rule that followed (August 1978–September 1979) and then the brief democracy of the Limann/People's National Party (PNP) governments were turbulent times both politically and in industrial relations.

The *coup d'état* by Jerry Rawlings and the Provisional National Defence Council (PNDC) in 1981 dramatically changed the political order in Ghana. Starting in June 1983, the PNDC began an Economic Recovery Program (ERP), backed by the IMF and the World Bank, and which later became a Structural Adjustment Programme (SAP). The programmes involved considerable liberalisation of the economy, as well as privatisations, and marked reductions in government expenditures in a variety of areas. As a result, public sector employment fell considerably, as did spending on education. However, the primary changes for labour unions came through the PNDC's efforts to secure support for its regime, and remove dissent. Part of the strategy of the PNDC involved organising the population into People's Defence Committees (PDCs) and Workers' Defence Committees, whose stated goals included attacking mismanagement and corruption. Dissident trade unionists were organised into an Association of Local Unions (ALU), which demanded the dismissal of all trade union leaders. There was a struggle between the ALU and the incumbent national and district unions for control of the union machinery. The end result was the formation of Interim Management Committees (IMCs) which were directed by the PNDC to undertake reorganisation of the unions, ostensibly to make them more responsive to the rank and file (Panford, 2001: 14).

While struggling with dissident trade unionists, at the same time the unions also found the Workers' Defence Committees to be a rival voice in workplaces, a voice that challenged both the unions and management in turn. As Krauss (1988: 195) notes, 'the union organisations encountered severe competition in their renewal from Workers' Defence Committees (WDCs), founded in many factories, offices, and business and state institutions. The WDCs carried out aggressive investigations into the existing and prior management. It soon became common for WDCs to eject senior managers, to seek their arrest or investigation, with WDCs attempting to take over the management of the organisation'. Before long, the PNDC worked to try to contain the WDCs given that their activism paralysed many institutions, and the independence of the WDCs and PDCs began to include criticism of the government. Therefore, in late 1984, the government renamed the PDCs and WDCs as Committees for the Defence of the Revolution (CDRs), and brought them directly under government control.

During the remainder of the PNDC era, the union leadership reasserted control of the unions in collective wage bargaining, and actively criticised PNDC policies, but there were very few strikes. The political strength of the TUC, coupled with its allies among churches, students, and teachers forced the PNDC to allow union autonomy and not to interfere in union elections, as previous governments had done. Still, the relationship between unions and the government became less favourable, reaching a nadir shortly before the return to democratic rule in 1992. Despite the generally tense relationship between the PNDC and unions, the PNDC made a remarkable legislative change shortly before the advent of Ghana's new Constitution in 1992. Since Ghana's independence, public sector workers had been denied the legal right to bargain collectively as unions. They were allowed to form associations that could engage in consultations with the government over conditions of service, but they were not deemed technically or legally to be trade unions. The PNDC changed that with the Public Service (Negotiating Committees) Law 1992, PNDCL 309. This law extended collective bargaining to most of the civil servants' associations in Ghana. This law was indicative of the further labour openness heralded in the Ghanaian Constitution of 1992.

The mechanics of industrial relations in Ghana

The collective bargaining machinery in Ghana prior to 2003

The predominant piece of legislation covering industrial relations in Ghana over the period from 1965 until 2003 was the Industrial Relations Act of 1965 (an amended version of the Industrial Relations Act of 1958). This Act was repealed and replaced with new legislation in September 1971, but this new legislation only lasted until January 1972, after which the 1965 Act was reinstated by the new military government (Anyemedu, 2000). Amendments have been made to the Act over the longer period, but perhaps the most significant changes have been with regard to its implementation, and in particular to the relationship between the Ghanaian government and the Trades Union Congress, as well as the degree of responsiveness of the TUC to its member unions, and the member unions to the rank and file, as outlined in the previous section.

The Act gave monopoly union status to the Trades Union Congress. That is, in order for a union to receive a collective bargaining certificate that enables them legally to engage in negotiations with the employer of an organisation or firm, it needed to gain official status, which could only be achieved through affiliation with the TUC. When, particularly during the latter part of the CPP (Nkrumah) period in Ghana, the government exerted significant control over the TUC, dismissing Secretaries General that fell out of favour, the government was able to exert control more broadly over unions in Ghana. More generally, the monopoly status of the TUC has been criticised as contravening ILO Convention No. 87, as well as the Constitution of 1992, which allows freedom of association.

With the formation of the Fourth Republic of Ghana under the Constitution of 1992, a number of legislative changes in industrial relations were ushered in. The constitution guaranteed workers' rights to associate freely both nationally and internationally, as well as the right to demonstrate against public policies. Although this constitutional provision did not get fully incorporated into Ghanaian legislation until 2003, in practice the monopoly status of the TUC was broken in 1993 under the legal protection of the Constitution when the Textile, Garment and Leather Employees Union (TGLEU) broke away from the Industrial and Commercial Workers' Union (ICU) to become the first union in Ghana that was independent of the TUC. Then, in 1998, a second national labour federation, the Ghana Federation of Labour (GFL) was formed, so that now unions could also choose to affiliate with either the TUC or the GFL.

Some aspects of the structure of collective bargaining have not changed with the Labour Act 2003, but are the same as under the Industrial Relations Act. That is, once workers at a given organisation become organised into a union, typically with the assistance of the relevant national union, the union can apply to the Labour Department[1] for a collective bargaining certificate in order to bargain with the employer of the organisation. The Chief Labour Office of the Labour Department then certifies the right of the union to bargain at a given organisation, specifying the class of workers at the organisation to which the certificate applies.

Once the Certificate is issued, the union and the employer are expected to negotiate a collective agreement, which could include any matters related to: (i) employment or non-employment, (ii) the terms of employment, (iii) the conditions of labour, of any of the employees of the employer that are subject to the bargaining certificate (Section 6 of the 1965 Industrial Relations Act and Section 98 of Act 651). Specifically, the collective agreements typically cover conditions of employment, discipline, conditions of work, wages, working hours, end-of-service benefits, as well as other benefits from the agreement. Since unions are organised along industrial lines, within some industries the employers come together to negotiate as a unit with the union to obtain a group collective agreement that applies across enterprises within the industry.

Since any negotiation is invariably influenced by the outside options of those involved in the negotiations, it is of course worth noting the actions and outcomes that were available to workers and management in the absence of collective agreement, as well as the tools available to enforce the provisions of the collective agreement under this regime (prior to Act 651). For example, after whatever means were specified within the collective agreement, or otherwise, for obtaining resolution of a dispute at the enterprise level were exhausted, either party could appeal to the Ministry of Labour for assistance. The Minister would initially appoint a conciliator to assist in resolving the dispute. If this action also failed, a more senior conciliator may be appointed, with the case thereafter going to arbitration, with the arbitrator appointed by the Minister. The arbitrator would have considerable power to gain access to information about the organisation, including account books and other information, and the decision of the arbitrator, once approved by the Minister, was final.

Therefore, while collective bargaining, check-off, and union shop provisions have been in place in Ghana for roughly forty-five years, the legal requirements that unions must satisfy before obtaining the legal right to strike are sufficiently onerous that Ghana has never seen a legal strike. Strikes have certainly been used nonetheless, with their frequency varying over Ghana's history according to the autonomous strength of the unions, as described in the previous section.

The Labour Act 2003 (Act 651) and collective bargaining

As already mentioned, the Industrial Relations Act of 1965 contravened the freedom of association that was guaranteed in Ghana's constitution in 1992. While making Ghana's industrial relations law consistent with its constitution was one factor driving the new labour legislation, another factor was the desire on the part of government to satisfy business demands for greater clarity and simplicity in Ghana's labour legislation, as well as business demands to make the labour legislation more amenable to business interests. This led to the Labour Act 2003 (Act 651), which was brought into effect in 2004. Some facets of the Act continue to be in the process of implementation in 2006.

In employment matters, the association that represents employer interests is the Ghana Employers' Association (GEA). This group advocates employer interests to government, and also advises employers in matters related to employment and labour law. For example, they held a number of seminars to familiarise employers with Act 651. The GEA has 350 members in a variety of sectors, including agriculture, fishing, banking, construction, services, education, health, hotels, information technology, insurance, manufacturing, mining, pharmaceuticals, petroleum, publishing, shipping, timber and utilities. It also represents employers at the ILO.

An overriding theme under the new act is the allowance freedom of association. As a result, the Trades Union Congress (TUC) is no longer the monopoly union umbrella organisation, and in particular, unions are no longer required to register as trade unions through the TUC. Instead, workers are free to create or join a trade union of their choosing, and, provided it follows general guidelines, have it registered by the Chief Labour Officer. Since workers are under any situation completely free to join the trade union of their choosing, it is entirely possible under the new Act to have more than one trade union at a given workplace. However, despite this fact, only one trade union will be given a collective bargaining certificate to allow bargaining with the employer for any particular class of workers at a workplace. While the Chief Labour Officer is free to choose which union at a workplace is to be given the Collective Bargaining Certificate, it is generally understood that this certificate is to be given to the union with the plurality of members at a workplace. This union will then bargain on behalf of its members, the members of any other unions at the workplace, as well as non-union members at the workplace that are subject to the bargaining certificate. Both the negotiating union and other unions at the workplace can request check-off of membership dues by the employer, but these no longer include agency fees for the non-union members. As a result, there certainly is potential under the new system for unions to suffer from the 'free-rider' problem where non-union members gain access to all of the benefits of union membership without the cost. To this point, union leaders to which I have spoken have not reported the 'free-rider' issue to be a problem, but whether this is inertia, or a permanent fact remains to be seen. The issue of multiple unions at a workplace and conflict over the negotiating union has arisen in at least one instance.

Trade unions are now free to associate with any trade union federation. To this point, five new unions have been created that have associated with the GFL. In addition, the Union of Industry, Commerce and Finance formed as a breakaway union from the Industrial and Commercial Workers Union (ICU) in 2003. Still, the historic unions of the TUC remain in force – membership changes notwithstanding.

A very significant change under the new legislation relates to public employees. Prior to 2003, associations of public employees were not formal unions under the Industrial Relations Act, although since 1992 they had been granted the right to collectively bargain. Under the new Act, and the freedom of association philosophy underpinning the Act, public employees are free to form unions. As a result, the major associations of public employees that had been formed prior to Act 651 have now registered (or are in the process of registering) as trade unions under the Act, including the Ghana National Association of Teachers (GNAT), the Civil Servants Association (CSA), and the Ghana Registered Nurses' Association (GRNA). While undoubtedly the official status as unions given these associations under the Act cannot but strengthen their hands, the change is not as dramatic as the introduction of their collective bargaining right in 1992. Moreover, a more significant change from the perspective of public-sector unions under the Act has to do with the mediation and arbitration of disputes under Act 651.

Despite the significant changes described above, many would argue that the major innovation under Act 651 has been the establishment of the independent National Labour Commission (NLC), which is charged with resolving labour disputes that were previously dealt with by the Minister of Labour. The Commission is designed to be a neutral body, and its membership reflects this. The chairperson of the commission is to be jointly nominated by the employers' organisation (GEA) and organised labour (currently the TUC). The six other members of the commission include two members nominated by Government, two by organised labour, and two by the employers' organisation, with the entire commission officially appointed by the President.

Under the new Act, when a grievance related to the application of a collective agreement (or any other dispute) cannot be handled through the mechanisms available at the organisation level, it is referred to the NLC for resolution. The NLC is empowered to resolve the dispute, and specifically empowered with the powers of the Ghanaian High Court to obtain documentation, compel testimony and enforce orders related to unfair labour practices (Sections 133 and 139 of Act 651). The Commission can (and typically does) appoint a mediator to resolve the dispute at its initial stages. However, if mediation is unsuccessful, the parties can choose jointly to submit the dispute to arbitration by the Commission, in which case the Commission appoints an arbitrator or arbitration panel. If the union and employer can agree on an arbitrator, an arbitration panel, or a method of appointment of arbitrator(s), then the Commission follows their joint wishes, but in the absence of such agreement the Commission will appoint its own arbitrator or arbitration panel (Section 156 or 157). The judgement of the arbitration panel is then final, and can only be appealed to the Appeals Court of Ghana.

Now, either side can refuse to submit to arbitration immediately, but this right merely delays rather than avoids the arbitration process. That is, unions are allowed to engage in strikes, and employers are allowed to engage in lockouts. However, the union or the employer must give seven days notice after the refusal to agree to voluntary arbitration before engaging in either a strike or a lockout (Section 159). More importantly, however, the strike or lockout is only allowed to last for seven days (Section 160 of the Act). At the end of seven days, the dispute is referred for settlement under compulsory arbitration. In this case, an arbitration panel is created, consisting of three members of the Commission: one member each representing Government, organised labour, and the employers' organisation. The arbitration procedure is swift, with the Commission making a judgement within fourteen days. This arbitration judgement is legally binding, can only be appealed to the Appeals Court of Ghana, and legally supersedes any previous aspects of the collective agreement that may conflict with the judgement.

Operationally, therefore, the first 'outside option' for both the employer and the union in the absence of agreement, negotiated or mediated, is the appointment of a mutually agreed upon arbitrator. The final legal 'outside option' for both employer and union is the decision of the arbitration panel set up by the Commission. To some degree, the exact nature of the outcome at this stage is somewhat difficult to determine, as very few cases have got so far. The outcome essentially depends upon the degree to which the members of the Commission act as professionals evaluating the dispute, and the degree to which they act as advocates for their respective parties (one for government, one for labour and one for the employer).[2] While this discussion might seem pedantic, it is important. Ultimately, a large portion of the influence of either side of a negotiation emanates from what that party can achieve in the absence of agreement, and so the careful analysis of the outcomes in the breakdown of negotiations (that is, through the compulsory arbitration process) helps us to understand the expected nature of the agreements achieved. That being said, since the NLC has been formed, a number of disputes have led to strikes, particularly in the public sector, before they went through arbitration.

In addition to the firm-level negotiations regarding wages, and conditions of employment, the three pillars of industrial relations in Ghana (government, unions, and employers) all have representatives on the National Tripartite Committee. This committee's primary functional purpose is to set the minimum wage in Ghana, but it also serves an important purpose as a clearinghouse for discussion of broader labour market and industrial relations issues. For example, other topics currently under discussion at the National Tripartite Committee include discussions of productivity (and how to both measure and improve it), as well as discussions about a 'living wage'.

Unions and unionisation in Ghana

While trade union membership has been declining overall in Ghana, and while union density remains a small fraction of the overall workforce, union density is relatively high within the formal sector. The most recent estimates of union membership for TUC affiliates are given in Table 15.1. These estimates come from a survey conducted by the TUC which covered most formal sector establishments, including all unionised establishments in Ghana in 2001, including 351,486 employees in 4973 workplaces. This survey should assist in constructing orders-of-magnitude estimates for union density. From this survey the total membership in TUC affiliates was at least 250,000. Other major unions in Ghana in 2001 which were not affiliated with the TUC include

Table 15.1 Trade union membership of TUC affiliates in 2001

Name of national union	Membership covered by survey	Membership as % of total
Industrial and Commerical Workers Union (ICU)	42,070	16.79
Teachers and Educational Workers Union (TEWU)	30,246	12.07
Public Services Workers Union (PSWU)	27,084	10.81
Ghana Private Road Transport Union (GPRTU)	26,901	10.74
Timber and Woodworkers Union (TWU)	22,758	9.08
Public Utility Workers Union (PUWU)	17,111	6.83
Health Services Workers Union (HSWU)	16,647	6.65
General Agricultural Workers Union (GAWU)	14,710	5.87
Construction, Building and Material Workers' Union (CBMWU)	11,676	4.66
Railway Workers' Union (RWU)	8,842	3.53
Ghana Mine Workers Union (GMWU)	8,379	3.34
Local Government Workers Union (LGWU)	7,521	3.00
Communication Workers Union (CWU)	7,124	2.84
Maritime and Dockworkers Union (MDU)	5,780	2.31
General Transport, Petroleum & Chemical Workers Union (GTPCWU)	3,247	1.30
National Union of Seamen (NUS)	256	0.10
Railway Engineman's Union (REU)	160	0.06
	250,512	100.00

Source: Membership Survey, Preliminary Report, TUC (Ghana), June 2001.
Note: Since the survey, the ICU disaffiliated with the TUC in 2003.

the Ghana National Association of Teachers, which had a membership of about 170,000 in May 2006, the Ghana Registered Nurses Association (9,000 in 2003), the Civil Servants Association of Ghana (76,000 in 2003), and the National Association of Graduate Teachers, as well as the Textile, Garment and Leather Employees' Union (which is associated with the Ghana Federation of Labour, membership about 16,500 in 2003).[3,4]

While obtaining exact estimates[3] of union density is challenging in the Ghanaian context, we can construct some order-of-magnitude estimates using combinations of union membership records, with employment estimates constructed from the 1999 Ghana Living Standards Survey, a national household survey which asked detailed employment information. The factors making this an approximation include the fact that the union data comes from the period 2001 through 2003, while the employment numbers are from 1999 and 2000. Overall union density among the employed workforce (not including unemployed, or those under the age of 15) in 2001 would have been between 5 and 8 per cent, depending on various assumptions made. On the other hand, union density within the formal sector varies between 45 per cent and 65 per cent depending on various assumptions, with union density higher within the public sector than in the private formal sector, although estimating union densities within these sub-sectors is even more difficult. Nevertheless, it is widely agreed that, since 2001, union density in the private formal sector has been declining, although it is difficult to say by how much. On the other hand, union density in the public sector has been holding its own, with for example, Ghana's largest union, the Ghana National Association of Teachers, growing from 150,000 in 2003 to 170,000 in 2006, even if overall public sector employment has declined since the mid-1980s.

The strength of unions is measured not only in their size, but also in their achievements and activities (Rigby *et al.*, 2004). The primary method of leverage for unions is the right to strike. As noted previously, the degree of strike activity has varied over the history of Ghana. In terms of union achievements, while naturally each union has a wide set of goals related to the interest of its members, one of the primary interests of union members, and certainly one of the easiest ones to measure is the union wage premium. For the Ghanaian context, Teal (1996) measured the union wage premium within the manufacturing sector at approximately 28 per cent. Blunch and Verner (2004) find that the size of this premium varies considerably across the wage distribution, being largest among the bottom 10 per cent of the conditional wage distribution. Unfortunately, we do not know how the union wage premium has been changing over time.

For a variety of reasons, unions are currently targeting the informal sector in Ghana for organising (see Croucher, in this volume). This is partly a recognition on their part that the informal sector forms the bulk of economic activity in Ghana, and that their capacity to influence the welfare of workers is dependent on reaching out to this sector. However, obviously, a major factor in their goal of organising the informal sector is the decreased absolute size of unions in the formal sector. Naturally, since many of those within the informal sector are self-employed, the role of unions within this sector has been different from its usual role in industrial relations. To this point, the primary actions of unions in the informal sector have involved acting as advocates on behalf of informal sector traders in their relationships with local government authorities. Union efforts in this area remain young, and whether the efforts prove fruitful will be determined in the coming years.

Trends in industrial relations in Ghana

While the Labour Act, 2003, was designed to achieve a number of different objectives, the pressure to pass the Act came largely from Ghanaian employers, and their organisation, the Ghana Employers' Association (GEA). While the Act achieved a number of objectives not limited to industrial relations, we shall limit out attention to the industrial relations provisions in the Act.

One major argument in favour of the Act was simply the dated nature of the industrial relations legislation prior to 2004. Since it was largely based on the Industrial Relations Act of 1965, as well as earlier labour-related ordinances, it was roughly 40 years old. More than that, however, the Industrial Relations Act only formed part of the labour legislation with which employers needed to become familiar. Specifically, the enactment of Act 651 involved the repeal of 15 earlier acts, decrees, laws, and ordinances. Prior to 2004, all of these legal instruments needed to be consulted before one would definitively know the Ghanaian labour legislation on a particular issue.

Therefore, a major purpose of the Labour Act, 2003, was simply to codify the legislation to make things clearer for everyone involved. In particular, a prime interest to the Ghanaian government over this period was to make Ghana a more attractive place for foreign investment. Irrespective of the content of Act 651, it achieved this purpose by making clear, in a very readable legal document, exactly what the labour rules are for Ghana. Any potential foreign investor wondering about investing in Ghana can obtain the legislation easily off the internet, and have a strong sense of what the legal expectations are of employers in Ghana on all matters of employment, not just industrial relations.

The Industrial Relations Act of 1965 had centralised much of the conciliation and arbitration process within the Ghanaian Ministry of Labour.[5] However, in a context where the government is a major employer, and therefore a number of the industrial disputes are between a government department and its workers, it is not surprising that there were calls for an independent body to solve industrial disputes. This is, of course, also consistent with the practice of many developed countries that have independent labour relations boards designed to rule in industrial disputes. As mentioned, one of the major initiatives of Act 651 is the creation of the National Labour Commission (NLC), which is designed to be the final, independent, arbiter in industrial disputes. Based on my conversations with unions and employers, there seems to be a strong desire on both sides of the employment relationship in seeing the NLC succeed. Naturally, a major goal of the NLC is to improve the speed and efficiency with which industrial disputes are handled, as outlined by the tight timeframes that are given the NLC in the Act for arbitrating disputes. While at times, either unions or employers can benefit from slow resolution to industrial disputes, increased efficiency in resolution of disputes naturally reduces uncertainty about the outcome, and as a result, both unions and employers support the goal of increased efficiency under the NLC.

Globalisation has increased competition in all tradeable industries. As a response, firms have responded to these competitive pressures by seeking ways to cut their costs, and at times lobbied governments to give them the regulatory flexibility to be able to do so. Since a substantial element of these costs include employment costs, the competitive pressures of globalisation have had considerable negative impact for unions. In the Ghanaian context, outsourcing has been one such outcome, at least partly related to the competitive pressures of globalisation; sub-contractors are rather less likely to make use of unionised labour, and are also more likely to be informal sector firms.

Other recent trends that unions cite as affecting employment levels in unionised workplaces include privatisations and new technologies. In a process that was begun by the PNDC government in the late 1980s as part of its Structural Adjustment Program, the government has privatised many state-owned enterprises. These privatised enterprises have frequently reduced employment, reducing the total number of unionised workers. In addition, new technologies have also made workers redundant.[6]

Conclusions

Trade unions have historically held a central role in Ghanaian political life. Much of that history has revolved around the Trades Union Congress (TUC). The TUC was extremely influential in the founding government of the Ghanaian republic. This influence translated into labour legislation that gave unions the right to bargain collectively, and finance their activities through check-off and union shop provisions. While the relative strength of the TUC varied over Ghana's first thirty-five years, its monopoly status as the union federation through which all unions were required to register ensured it kept a prominent place in Ghanaian affairs. This prominence would frequently benefit workers who were not TUC members, or even union members, as the TUC had the strength and the capacity to take broader policy positions that advocated on behalf of workers more generally.

Still, things have changed considerably since 1992 in the industrial relations landscape in Ghana. Several of these changes have been institutional. The first institutional change involved the legal recognition of the right of public sector associations (including teacher unions, for example) to collectively bargain, in 1992. This raised the prominence of public sector unions within the Ghanaian landscape. The second involved union plurality and freedom of association, which was guaranteed in the 1992 Constitution, and operationalised with the formation of the Textile, Garment and Leather Employees Union (TGLEU) in 1993, and later with the establishment of the Ghana Federation of Labour, as a rival to the TUC in 1998. This union plurality was not codified into Ghanaian law until Act 651 in 2003. The third major institutional change involved the creation under Act 651 of the National Labour Commission (NLC), an independent, professional labour relations board charged with the settlement of industrial relations disputes. Whether the NLC will have the resources, the capacity (given the demand for its services), and the impartiality to perform its tasks effectively remain to be seen.

At the same time as these institutional changes have been happening, other processes have also been at work affecting the industrial relations landscape. Globalisation has increased the competitive pressures on private sector employers. This has increased the pressures on unions and workers, both directly, as well as indirectly, through reduced union membership as a result of outsourcing and privatisation.

Despite these facts, unions remain a significant power in Ghanaian political life. The constitutional right of workers to form unions, coupled with the historic strength of unions, has ensured that even though unionisation levels have dropped significantly over the past fifteen years, primarily through reductions in employment at unionised workplaces, union density remains significant within the formal sector, and is still non-zero within the economy as a whole.

In short, the Ghanaian industrial relations system is shifting. For its first thirty-five years, industrial relations in Ghana was centred around the TUC. Currently, the system is shifting to a new systemic equilibrium, one that is pluralistic, and is certainly intended to be more professional in the handling of disputes. Since the shift is very much ongoing, and therefore the final equilibrium outcome far from certain, Ghana will be of considerable interest to students of African industrial relations in the coming years.

Notes

1. The Labour Department is part of the ministry within the government responsible for labour. This ministry has taken on various names over the course of Ghana's history. Currently, the title is the Minister of Manpower, Youth, and Employment.
2. At the time of writing this article, the single case that had gone to compulsory arbitration was adjudicated through the unanimous decision of the three-member panel. If one can conclude anything from a single data point, the first case might be suggestive of the independence of the panel.
3. The data for the Ghana Federation of Labour, the Civil Servants Association and the Ghana Registered Nurses Association were taken from Gockel and Vormawor, 2004.
4. Technically, the civil servant associations were still not formal unions, in that they were not associated under the law with the Trades Union Congress in 2001. However, as already noted, they had been granted legal collective bargaining status by the PNDC in 2002, and so we are treating them as unions for the purposes here of calculating union density.
5. As mentioned, this Ministry has changed title several times over Ghana's history.
6. For example, the Bank of Ghana had thousands of cash counters in its employ before they were made redundant, and replaced with automatic cash counters.

References

Anyemedu, K. (2000), 'Trade Union Responses to Globalization: Case Study on Ghana', Discussion Paper 121, ILO Labour and Society Programme.

Blunch, N.-H. and Verner, D. (2004), 'Asymmetries in the Union Wage Premium in Ghana', *World Bank Economic Review*, 18, 2: 237–52.

Damachi, U.G. (1974), *The Role of Trade Unions in the Development Process: With a Case Study of Ghana*. New York: Praeger.

Ghana Statistical Service (2000), 'Ghana Living Standards Survey – Report of the Fourth Round'. Mimeo.

Gockel, A.F. and Vormawor, D. (2004), 'FES Trade Union Country Reports: The Case of Ghana', a Background Paper prepared for Friedrich Ebert Stiftung.

Jeffries, R. (1978), *Class, Power, and Ideology in Ghana: The Railwaymen of Sekondi*. Cambridge: Cambridge University Press.

Kraus, J. (1988), 'The Political Economy of Trade Union-State Relations in Radical and Populist Regimes in Africa', in Southall, R. (ed.), *Labour and Unions in Asia and Africa*. London: Macmillan Press.

Kusi, Nana, T.A. and Gyimah-Boakye, A.K. (1994). 'Collective Bargaining in Ghana: Problems and Perspectives'. In Political Transformation, Structural Adjustment and Industrial Relations in Africa: English-Speaking Countries. Geneva: International Labour Office.

Panford, K. (2001), *IMF–World Bank and Labor's Burdens in Africa: Ghana's Experience*. Westport, Conn: Praeger Publishers.

Rigby, M., Smith, R. and Brewster, C. (2004), 'The Changing Impact and Strength of the Labour Movement in Europe', in Harcourt, M. and Wood, G. (eds), *Trade Unions and Democracy: Strategies and Perspectives*. Manchester, Manchester University Press.

Roper, J.I. (1958), *Labour Problems in West Africa*. Harmondsworth, Middlesex, England: Penguin Books.

Teal, F. (1996), 'The Size and Sources of Economic Rents in a Developing Country Manufacturing Labour Market', *The Economic Journal*, 106, 437: 963–76.

16
Industrial Relations in Francophone Africa – the Case of Niger
Richard Croucher

Introduction

This chapter examines industrial relations in the ex-French colony Niger, one of the world's poorest states. An enormous land-locked country in the interior of West Africa, the great majority of its population of around ten million is engaged in subsistence agriculture. The economy is trifurcated: the state sector coexists with islands of modern production in a sea of 'informal', precarious economic activity. Many of the skilled and able-bodied have historically emigrated to the coastal states; the process has accelerated over the past few years, with significant consequences for its trade union movement (given the importance of skilled workers to trade unionism) and civil society. A succession of natural disasters, and particularly the 2004–2005 famine and locust invasion, has led many to despair of Niger's situation.

How far may one speak here of 'industrial relations' in the conventional sense, whereby workers' organisations deal with employers with a certain power balance between the parties? In the trifurcated economy's first branch, the state bargains with relatively stable unions in the public services, utility and transport sectors. In the second, bargaining occurs with individual employers, notably with a few multi-national enterprises, as provided for in the Labour Code. A third branch involves far more people: 'informal' work, where workers are too weak to bargain collectively although unions have attempted to organise. These workers regard those in the other sectors as highly privileged. In this branch, as Wood and Frynas (2006) argue, management is essentially patriarchal and little scope exists for institutional industrial relations. The limited collective bargaining possibilities are one reason for Niger's unions being arguably most effective as political agents, when they have overcome perceptions of themselves as defenders of a privileged 'labour aristocracy' to take on the mantle of defenders of the national interest and of working people beyond their limited membership.

Niger is a significant case because it shows both a state and a trade union movement labouring under enormous objective difficulties. Both confront acute versions of wider problems brought by 'globalisation', and the state has increasingly sought to divide and repress trade unionism as an obstruction to Structural Adjustment Programmes and foreign investment. Yet despite these massive difficulties, the unions continue to make serious efforts to defend the interests both of their own members and of working people more generally. If trade unionism can sustain or renew itself in Niger, that will indeed be a significant achievement auguring well for trade unionism internationally.

The chapter begins by outlining the history of Niger's unions in the context of their most important relationship, i.e. that with the state. It then discusses the evolution of the Nigerien economy, focussing on the recent devastating effects of Structural Adjustment Programmes. It concludes by looking at the ways that unions have attempted, with international assistance, to improve their position.

History: dependence and independence

An important reason for the persistence of trade unionism despite massive problems lies in its deep roots in Nigerien society. The origins of African trade unionism generally lie in antecedent social formations and traditions rather than in colonial legislation seeking *post hoc* to shape their nature during the initial period of institutionalisation. These prior formations underpinned solidarities and constituted resources for early forms of self-help and trade unionism often dubbed 'native unionism' by colonial administrators (Croucher, 2003). They continue to do so, providing networks of support constituting vital links between urban and rural societies and assisting personal transitions from rural to urban society (Falola, 2002).

Trade unionism in Niger began to develop institutionally in 1937, when the French permitted very limited forms of unionism for white-collar 'cadres'. In Francophone West Africa, trade unions developed along fundamentally different lines from their counterparts in the Anglophone countries because the colonial power regarded the colonies as an extension of France. The unions, which expanded in membership and influence during the Second World War, were formally therefore branches of their metropolitan 'parents', who attempted actively to direct them. The French legacy remains significant for several reasons. First, French law is based on constitutional and civil law rights, according a specific position to collective organisations of citizens and workers with no direct equivalent in British law where unions have 'immunities'. As La Porta *et al.* (2000) argue, civil law régimes provide a more solid basis for institutions than their common-law counterparts, *inter alia* by limiting judges' power. More broadly, trade unionism was recognised as an integral part of the polity in a sense that was not the case in British colonies and this solid politico-legal foundation remains of fundamental importance. Secondly, trade unionism was and remains a politically-driven and broadly-conceived social project. The French legacy embedded ideas of universal rights, concepts acting as an important resource for unions. Thirdly, the French state and companies make strong efforts to maintain relations with Niger, efforts matched by the French unions. Niger's unions still gain assistance from their French counterparts. However, in one significant respect, the French legacy was transcended by Niger's unions, which were for many years able to resist reproducing French unions' political fragmentation.

Niger's unions developed in a symbiotic relationship with the nationalist movement for independence. In some senses, the unions were the senior partner in the relationship since the tiny group of (French-educated) intellectual nationalists had negligible links to the population and the unions were therefore indispensable in providing roots in the population. The unions themselves had small membership, with less than three thousand members in 1954, but occupied strategic positions in the economy and like their French counterparts enjoyed mobilisation capacity well beyond their members (Duerster and Fenner, 1980). The nationalist contribution was to impress on unions the need to maintain their unity through one national centre and to link Niger's unions to their counterparts in Francophone Africa through the international *Union Générale des Travailleurs de l'Afrique Noire*.

At the end of the Second World War both unions and nationalists challenged the French labour tax which, like the Portuguese, it levied on the indigenous population. This tax, the '*indigénat*' constituted a clear focus for the nascent nationalist movement because it constituted a universal grievance that the unions could exploit (Cooper, 1996). The *indigénat* was soon abolished, in a major victory for the nationalist–union alliance (ibid.). In November 1952, unions in Francophone West Africa took a further step forward when they conducted a general strike to compel the French to institute a uniform Labour Code (*Code du Travail*) in the colonies (Pedder, 1979). This was the origin of relatively favourable labour laws that support unions (Panford, 1994) and remain the basis for current labour legislation. The unions were able sufficiently to impress a weakening colonial power to encourage them to make concessions of enduring significance. The point was not lost on the nationalists, who had begun to understand the potential problems posed by union power after independence.

Niger became independent from France in 1960, but independence for Niger brought immediate subordination for the unions. The initial post-colonial period stamped unionism with a 'transmission belt of the state' legacy that took many years to overcome. Harman Diori's long rule brought the dissolution of Niger's section of the *Union Générale des Travailleurs de l'Afrique Noire* as he sought to promote a rival union dominated by his *Parti Progressive Nigérien*, the *Union Nationale des Travailleurs du Niger* (UNTN, formed in September 1960). Its General Secretary, René Deleanne, was a member of the Cabinet and General Secretary of the National Assembly. The UNTN depended on state funds and the state encouraged its growth. In 1974, the first of a series of military putsches overthrew Diori. Initially, only small moves to independence occurred in the UNTN, though in 1976 it took the process further with a new General

Secretary (Duerster and Fenner, 1980). In the early 1980s, Niger's economic position improved somewhat with uranium prices and unions recovered with it. However, uranium prices declined after a few years and government weakness in the face of mounting external economic problems encouraged the UNTN to argue openly for an end to military rule. In 1990, 1991, 1992 and 1994, the unions initiated widespread strike action to demand and defend democracy when that was at first resisted and the Government, once instituted, was threatened by the military (Adji, 2000). Such demonstrations of union power have not been repeated in the 21st century, possibly because of the union movement's fragmentation as three rival confederations have emerged to challenge the USTN. The government, seeking to divide and rule, has encouraged this fragmentation. The government has implemented Structural Adjustment Programmes since the early 1980s, and these have showed the USTN's incapacity to defend the interests of its mainly public sector membership as large numbers of public sector workers were dismissed. Reliable membership figures do not exist and many members cannot pay subscriptions, but an external source (County, 2005: 247) recently suggested that the USTN has 60,000 members, a total matched by its three rival confederations. The main rival confederation is the *Confederation Nigérien du Travail* (CNT), representing mainly private sector workers but with membership in all sectors (Adji, 2000; County, 2005).

Thus, until recently the unions demonstrated remarkable resilience and mobilisation capacity especially when advancing and defending democratic values. With the exception of the immediate post-independence period, when the state enjoyed great legitimacy, neither the colonial nor the independent state have been able entirely to bend unions to their will. More recently, however, unions' achievements have been threatened by world financial institutions.

The economy: from national construction to impoverishment and dependence

Niger's economy was until the 1970s almost exclusively agricultural, centred on groundnut cultivation, providing little basis for the development of trade unionism. Groundnut cultivation has practically disappeared but around Independence hopes were pinned on the development of the uranium mines. This offered the government the prospect of national development from the resultant revenue, and simultaneously gave rise to improved hopes for trade unionism.

The government's hopes were to some extent realised until world uranium prices collapsed in the 1980s. Niger produces some three thousand tonnes of uranium a year, sold mainly to France and Japan. Both the mines involved are operated by the French company Cogema, one in a joint venture with a local company and the other with a state-owned concern. These mines are regulated by the French atomic energy commission. Syntramin, the miners' union, had considerable mobilisation capacity even during the depression, launching a major strike to improve wages, conditions and safety in 1995 (*L'Humanité*, 1995). They continue to highlight dangerous conditions and the difficulties the union experiences in enforcing adequate safety standards.

Some gold mining is also carried out, and there is the prospect of oil revenues if exploration is successful. In addition, there has been limited development of industrial production also offering some basis for unionism. Nevertheless the state, supported by extensive US and European aid, has been a major employer, magnifying the effects of their attempts since 1981 to follow policies prescribed by Structural Adjustment Programmes (SAPs). This has led to an expansion in 'informal' working, bringing it currently to around 80 per cent of the workforce.

These neo-liberal policies confronted the essentially French model of social relations embodied in its Constitution and norms. The last decade has seen persistent attacks on unions and their rights in efforts to meet the requirements of SAPs. One effect has been a reduction in the number of state employees, in health, education and elsewhere. Public sector salaries were cut across the board: in 1997, public sector salaries were reduced by 30 per cent and automatic increments for civil servants removed, bringing sizeable but ineffective demonstrations. The unions appeared as defenders of privileged workers enjoying benefits denied to the great majority of the population. The check-off system for union subscriptions, previously unchallenged, has been queried and undermined by the Ministry of Finance. The state has disbanded two police unions and has encouraged unions favourable to its policies (Adji, 2000). Increasingly, pay arrears have developed, creating a new and acute problem for unions, a problem hitherto largely confined to the Russian speaking world unknown even in Anglophone West Africa.

There has been a shift within state rhetoric and policies towards an acceptance of neo-liberal ideas depicting trade unionism as an obstructive force. Nevertheless, the state has been constrained in its attacks on the unions in comparison with those made in some other African countries. Thus, there is no equivalent to the Senegalese President, who argued that the USA provides 'a model of rapid development that neither France nor Europe can offer' (*L'Express*, 10 November 2005). Moreover, recent attempts to victimise trade union leaders have brought decisions in favour of trade unionists in the Court of Appeal (ICFTU, 2006), supporting La Porta *et al.*'s (2000) arguments about the advantages of civil law régimes. The country's legal system both reflects and helps to defend a wider consensus that recalls the constitution and reinforces the governing elite's reservations in relation to fully internalising US-style neo-liberalism.

SAPs: consequences for unions

SAPs and associated policies have had two main consequences for the trade union movement. The first and most fundamental has been a growth in informal working and a consequent catastrophic decline in revenues to the

Table 16.1 Changes in USTN revenue (in CAF)

	1993	1994	1995	1996	1997	1998
Revenue from union cards bought and union contributions	3,380,000	2,338,000	209,000	1,209,000	400	433
Overall union receipts	128,173,861	55,963,585	67,110,585	43,644, 591	69,688, 857	42,985, 818

Source: Adji, 2000: 9.

USTN. This contributed to the second, namely the development of significant breakaway union confederations.

Unfortunately, up to date figures for union income are not available. However, Table 16.1 shows that the USTN lost a large proportion of its income between 1993 and 1998. Although equivalent figures for the CNT are not available, it seems likely that it also experienced losses in the same period.

Table 16.1 shows a disproportionate reduction in subscription income; overall income includes income from internationally-funded projects. Subscription income is unlikely to be increased by organising impoverished informal sector workers. This underlines the increasing dependence of USTN affiliates on non-subscription income, threatening consequences for union democracy. Union leaderships deriving little income from membership are unlikely to feel strongly encouraged to respond to members. Thus although the mandates of the great majority of union leaders have long expired, they nevertheless remain in office (Adji, 2000). Equally, it underlines the increasing importance of international assistance, funds from organisations such as the Dutch FNV Mondiaal brokered by Global Union Federations or provided directly from organisations such as the International Labour Office.

During the 1990s, when the USTN experienced this massive decline in income, new confederations were formed. This was in part a consequence of its reduced ability to provide services to affiliates, which in turn led to a crisis of confidence in USTN. In 2000, it was reported that the four confederations had little contact and made no effort to co-ordinate their activities (Adji, 2000).

Union responses, national and international

The divided unions are therefore faced with having to undertake strategically important but difficult and labour-intensive tasks, notably campaigning against neo-liberal policies and organising 'informal' workers, with greatly diminished resources. Niger's unions have nevertheless continued to conduct vigorous rearguard actions against privatisation, especially where they remain relatively well-organised. Thus, the alliance of Telecom unions has linked effectively with French organisations to perform a political 'watchdog' role in relation to the long-running and difficult privatisation of their industry involving France Télécom. The Nigérien unions have produce extensive critiques of the arrangements, and linked effectively with their French counterparts (Co-operation Solidarité Développement, 2005). This illustrates the way in which the country's unions can draw strength from their association with their French counterparts.

International assistance has also been vital in approaching the task of organising informal workers. Both the International Labour Organisation and the Global Union Federations have a long history of providing assistance to African unions. In the light of the worsening situation in Niger, these efforts have in some respects intensified. The ILO initiated a project (DANIDA) that included co-ordinating efforts to organise workers in the informal economy in the four trade union centres. The possibility of an alliance or federation of 'informal workers' with the possibility of direct affiliation to a Global Union Federation has been discussed. However, there still appears to be resistance to the confederations working together (StreetNet News 5, 2006). The DANIDA project has given way to a project funded by the Danish LO/FTF to extend organisation in the informal sectors.

It has been claimed that a 'massive upsurge' in unionisation of 'informal' workers has occurred recently (ICFTU, 2006b). SNTIN (*Syndicat National des Travailleurs de l'Industrie du Niger*) have organised vendors of purified water into the Association 'Pure Water' arranging micro-finance for members, and improving expertise in marketing and distribution, import and export. It has received assistance from SNTIN in training and capacity-building (StreetNet News 5, 2006). Some progress has been made in recruitment but no figures are quoted by the sources used above. The depth of male influence in the unions is an important limiting factor in efforts to organise the large numbers of women involved in 'informal' work.

Conclusion

Niger's industrial relations have been deeply stamped by the country's economic and political history, since severe under-development has meant that state-union relations have taken centre stage. The nature of French law and political norms was helpful to unionisation but unionism, deeply rooted in local communal traditions and practices, both drew on and transcended the French colonial legacy. Unions reached the apex of their influence towards the end of colonial rule, but after independence the state attempted to subordinate the unions to their will and for a period it was successful. By the late 1980s the unions re-asserted their independence by taking industrial action to advance and defend democratic values and this represented a second pinnacle of their historic achievement. In both cases, their political role was paramount. The intervention of global neo-liberal institutions brought a much less effective response and Structural Adjustment Programmes destroyed a major historic achievement by bringing about the union movement's fragmentation. As a result, the unions have become increasingly dependent on international solidarity and the dilemma for Niger's unions, as for many others, is to seek and use international support without compromising their independence and capacity for self activity.

References

Adji, S. (2000), *Globalization and Union Strategies in Niger*. Geneva: International Institute for Labour Studies.
Cooper, F. (1996), *Decolonization and African Society: The Labour Question in French and British Africa*. Cambridge: Cambridge University Press.
Co-operation Solidarité Développement (2005), '"Niger: l", autorité de Régulation met en demeure les operations de télephonie mobile . . . de respecter leurs obligations contractuelles'. Posted 8 October 2005, downloaded 9 November 2006.
County, B. (2005), 'Niger', in *Trade Unions of the World*, 6th edn. London: International Centre for Trade Union Rights and John Harper Publishing.
Croucher, R. (2003), 'African Labour', *Historical Studies in Industrial Relations*, 15: 95–112.
Duerster, H. and Fenner, M. (1983), 'Niger', in Mielke, S. (ed.), *Internationales Gewerkschafts Handbuch*. Opladen: Leske.
L'Express (2005), 10 November. 'Entretien avec le Président du Sénégal'.
Falola, T. (ed.) (2002), *African Politics in Post-Imperial Times: The essays of Richard J. Sklar*. Trenton, New Jersey: Africa World Press.
Henley, J.S. (1989), 'African Employment Relationships and the Future of Trade Unions', *British Journal of Industrial Relations* 27, 3: 295–310.
L'Humanité (1995), 31 January 1995.
International Confederation of Free Trade Unions Online (ICFTU) (2006a), 'Niger: Court of Appeal Orders the Reinstatement of an Unfairly Dismissed Union Leader under Pressure from the International Trade Union Movement'. Filed 8 February 2006, downloaded 9 November 2006. www.icftu.org
International Confederation of Free Trade Unions Online [ICFTU] (2006b), 'Interview with Abdou Maigandi, USTN'. Filed 4 July 2006, downloaded 9 November 2006. www.icftu.org
La Porta, R., Lopez-de-Silanes, F., Shleifer, A. and Vishny, R. (2000), 'Investor Protection and Corporate Governance', *Journal of Financial Economics* 58: 3–27.
Organisation of African Trade Union Unity (2000), 'The OATUU/SASK/FNV OHS Project for West Africa. An Up-dated report of activities from 1998 to December 1999'. Report. Accra: OATUU.
Panford, K. (1994), *African Labour Relations and Workers' Rights: Assessing the Role of the International Labour Organization*. Westport, Connecticut: Greenwood Press.
Pedder, F. (1979), *Main Currents of West African History, 1940–1978*. London: Macmillan.
StreetNet News 5 (2006), 'StreetNet-UNI fact-finding mission to Francophone West Africa'. Downloaded 9 November 2006. www.streetnet.org.za
USTN (2001), 'Seminaire USTN/OUSA/FNV/SASK'. Thème: Formation de base des cadres syndicaux en matière de santé et securité au travail'. Report. Niamey: USTN.
Wood, G. and Frynas, J.G. (2006), 'The Institutional Basis of Economic Failure: Anatomy of the Segmented Business System', *Socio-Economic Review*, 4, 2: 239–77.

Part IV
Trans-Continental Trends and Issues

17
Organising the Informal Economy: Results and Prospects – the Case of Ghana in Comparative Perspective

Richard Croucher

Introduction

Most of the world's population earns a living outside formal employment relationships, in the 'informal economy'. ILO figures suggest that the African informal economy is growing: in most African nations at least half and frequently 90 per cent of the working population is occupied within it (ILO, 1999a; Croucher, 2003: 101; Ghana Trades Union Congress, 2006); it is where many precarious workers engage in a daily battle for survival. This chapter examines Ghanaian union experiences of organising the informal economy.

De-regulation has increased 'informalisation' globally, impacting trade unions world-wide (ICTUR, 2005). 'Informalisation' is a wider process, impacting formally employed workers and trade union organisations, affecting organised workers' capacity to extend their capacity to organise workers. The Ghanaian case is relatively favourable to organising 'informal' workers, since Ghana has experienced stable political, social and economic circumstances in recent years. Proceduralised industrial relations exist in parts of the economy, but union membership loss has been severe, damaging confidence and reducing resources (Konings, 2002). A reliable recent international source offers no membership figures for Ghanaian unions (ICTUR, 2005).

There has been considerable discussion of attempts to stimulate union renewal across the world (Fairbrother and Yates, 2003a,b; Fantasia and Voss, 2004). The equally important debate on precisely how unions organise in the developing world's informal economy has made less progress, despite some significant contributions. The Ghana Trades Union Congress (2006) has called for intensified research, but relatively few experts discuss practical union organising activity in the global South; a recent volume on strategies for union revitalisation in a globalising economy contains no examination of the Southern hemisphere (Frege and Kelly, 2004). Yet the African experience is clearly relevant to trade unionists internationally.

The chapter's overall argument is as follows. Informalisation affects unions as well as those in the informal economy. Unionisation is desirable both for representational purposes and for national economic development, but is hindered by a lack of union resources. Organising 'informal' workers is difficult for unions geared to other purposes and the most successful unionisation effort among them arose initially from self-organisation, was supported by the state and only later transformed into unionisation.

Defining the informal economy

Competing conceptualisations of the less regulated parts of economies exist (for a critical review of discussions, see Feldman and Ferretti, 1996; for a conceptualisation of different approaches to definition, see Chen et al., 2002). We use the 'informal economy' concept rather than the 'extra-legal' alternative, because of the continuing significance of statutory regulatory agencies to precarious workers (Lourenço-Lindell, 2002). How to define the informal economy's boundaries has generated much debate since it has significant links with the formal economy. Informality may best be conceptualised as *both* a wider process and an 'economy' or a 'sector' despite its fuzzy boundaries (Croucher, 2003: 108). Those working in it share certain characteristics. They are in casual, marginal or precarious occupations; they are often not employees, but are 'self-employed', or work as agricultural producers or in family undertakings (War on Want, 2006). They usually lack insurance of any kind (Selcuk, 2005). Some suggest that the defining quality of employment relationships in the 'informal' economy is an absence of contact with regulatory agencies. Lourenço-Lindell (2002) demonstrates however that many actors in the informal economy have considerable contact with governmental agencies, creating problems by harassing them and demanding bribes. A more accurate defining characteristic of those occupied in the informal economy is therefore that they lack enforceable rights. According to Selcuk (2005) their defining characteristic is that they lack enforceable contractual rights, but this definition illustrates the difficulty in defining a specific informal economy since many workers with formal legal rights cannot enforce them. Thus, although there is a recognisable informal economy, the wider economy is also increasingly 'informalised'.

The informal economy: in need of extension or regulation?

Is increased regulation of the informal economy in African countries' national interests? The argument that regulation ensures certain national minimum labour standards and, in turn, improves economic efficiency, stretches back to the British theorists the Webbs (Webb and Webb, 1897: 773). The state had to act with unions to reduce low-paying employers' social impact and a similar position is currently advanced by the ILO (2002a).

However, there has also been a contrary tradition of argument holding that the informal economy is to be encouraged as a seed-bed of entrepreneurial activity and therefore an engine for development. De Soto (1989: 255) suggested that 'the real problem is not so much informality as formality'. For Sauvy (1984), so-called 'black working' (*sic*) prefigured a future neo-liberal 'utopia'. For these writers, *de*-regulatory approaches towards the formal economy are required and they view the reduced role for the state and unions that this would entail in a positive light. Such arguments underpinned Structural Adjustment Programmes in Africa and though these viewpoints enjoyed a heyday in the 1980s, they are still advanced (see, for example, Browne, 2004).

Much recent work suggests that the state is in fact a vital actor in leading economic transitions in Eastern Europe, implying a need to extend its regulatory capacity (Negoita, 2006). Wood and Frynas (2006) show that the informal economy is a central component of what they describe as African 'segmented' business systems that generate benefits for local elites, but which constitute a *barrier* to development. Segmentation implies a lack of productive complementarities between employers and sectors, which unions' cross-employer organisational form helps promote.

Unions and the informal economy

Unions can build workers' confidence explicitly to improve efficiency through their exercise of voice and can shift employers away from 'low road' perspectives by 'educating' them (Streeck, 2004). Moreover, they can themselves take relevant initiatives, especially by directing education at workers and this has been a major function for them in Africa (Croucher, 2003). Unions' educational traditions mean that they can educate workers in ways other organisations cannot replicate. As organisations capable of drawing workers into and conducting experientially-based education, they can *themselves* make significant contributions to raising skill levels and to building workers' capacities as economic and political actors. Thus, they can both indirectly stimulate vital investment in workers' capacities and themselves further it directly (Feidel-Merz, 1964; Croucher, 2004). As Joseph Stiglitz argues, they are 'key to democratic economic development' (Stiglitz, 2000: 20). Unions embody and propagate ideas of collective organisation, representation and bargaining often reflected in other social movements and provide a non-tribal, secular model of collective organisation. Unions also have international links to attract foreign assistance and attention (Croucher, 2003).

Union membership in the informal economy is hard to establish, but is certainly small (War on Want, 2006; Croucher, 2003: 102). In West Africa, union membership and activity has centred on the state sector, and transport, manufacturing and extractive industries. Unions' positions were drastically undermined during the period of Structural Adjustment Programmes such as those imposed in Ghana in the 1980s and 1990s (Konings, 2002). This stimulated interest among some unions in the informal economy, but such interest has been uneven. In some cases, unions sustained their membership and industrial influence despite massive re-structuring, as for example in the Nigerian textile industry (Andrae and Beckman, 1998); in these cases unions have made minimal effort because their finances are stable. This hints at a general problem: that individual unions either have the resources derived from a stable core membership to organise in the informal sector, in which case they see no need, or see the need but lack resources. Moreover, pressure from existing members means that resources will tend to be spent on them rather than on prospective members. Union confederations have therefore played a significant role in helping establish informal economy organisations and also have these organisations as affiliates (War on Want, 2006). The ILO and the Dutch FNV fund the Pan-African Organisation of African Trade Union Unity to work with unions to try to increase womens' participation in internal union democracy, acting as a vehicle for involving them more fully in wider democratic processes (GEPATU, 2006).

Those active in the informal economy have themselves sometimes formed collective self-help bodies. These organisations of women, street traders and others fulfil a wide range of functions including mutual assistance and rights training (War on Want, 2006). Though some bodies have a national remit, most are local organisations with small memberships. They have a range of different forms, often complementary, similar to, or linked to, unions. They can exercise political influence, but unions are much larger, national organisations with greater mobilising and power resources than informal economy organisations. Yet how far unions are able and willing to assist informal economy workers remains an open question.

Difficulties of unionising the informal economy

Union organising in the informal economy has long been widely advocated but it faces formidable barriers (Gallin, 2001). Workers 'walking the tightrope', engaged in a daily battle for survival, can rarely afford risky experiments (Lourenço-Lindell: 254). Fierce competition between individuals can make collective action to bring that competition within acceptable limits necessary but difficult to develop (Wood and Frynas, 2006). The heterogeneity of the informal economy makes it difficult to organise large groups (Gallin, 2004) while short enterprise life-spans and 'hard-line patriarchal attitudes' from employers constitute further obstacles (Wood and Frynas, 2006: 256).

Unions generally only fund the task when supported by the ILO, international or national union confederations, NGOs or other agencies. Even where unions undertake these new, difficult, labour-intensive and necessarily long-term activities (Ghana Trades Union Congress, 2006), the work is problematic. Some of the methods adopted such as dealing with product suppliers or purchasers are unfamiliar to unions since structures and cultures are attuned to the more collective bargaining needs of their existing constituencies.

How far new constituencies can in fact assert their agendas within unions in relation to well-established majority constituencies remains unclear.

The informal economy is an archipelago, and each island within it has a different environment. Each group of workers in the informal economy has its specific needs that unions need to understand (Ghana Trades Union Congress, 2006). War on Want revealingly calls for unions, as well as the ILO and governments, to bring informal economy organisations more fully into policy making processes (ibid.). Feminists have pointed out the limited participation possible for women in unions (Clean Clothes Campaign, 2005).

Detailed case studies such as those conducted by Cross (1997) identify Mexican relatively well-organised informal workers and uncover the reasons for their success. Cross found that those groups in constant conflict and negotiation with the state (such as taxi drivers) tended to be well organised. Rossignotti (2006) identifies and elaborates general principles for informal sector organising: building a consensual and bottom-up process; adaptation of traditional union recruitment strategies; good quality education and communication policies; building coalitions with other organisations and intensifying international co-operation on advancing rights in the informal economy. Thus, Cross and Rossignotti indicate the considerable demands of organising informal workers both in terms of the effort required and the need to sustain that effort across long periods to achieve success. Whether Ghanaian unions outside of those such as the General Agricultural Workers Union for whom it is a particularly important activity are willing to invest in this way is unclear.

'Informal sector' organisation in Ghana

Ghana represents one of the most positive African cases of collective organisation outside of stable employment. It has also been an exceptional country in that it has taken some measures to integrate those in the informal economy into the social security and health systems as advocated by informal economy bodies and unions (War on Want, 2006). The Ghana TUC has, through its Informal Economy Desk, played an important part in helping to establish and assist organisations in the informal economy for over a decade. In Ghana, government has developed a corporatist exchange relationship with unions that has proved mutually favourable and raised incentives to co-operation on both sides. The channels for political advocacy with government are relatively well developed there partly because the state has historically played a particularly important part in shaping trade unionism (Panford, 1994). We now examine three cases of such organisations to understand their *raisons d'être* and how they function.

Our first example is the Ghana Private Road Transport Union (GPRTU), frequently cited as an example of unionism among 'informal sector' workers, although little detail is usually provided (see, for example, Anyemedu, 2000). It is Ghana's fifth largest union with a membership of 37,400 in 1998 (Anyemedu, 2000). The GPRTU has been used by the government to collect taxes, enabling the government to raise tax revenue in the informal economy in return for trade-offs for GPRTU. GPRTU began as an unofficial association that later joined the Ghana TUC and which is now one of its largest and most stable affiliates. A recent detailed study (Reinking, 2006) clarifies how it functions by investigating a branch in Accra. The Tro-tro (minibus) branch examined by Reinking includes both Tro-tro owners and drivers. Its function is described as:

> ... to organise owners, owner/drivers, employed professional drivers, porters and lorry guards who are engaged in the road transport industry of the private sector into one organisation for them to protect, sustain and promote their common interests. . . to regulate relations and to settle disputes between employees and employers (Reinking, 2006: 1).

The union restricts the supply of labour; membership of an informal social network permits entry. Car owners seeking drivers approach the union and are referred to one of their members. The branch has considerable internal formalisation, with elected office holders including trustees, positions held exclusively by car owners despite democratic elections. This formalisation reflects its functions and the monopoly that they impose over parking and hiring places and which appears to have been instituted with the introduction of the 'income tax', or daily fee compulsory for all Tro-tros. The union offered to collect this tax for the authorities who were themselves unable to do it, and from that point the monopoly appears to have been established. The union acts to control the quality of taxis, and as an unemployment relief scheme for long-term unemployed drivers. The latter police existing routes, preventing other drivers from using them. It also acts as a distributor of work, providing occasional work for unemployed members when other drivers need time off. Complaints from passengers are dealt with by the union, which may fine drivers. It therefore operates as a professional guild, a mutual benefit society, a craft union, a labour agency and a tax collection body. Reinking (2006) expresses serious reservations in relation to the GPRTU: how far is it, since it includes both drivers and owners, an independent union and how far is it a government agency? Moreover the union is essentially male, and restricts membership by means of informal networks. However these difficulties illustrate the problems faced by workers in the informal sector. The trade-off for members is freedom from harassment by state officials in return for union tax collection, vehicle inspection and discipline.

The GPRTU, like six other unions, is affiliated to an umbrella organisation, Street Net Ghana Alliance (SGA), an organisation whose activities have been documented by War on Want (2006), and whose extensive case study we use here for our second example. The GPRTU provides an element of organisational stability for the SGA. The SGA was originated and supported by the Ghana TUC's Informal Sector Desk. It is accommodated in the GTUC building and has access to its resources, although the aim is for it to become independent.

Its constitution stresses several functions: to expand such networks, to gather information on street traders' situations and to empower them. The SGA has organised some vendors, hawkers and traders in street markets in Accra and Takoradi and has nineteen traders' associations (although only a few pay dues) with a total membership of 5,810 individuals (mostly women) together with the unions mentioned above. Two central organising strategies were initially envisaged, training and micro-loans, but neither has been implemented due to a shortage of resources and membership has decreased. A further function has been advocacy to metropolitan and state authorities and in Takoradi the SGA has organised women to participate in a health insurance forum. It has also enrolled three hundred women in the state pension scheme, previously the province of formal sector workers. In summary, the SGA is an umbrella organisation initiated by the GTUC, that has conducted some advocacy and organising work. Its notable successes in terms of involving women street traders have been on health, insurance and pension issues but its major problem has been a lack of resources. Its reliance on the GTUC, was also cited by a War on Want respondent as a difficulty causing delays in decision-making.

Our third example is from an initiative outside of the GTUC, typical of the small and local organisations that are scattered throughout the 'informal economy'. Our account of the local Yeji branch of the National Inland Canoe Fishermen's Association (NICFA) derives from Britwum et al. (2006), who describe several such bodies in detail. Nationally, the Association appears not to have members affiliated in some important inland fishing areas, but in Yeji there is an active branch with 700 men and 25 women involved, described as associate members and paying an annual subscription. Almost all inland fishing enterprise operators are in membership. The association was 'quite active' (Britwum et al., 112), with regular meetings to discuss issues of collective concern. Local executive officers are elected, subject to their removal before the end of their term of office if the membership wishes. The organisation has two main functions: buying goods in bulk and providing education on efficient and environmentally friendly fishing methods. It is characterised by a high level of involvement and direct democracy, but, like the GPRTU, is essentially a male organisation.

Conclusion

As we argued initially, improved union membership in the informal economy would aid national development through the direct contribution notably to educational levels. However, union educational activity is expensive (Sogge, 2004).

The GPRTU experience supports Cross's (1997) suggestion that high levels of organisation are most in evidence where 'informal' workers come into conflict with the state. However, most workers in Ghana's informal economy do not have this relationship to the state. Moreover, they are not urban men, but women working in agriculture, a difficult-to-organise sector world-wide.

Anyemedu (2000) identified three key problems for unions: high organising costs in relation to income from informal sector workers, the absence of a package of benefits to attract informal sector operators, and lack of previous experience in union organisation among these workers. Anyemedu suggests that the first is crucial, since organising informal sector workers could worsen unions' weak financial position. In our three cases, the only one with a major problem with payment of subscriptions was the SGA, which was not initiated from below but by the GTUC. Furthermore, the principal example of a successful informal economy organisation, the Indian Self-Employed Women's Association, includes both well-off and poor women, enabling cross-subsidy.

Unions world-wide face great organisational and cultural problems in making major changes; how far they are in fact prepared to make such risky investments? Informalisation has reduced union income: the problem that they are addressing simultaneously limits their capacity to address it. The running in the informal sector has not been made by unions, but rather by international organisations, notably the International Labour Organisation, by funding pan-African projects such as GEPATU. Beyond the ILO, Global Union Federations have also obtained funding from their European funders. These projects have been predominantly elicited by Pan-African organisations or national trade union centres for whom external funding may constitute an important resource. However, national unions have very limited capacity to build on internationally-funded projects.

Ultimately it is less a question of unions' survival and more one of how these workers protect themselves. *Self*-organisation of 'informal' workers is difficult and may carry a high cost in terms of the compromises that have to be made. Yet its existence shows that it can be achieved. Organising informal workers from the outside, experience shows, is difficult and resource-intensive. The GTUC has been most successful when it has integrated an existing body, i.e. the GPRTU. This suggests that internationally-funded projects are likely to be most effective when they target direct organisation of promising groups in the informal economy to develop viable models of organisation. Unions could also investigate other strategies that offer ways of circumventing the problems. These might include examining how they can tap into social questions with widespread appeal, especially in relation to Africa's major health issues, in ways that provide practical assistance to people. Unions could broker overlapping interests between international organisations, the Ghanaian state and the population in ways that could raise their profile.

References

Andrae, G. and Beckman, B. (1998), *Union Power in the Nigerian Textile Industry: Labour Regime and Adjustment*. Uppsala: Nordiska Afrikainstitutet.

Anyemedu, K. (2000), *Trade Union Responses to Globalization: Case Study on Ghana*. Geneva: ILO; International Institute of Labour Studies.

A.O. Britwum, N.K.T. Ghartey, Agbesinyale, P. (2006), *Organising Labour in the Informal Sector: the Conditions of Rural Agriculture in Ghana, Accra.* Published for Ghana Trade Union Congress by Ghana University Press.

Browne, K.E. (2004), *Creole Economics: Caribbean Cunning Under the French Flag.* Austin: University of Texas.

Chen, M., Jhabvala, R. and Lund, F. (2002), *Supporting Workers in the Informal Economy: A Policy Framework.* Working Paper. Geneva: ILO.

Clean Clothes Campaign (2005), *Made by Women.* Amsterdam: CCC.

Cross, J. (1997), *Informal Politics: Street Vendors and the State in Mexico City.* Stanford: Stanford University Press.

Croucher, R. (2003), 'African labour', *Historical Studies in Industrial Relations,* 15: 95–112.

Croucher, R. (2004), 'The impact of trade union education: a study in three countries in Eastern Europe', *European Journal of Industrial Relations,* 10, 1: 90–109.

De Soto, H. (1989), *The Other Path: The Economic Answer to Terrorism.* London: Harper and Row.

Fairbrother, P. and Yates, C. (eds) (2003a), *Trade Unions in Renewal: A Comparative Study.* London: Continuum.

Fairbrother, P. and Yates, C. (2003b), 'Unions in Crisis, Unions in Renewal?', in Fairbrother, P. and Yates, C. (eds), *Trade Unions in Renewal: A Comparative Study.* London: Routledge.

Fantasia, R. and Voss, K. (2004), *Hard Work: Remaking the American Labor Movement.* California: California University Press.

Feidel-Merz, H. (1964), *Zur Ideologie der Arbeiterbildung.* Frankfurt: EVA.

Feldman, S. and Ferretti, E. (1996), *Informal Work and Social Change: A Bibliographic Survey.* Ithaca, New York: ILR Press.

Frege, C. and Kelly, J. (2004), *Varieties of Unionism: Strategies for Union Revitalization in a Globalizing Economy.* Oxford: Oxford University Press.

Gallin, D. (2001), 'Propositions on Trade Unions and Informal Employment in the Time of Globalization', *Antipode,* 19, 4: 531–49.

Gallin, D. (2004), 'Organizing in the Global Informal Economy', report of the Bogazici University Social Policy Form: Changing role of unions in the contemporary world of labour. Geneva: Global Labour Institute.

GEPATU (2006), 'Gender Mainstreaming Project for African Trade Unions'. Accra.

Ghana Trades Union Congress (2006), '*Organizing in the Informal Economy: Ghana, Trades Union Congress Experience*'. Downloaded from GEPATU web-site, 17 July 2006.

ICTUR (International Centre for Trade Union Rights) (2005), *Trade Unions of the World.* London: John Harper.

ILO (International Labour Organization) (1999a), *Trade Unions and the Informal Sector: Towards a comprehensive Strategy.* Geneva: ILO Bureau for Workers' Activities (BP/TUIS 99).

ILO (1999b), *Labour Education* Special Edition: 'Trade Unions in the Informal Sector'. Geneva.

ILO (2001), *Promoting Gender Equality – A Resource Kit for Trade Unions.* Geneva.

ILO (2002a), *Decent Work and the Informal Economy.* Geneva.

ILO (2002b), *Labour Education* special edition: 'Unprotected Labour: What Role for Unions in the Informal Economy?'. Geneva.

Joshi, A. and Ayee, J. (2002), 'Taxing for the State? Politics, Revenue and the Informal State in Ghana', *Income Data Services Bulletin,* 33, 3: 90–7.

Konings, P. (2002), 'Structural Adjustment and Trade Unions in Africa: The Case of Ghana', in Gilberto, F. and Riethof, M. (eds), *Labour Relations in Development.* London: Taylor and Francis.

Lourenço-Lindell, I. (2002), *Walking the Tightrope. Informal Livelihoods and Social Networks in a West African City.* Stockholm: Acta Universitatis Stockholmiensis.
Martens, M.H. and Mitter, S. (1994), *Women in Trade Unions: Organizing the Unorganized.* Albany, New York: ILO Publications.
Negoita, M. (2006), 'The Social Bases of Development: Hungary and Romania in Comparative Perspective', *Socio-Economic Review*, 4, 2: 209–38.
Panford, K. (1994), *African Labour Relations and Workers' Rights: Assessing the Role of the International Labour Organization.* Westport Ct.: Greenwood Press.
Reinking, J. (2006), *Taxi- and Trotro- Enterprises in Accra.* Lehrforschungsberichte, Berlin.
Rossignotti, G. (2006), ' "Unionizing the informal sector"; Interactive Conference on Organiszed Labour in the 21st Century'. International Institute for Labour Studies: http://www-ilo-mirror.cornell/edu. Downloaded 10 July 2006.
Sauvy, A. (1984), *Le Travail Noir et l'Economie de Demain.* Paris: Calmann-Levy.
Selcuk, F.U. (2005), 'Dressing the Wound: Organizing Informal Sector Workers', *Monthly Review*, 57, 1: 1–8.
Sogge, D. (2004), *Turning the Problem Around.* Amsterdam: FNV.
Stiglitz, J. (2000), 'Democratic Development as the Fruits of Labour', Keynote address to the International Industrial Relations Association, Boston.
Streeck, W. (2004), 'Educating Capitalists: A Rejoinder to Wright and Tsakalatos', *Socio-Economic Review*, 2, 3: 425–38.
Webb, S. and Webb, B. (1897), *Industrial Democracy.* London: Longman Green.
Whitley, R. (1999), *Divergent Capitalisms.* Oxford: Oxford University Press.
Wood, G. and Frynas, G. (2006), 'The Institutional Basis of Economic Failure: Anatomy of the Segmented Business System', *Socio-Economic Review* 2006, 4(2): 239–77.
War on Want (2006), *Forces for Change: Informal Economy Organisations in Africa.* London: War on Want.

18
Cross-Continental Trends and Issues in Employment Relations in Africa
Frank Horwitz

Introduction

There are many challenges facing workers and managers in Africa today. Forced to open their markets as part of World Bank and IMF structural adjustment programmes (SAPs) and finding many foreign markets closed to their products, organisations have borne the brunt of globalisation, resulting in plant closures and high unemployment. In the worst cases countries like the Democratic Republic of Congo and Somalia have been so ravaged by war that they have no real economy, ceasing to function as modern nation states. However, there are more democratic elected governments in Africa today than fifteen years ago. Matanmi (2000) summarises the major elements of industrial relations in emergent or transitional economies as having elements of colonial impact, nationalism, post-colonial states and crises of development; an impact of structural adjustment programmes; the democratic challenge; and the emergent demands of social partnership. (Matanmi, 2000: 95–6). Industrial relations (IR) problems and challenges in Africa have not been adequately addressed in the mainstream literature. (Kamoche *et al.*, 2004a). In many cases the State still plays a predominant role in driving industrial and economic development though institutional State directed industrial relations systems, investing through parastatal organisations, soliciting foreign aid and public works programmes seeking to improve employment creation. When most African countries were gaining independence, particularly in the 1960s and 1970s, these measures proved critical as colonial administrations of the time had failed to establish a broad-based and thriving private sector.

Analysts make broad generalisations about industrial relations in Africa ignoring the unique features in each country. Table 18.1 shows the relatively low, but also uneven Gross Domestic Product (GDP) for selected African countries. The diversity of Africa cuts across many dimensions: ethnically, with some 2000 different ethno-cultural communities; historically, with effects going back to whether the country is a former colony of Britain, France, or Portugal for example; politically, with dictatorships and democracies; and economically,

Table 18.1 Gross Domestic Product (GDP in US$ billion) and per capita GDP (US$) for selected African countries

South Africa	104.3	2620
Nigeria	43.5	335
Kenya	12.1	371
Zimbabwe	8.3	706
Ghana	6.0	269
Uganda	5.9	260
Botswana	5.2	3066
Mozambique	3.9	200
Malawi	1.9	166

Source: The World Bank, 2002.

with several high-income countries amidst a poverty-stricken majority. It is erroneous to assume homogeneity within specific countries too, since many African countries have diverse ethno-cultural communities (Kamoche et al., 2004a: xvi). In countries like Zambia and Ghana, with extensive privatisation of state-owned enterprises (SOEs), the IR landscape has been reshaped in significant and enduring ways. Many Zambian SOEs, for instance, have been bought by South African companies, whose managers apply employment practices based on those of the parent company. The Southern African region (in particular Botswana and South Africa) has emerged as a catchment area for talent from other parts of Africa, in particular East and Central Africa. In South Africa itself, a brain drain, in part, reflects the neglect of education and training during the apartheid years.

In this economic context, industrial relations regimes in these countries are relatively new and evolving. The International Labour Organisation (ILO) for example, has a number of advisors working with African country governments to establish industrial relations systems, legislative frameworks, collective bargaining and dispute resolution systems based on ILO Conventions. Since its launch in 2000, the ILO/SWISS Project based in Pretoria has made considerable progress in initiatives to strengthen social dialogue in countries such as South Africa, Namibia, Botswana and Zimbabwe by seeking to create tripartite forums and designing industrial relations and dispute resolution systems (Anstey, 2004: 59). It has also made progress in this regard in Nigeria. The ILO project has for example helped to develop some 23 codes and guidelines for best practice for social partners in Botswana. Extensive training has been provided for arbitrators and conciliators. In South Africa the project supports the bi-partite Millennium Council, which focuses on macro-economic and social policy issues. This has been vital in revitalising social dialogue.

As emergent economies, many African countries show uneven patterns of development and under-development, with low average per capita national income, low living standards and poorly developed social welfare. In IR terms

African countries are not monolithic. The contiguous sub-Saharan African countries differ in levels of infrastructural development or acquisition for expanding wage-employment and industrial sectors. Unevenness in this regard widens when comparing regional faster-growing and more rapidly industrialising South Africa with other African countries like Ethiopia (Matanmi, 2000: 96). Industrial relations in Africa are often rooted in colonial or apartheid (South Africa) regimes which created wage work in the exploitation of primary natural resources such as gold, diamonds and emergent manufacturing sectors such as clothing and textiles in countries such as Kenya and South Africa. Political independence expanded wage-employment sectors (largely public, but also private sectors), creating legislative frameworks legitimising, to varying degrees, trade union rights.

The role of government

The role of government in African IR varies from State control in formally socialist states such as Ethiopia and Mozambique, to State direction in countries like Zambia, to a strong legislative framework permitting more voluntarist systems such as in South Africa and Namibia. Under colonialism or apartheid, trade union movements could be characterised in part as social movements, often mobilising workers against an existing political regime. South Africa was a good example of this. Leadership development emerged from trade union movements to subsequently assume prominent political and business leadership roles following democracy. But when government becomes hegemonic, for reasons of ineptitude or malfeasance, labour policies are sometimes inconsistent and un-enforced (Fashoyin et al., 1994).

In most cases, newly independent sovereign states, though pluralistic, lacked a democratic culture and tolerant political leadership to carry along the wider populace. The pursuit of often parochial interests in the face of widespread poverty and scarcity soon fanned the embers of inter-ethnic confrontation. However, there are pressures for significant change through democratisation and good governance. The New Partnership for African Development (NEPAD) initiative for peer review is a potentially important development in Pan-African democratisation. It is premised on the notion of a self-directed social, economic and political Renaissance for Africa.

'Weak private sector development has left the state as the major economic actor and employer in most economies. Whilst the state may be dominant in many African countries, it is also often itself in crisis' (Anstey, 2004: 58). Anstey argues however, that a more positive picture is emerging. South Africa's political transition was managed through social dialogue and the basis for political discourse was set through a decade of vigorous exchange in civil society, for example through collective bargaining in the private sector. Elsewhere in Africa, conditions of scarce resources, political instability and weak institutions will test the resilience of such initiatives within individual nation states – and at regional level they will prove a major challenge for co-ordination and co-operation within SADC (South African Development Community) arrangements (Anstey, 2004: 59).

Structural adjustment programmes

One key potential area for social dialogue is around structural adjustment programmes (SAPs). Many emerging economies in Africa were under one form of structural adjustment programme or another by the mid-1980's, comprising several policy measures aimed at finding effective solutions to macroeconomic problems. The problems generally include a lack of self-reliant growth and development, low productivity and stagflation, serious imbalance of payments, huge external debts, and government budget deficit. Moreover, the SAPs have often been prescribed by the Bretton Woods institutions (the International Monetary Fund and the World Bank), on whom the crisis-laden economies of these nations are dependent for development credit and finance (Matanmi, 2000: 100). The prescriptions are usually comprised of devaluation, removal of subsidies on basic commodities, reduction of government expenditure, labour market reforms, reduction of trade protection, and increased incentives for the traditional sector (agriculture and mining). Globalisation has not seen many positive benefits for the poor in Africa. 'For decades those who have laboured for the poor in Africa and other developing countries say 'conditionality' – the conditions that international lenders imposed in return for their assistance – undermined national sovereignty' (Stiglitz, 2002: 9). These measures have so far not jolted the countries into clear signs of possible recovery. In African countries such as Botswana, Ethiopia and Uganda some measure of success has occurred in developing alternative strategies with recognition of the need for a paced market reform, land reform competition policies before privatisation ensuring job creation with trade liberalisation (Stiglitz, 2002: 87).

Matanmi (2000) concludes that the effects of SAPs on industrial relations too have been unfavourable. These include union membership decline with contracting formal employment, growing informalisation and casualisation, a toughening of collective bargaining with increasing precarious, unprotected and insecure employment. Whilst civil strife in Africa has retarded development, it has also limited moves towards developing industrial relations institutions. There is a vital need for institution building in African countries to strengthen industrial relations systems. This underlines a need to extend the IR agenda to arguably the most important challenges facing Africa: that of human resource development, building managerial capacity, investing in training and development and sound human resource management practices.

African organisations and trade union density

Many African economies are experiencing a transition from large and often over-staffed public corporations to enterprises that have to compete globally and be profitable (Jackson, 2002). Modern organisations in Africa fall into three categories (Fashoyin, 2000). The first comprises public enterprises, in which the state controls 50 per cent or more of the share capital. Organisations in this category are set up to discharge specific functions and attain objectives which are more readily achievable outside the civil service system. In most African economies this is the dominant type of organisation in the modern sector. Extensive privatisation programmes have substantially reduced the role of the state in business enterprises in this category. The second category includes private indigenous enterprises, an area in which African entrepreneurs are dominant. Enterprises in this category are comparatively small in size and are prominent in certain industrial sectors such as commerce, manufacturing and service. In this same category are a large number of micro-enterprises in the informal sector In this category of African businesses, management principles are marginally or informally practised. The third category includes multinational companies, foreign subsidiaries and joint-venture organisations. Organisations in this latter category occur in all sectors, particularly in manufacturing, textiles and automobile assembly.

Implementation of ILO conventions, even where formally subscribed to, is often not strongly supported. Trade unions are sometimes restricted in the scope of their activities due both to the limited spread of wage or paid employment and to unfavourable state policies which impede their ability to effectively use bargaining machinery. Bearing in mind an authoritarian–paternalistic style of management, collective bargaining does not always receive the approval of management (Fashoyin, 2000: 172–3).

The effects of ethnicity are not well documented regarding organisational impacts on IR in Africa (Nyambegera, 2002). Managerial styles, human resource management (HRM) practices and preferences for particular types of conflict resolution, may be mediated by ethnic factors, including the degree of cultural ethnocentrism, and tolerance or intolerance of diversity. Firm level employment practices in some countries like Kenya and South Africa have sometimes reflected preferences for particular ethnic groups or family members of an ethnic group. Political-historical factors such as Apartheid and colonialism have seen post independence governments promoting policies variously referred to as Africanisation, localisation and employment equity. In South Africa for example, trade unions have to be consulted by employers on the latter's employment equity plans, in terms of the Employment Equity Act (1998).

Developing countries have generally shared the trade union decline seen in the West (Verma *et al.*, 2002) despite the notion that increasing political democratisation would be accompanied by stronger independent labour movements. In very few African countries is more than 15 per cent of the labour force in formal wage employment (Anstey, 2004: 54) and never more than 25 per cent (table 18.2). South Africa is one of the few countries to have shown a countervailing trend. Union density rose by no less than 40 per cent, between 1950 and 1997 but was still relatively low at 19 per cent in 1997, and

Table 18.2 Statistics on trade unions in selected African countries

Country	Pop. (000s)	HDI	Labour force (000s)	TU members (000s)	% of labour force	% non-agric labour force	% formal sector wage earners
African states							
South Africa	42 393	71	16 635	3 154	18.9	21.8	51.9
Botswana	1 484	67	654	45	6.8	11.5	19.3
Namibia	1 575	64	650	55	8.4	22	
Zimbabwe	11 439	50	5 281	250	4.7	13.9	21.7
Ghana	17 832	47	8 393	700	8.3	25.9	
Kenya	27 799	46	13 953	500	3.5	16.9	33.3
Nigeria	115 020	39	45 565	3 520	7.7	17.2	
Zambia	8 275	37	3 454	273	7.9	12.5	54.5
Senegal	8 532	34	3 815	184	4.8	21.9	54.8
Uganda	20 256	34	10 084	63	0.6	3.9	
Malawi	9 845	33	4 807				

Source: ILO (1997). The ILO Swiss Project in Pretoria (2003) advised that these are its most updated statistics.

subsequently has stabilised and declined in some sectors such as building, construction, clothing, textiles and mining. Unions tend to be more representative of the formal wage sector economy than of the large informal and casual work force.

In South Africa it is estimated that employment losses in traditionally highly unionised industries have resulted in a drop of union membership by over 20 per cent in the past three years, mainly as the result of an increasing use of labour-only sub-contractors and casual and short-term contracts. In the mining industry, coverage by collective agreements has dropped to below 50 per cent from 58 per cent in 1997 (Theron & Godfrey, 2000: 116).

The State, collective bargaining and dispute resolution

Siddique (1989: 385) points out that most developing countries exhibit a dualistic economic structure, where a pre-capitalist economic system dominates the scene, with a small industrial sector and a related small working class. Other features include a segmented labour market, with a sharp dualism both between modern and traditional manufacturing sectors and between large and small firms. Siddique (1989) argues that IR in developing country settings can be explained partly by the role of the state. The State's influence is manifest through its dominant role in industrialisation and the labour market and its dominance in the industrial sector; with weak trade unions and collective bargaining.

The emergence of seemingly powerful industrial unions in critical sectors in countries such as Ghana, Nigeria and Zimbabwe has also influenced the proliferation of employers' associations and federations. It is significant that tripartite organisations have increasingly included members of unions, employers associations and government. A further development has been the deregulation or decentralisation of collective bargaining. The original centralised structures of bargaining have been strained and rendered unviable, with the implication that aspects of national labour contracts, even under multi-employer bargaining, are increasingly being subjected to individual employer conditions. Although this is one dimension of a new flexibility in the labour markets, it is an important instrument of the ascendancy of concession bargaining, and the new economy-imposed challenge of employer-employee cooperation, in these countries (Matanmi, 2000: 100).

Since the 1980s an increasing number of enterprises in Africa have taken a more accommodating stance towards worker's unions. Increasingly, managers are realising both the positive role of the union and also the inevitability of workers' organisation for providing a voice for workers. Thus, what the future portends for labour relations is how to balance the organisational interests of the workers with the commitment to corporate effectiveness and competitiveness (Fashoyin, 2000, p.173).

Public sector industrial relations

In Southern African countries the level of unionisation in the public sector is generally similar to that in the private sector. Some countries, such as Zambia, have experienced considerable privatisation, but the continuous fall in the size of the public sector does not seem to have affected the level of unionisation. Where trade unions are replaced by associations of civil servants (as in Zimbabwe, Botswana and Lesotho), the level of membership of such associations does not suggest a different level of unionisation (Kalula and Madhuku, 1997). Southern African countries may be placed in two groups, in respect of public sector IR (Kalula and Madhuku, 1997: 4–5):

- countries in which trade unions are allowed to operate freely in the public sector: including South Africa, Namibia, Zambia, Mauritius and Malawi;
- countries that do not provide for the registration of recognised trade unions for government employees: including Zimbabwe, Botswana and Lesotho. Government employees in this group are permitted to form workers' associations to represent their interests, but these associations are not as privileged as trade unions.

The trend in Southern Africa, however, is towards recognition of freedom of association of all workers, including those in the public sector.

In all Southern African countries, there is a decline in unilateralism in the centralised or decentralised bargaining. Even where the law does not provide for collective bargaining, either law or practice has entrenched some form of consultation between workers' bodies and government before the promulgation of terms and conditions of employment. South African legislation provides for the establishment of different bargaining councils for different sectors in the public service, but also for a central Public Service Co-ordinating Bargaining Council dealing with certain uniform rules.

Zambian legislation has no specific structure for public service collective bargaining but the system of joint councils is based on sectoral bargaining. Most unions in Zambia belong to one umbrella organisation, the Zambia Congress of Trade Unions (ZCTU). Contentious issues between unions and management usually centre around pay rates, cost of living adjustments (COLAs), health care, allowances (e.g. housing), layoff procedures, leave (e.g. sick leave and maternity leave), training and promotion, pension plans, and disciplinary cases (Muuka and Mwenda, 2004). The country has experienced high levels of unemployment and underemployment. Zambia has had a relatively strong and highly unionised IR system, with union density averaging 56 per cent over the period 1995–2000. Total union membership has, however, dropped steadily – from a high of 289,322 unionised employees in 1995 to 234, 522 in 1999, (ZCTU, 2004). Job and union membership losses have affected sectors like airlines, agriculture, banking, education and mining. For the Mineworkers' Union of Zambia and the National Union of Public Service Workers, declining numbers have been largely due to the impact of SOE downsizing as privatisation of those SOEs takes root. A more serious factor has been the impact of HIV and AIDS in sectors such as financial services, as well as the prolonged periods of drought. The decline in trade union membership can also be attributed to a lack of capacity by unions to organise in the new and increasingly hostile environment, particularly in the emerging private sector after privatisation.

Contemporary employment relations and labour markets

Labour market negotiations in many African countries are governed by rules contained in labour codes and in collective agreements which vary considerably in their efficacy. In Tunisia, for example, these are negotiated by tripartite committees every three years. Labour disputes are rare. Tunisian unionism has been characterised by the domination of a single national organisation – The Tunisian General Employment Union (UGTT) – established in 1946. It represents 30 per cent of the Tunisian workforce; with 60 per cent of members in the public sector. The UGTT is composed of 7,000 unions distributed throughout the country, of which 23 are regional unions, 20 are professional federations, and 30 are national unions, with the rest being local unions. As in several other African countries, pre-independence unions had strong features of a social movement collaborating with nationalist political organisation by mobilising workers in a struggle for independence (Yagoubi, 2004). After independence, the UGTT became more an administrative institution than an independent organisation of workers, and its leaders belonged to the government structure occupying functions in national and regional administration. Today, Tunisian unionism is undergoing a transformation. While strikes used to be an instrument of the union struggle, the union is also involved in contractual policy, through periodic negotiations with an employers' association. At the enterprise level, despite social and economic changes, the union still occupies a less important place. Conflict resolution occurs primarily at the workplace, not necessarily involving an independent union.

Ethiopia shows how an initially independent union movement can become subsumed under a state directed system where various governments over time including military and 'imperial' regimes required the union movement to support their particular aims. In 1962, the government in Ethiopia issued a Labour Relations decree, which allowed the establishment of trade unions. The first trade union, the Confederation of Ethiopian Labour Unions (CELU), was recognised by the authorities in 1963. CELU was made up of 22 industrial labour groups. The lack of national structure and constituency has affected its effectiveness (Mekonnen and Mamman, 2004). The failure to follow government's demands lead to its abolishment. It was replaced with the Ethiopia Trade Union (AETU) in 1977. The intention of the government was made clearer when it declared that the main purpose of AETU was to educate workers about the need to contribute their share to national development by increasing productivity and building socialism. Following the overthrow of the socialist government in 1991, trade unions in Ethiopia have become relatively more independent. However, they still remain polarised and ineffective, largely due to internal strife, national economic problems, and the increasing marketisation of the economy. High unemployment and the growing privatisation of state-owned enterprises have also resulted in lower trade union membership (Mekonen and Mamman, 2004: 111).

Zambia, under former President Dr Kenneth Kaunda, operated a policy called industrial participatory democracy. Aimed at active involvement of workers at industry levels with the establishment of works councils, it occurred against a backdrop of decentralisation and local government reforms (Muhandu, 2000). In Zimbabwe the trade union movement grew to some 1.5 million members. Minimum wages are legislated and labour representation has to some extent enhanced fair labour practices and negotiation skills (Tamanyani and Muranda, 2000). However, in contemporary Zimbabwe the union movement has strongly opposed aspects of government policy and has been viewed as a social movement increasingly under pressure to conform to, rather than oppose, state interests. The general secretary of the Zimbabwe Congress of Trade Unions, Collin Gwiyo is quoted as saying that 'Zimbabwe is still being run by a national liberation movement and that this liberation project was never turned into a democratic one. Hence the institutions of state began to mirror the practices inherent in liberation movements and not democratic ones' (Gwiyo, 2004).

Countries like Egypt and Somalia, for example, have fully-fledged labour codes. Ghana, Nigeria, Kenya, Zambia and Mauritius – to mention just a few – have adopted specific industrial relations Acts that also recognise various rights (ILO, 1997: 28–9). The scope of both labour policy or legislation and collective relations was rather limited until the 1970s or 1980s, depending on the individual country. For example, in Africa even now, with the exception of Egypt, Ethiopia, Libya, South Africa and Tanzania, existing legislation has yet to include the rural (traditional) and the urban-skewed wage-employment sector (Matanmi, 2000).

Collective bargaining limitations include inequality in bargaining power relations, especially in the context of uneven socio-economic development and largely unfavourable economic trends, together with governments' predilection to create obstacles in the way of development of collective bargaining. In the long term, sustained stewardship training and general labour education would serve the workers and their unions well (Matanmi, 2000: 99). Another common and comparatively new pattern in emerging countries is industrial unionism, whereby workers in the same industry, irrespective of occupational or skill differentiation, belong to the same union.

In Mauritius the history of the labour movement dates to the plantation days of tyranny, where repression and even execution were the lot of assertive workers, especially in the 1970s. The socio-political environment has much changed since, with the flourishing economy and quasi-full employment lasting two decades. The Industrial Relations Act and the Trade Unions and Labour Relations Act provide mostly for an interventionist approach, regulating the legal environment within which unions operate. However, this legislation itself has been contentious for decades now, with successive governments promising to review it (Ramgutty-Wong, 2004). Unions in Mauritius lack concerted action around essential issues, with falling union density. Another characteristic is the small membership size, with a high proportion of unions with less than 100 members. Union membership is widely spread across sectors, industries, and occupations although, generally speaking, union activities are not backed by popular support, and their role as political change agents has not so far carried much weight either. As in some other African countries, negotiations for annual salary compensations are conducted in a tripartite system with the state and employer groups involved, although the union groups tend not to be equal players. Fragmentation within the union movement makes it difficult to exercise much bargaining power. Thus, the current framework of industrial relations in Mauritius is neither adequately enabling nor particularly repressive (Ramgutty-Wong, 2004). Union membership appears to be weakening through some anti-union sectors, individualistic cultural values and a new found and materialistic orientation, though that state sector is more tolerant of unions (Ramgutty-Wong, 2004: 66).

Like Mauritius, there are several unions in the Ivory Coast, and a tradition of employer-union adversarialism. The major unions are UGTCI (General Union of Workers of Ivory Coast), Centrale Dignite (Dignity Central), SYNARES (a union of university professors), and the SYNESCI (a union of middle school and high school teachers), to name the most popular. Although these unions did not play a key role during the independence struggles, they were instrumental in contributing to multi-party elections and democracy in the early 1990s. Specifically, SYNARES and the SYNESCI were instrumental in allowing the multi-party elections in 1990 and the liberalisation of the political discourse. The labour–management relationship may symbolise a cultural pattern in that it helps understand how those who have power and control resources view employees in the workplace. In countries where labour-management relations are adversarial, one may expect a 'them versus us' mentality (Buegre, 2004).

As in South Africa, the trade union movement in Tanzania was actively involved in the anti-colonial struggles. However, after independence, relations between the trade union leaders and the government were strained over the future role of the labour movement. Following a military mutiny in 1964 and the alleged involvement of some prominent trade union leaders, the government dissolved and banned the Tanganyika Federation of Labour (TFL). In its place, the government created an economic development oriented/state institution union called the National Union of Tanganyika Employees (NUTE). In 1997, the merger of the political parties on the Tanzania mainland (formerly Tanganyika) and Zanzibar was accompanied by the merger of the trade unions in both places. The new labour movement was subsequently integrated into the new political party. With multi-party politics, the Tanzanian labour movement freed itself from the state apparatus and become autonomous. In 1998 it gained legal status with the enactment of the Trade Union Act which allowed freedom to form trade unions and evolved into a number of trade unions under one umbrella organisation in April 2001. By April 2002 17 trade unions on the mainland had registered with the registrar of trade unions. Although trade unions are recognised, the complex dispute settlement procedures make it extremely difficult for unions to call strikes in the public sector and many work stoppages are considered illegal by public authorities and tribunals. There are procedures for compulsory arbitration or adjudication when bipartite negotiations between employer and employees fail.

Unions have increasingly in the current decade focused their attention on addressing problems arising from enterprise restructuring programmes and privatisation, child labour, and the impact of HIV/AIDS on employment. As in Kenya, Botswana and South Africa, HIV/AIDS is a serious problem. Trade unions are working in conjunction with the government and NGOs to educate workers on prevention measures. Tanzanian trade union leaders have mounted vociferous attacks on the negative impacts of the ongoing privatisation program. Since the initiation of the privatisation program in the 1990s, there has been massive retrenchment of workers in the public sector in Tanzania.

The privatisation program has resulted in changes in conditions of service, deterioration and lack of enforcement of minimum employment standards legislation. Market oriented reforms like in many other African countries have weakened the ability of trade unions to successfully contest policies and practices detrimental to workers interests (Debrah 2004).

Analysis and conclusion

African employment relations have been affected by several complex trends. The impact of structural adjustment programmes (SAPs) which, except for Libya and South Africa, have been implemented in most countries assessed here as part of World Bank and IMF economic reform measures have been adverse to employment relations. Liberalised economies with privatisation and deregulatory measures have seen a drop in formal employment and deterioration of labour standards. This is exacerbated by the fact that Africa receives less than one per cent of the world's foreign direct investment. Whilst there is some evidence of a concomitant rise in employment relations institutions such as collective bargaining and dispute resolution as democratisation occurs, strong independent trade unions not linked to the state or employers are rare. Positively however, tripartite corporatist engagement has emerged in some countries such as South Africa.

A second theme is that of HIV/AIDS which, especially in sub-Saharan Africa, has had a devastating impact on employment, on employment and health care costs and on union membership decline. HIV/AIDS also has a deleterious effect on absenteeism, training, career and succession planning, with adverse effects on State and union negotiated medical schemes.

A third theme is significant change in labour market policy and structures with both the State and employers in many countries either turning a 'blind eye' through ineffective monitoring of legislative protective and collective agreements, or actively promoting more flexible arrangements. The aim is increased cost reduction and flexibility: the effect is a deterioration in employment standards, social protection and rising informalisation and casualisation in labour markets. Examples include the decline of regional centralised bargaining structures in the building and construction industry in South Africa.

A fourth theme relates to trade unions' strategic capacity. In a case study analysis of trade unions in the garment industries in Kenya, Lesotho, Swaziland and Malawi, Koen (2004) found that trade unions lacked strategic leadership, sound organisational practices, capacity and regional co-ordination, sometimes resulting in significant power imbalances and dependency relationships with employers and the State. Tougher stances by employers in Kenya, for example, where a well-established tradition of industrial unionism has occurred, have affected organisational efforts of the union, though this did not prevent spontaneous work stoppages by non-union members in January 2003. Driving the conduct of industrial relations and unionisation trends in African countries, is a combination of macro-economic and trade policies using import and substitution, export processing zones, cheap labour and tax incentives to attract foreign direct investment, often from Asian countries like Taiwan. One of the consequences is the migrancy of clothing and garment operations from one country to another. Attempts at militant union action and organisation have elicited harsh responses including factory closures and relocations. Conditions in factories organised by unions are exploitative often because of increasing pressures from the retail top-end of the supply chain for profit margin squeezes, low cost products and stringent delivery times of suppliers (Koen, 2004: 56).

Cross border trade union solidarity in Africa is as rare as it is politically restricted. Recent attempts by COSATU in South Africa to meet with its Zimbabwean counterpart, the Zimbabwean Congress of Trade Unions prior to that country's 2005 elections saw the COSATU delegation twice prevented from entering Zimbabwe. The ILO and ICFTU-Afro, the Southern Africa Trade Union Co-ordinating Council (SATUCC) and the Union Network International (UNI) have all protested to the Zimbabwean government calling for an end to the harassment and repression of union leaders, and calling on the ILO to intervene. With the deterioration of the economy, erosion of human rights and concomitant employment rights such as freedom of association and independent collective bargaining in Zimbabwe, workers' have become increasingly desperate (Musonda, 2004).

Bahadur (2004) notes a relationship between the African Growth and Opportunity Act (AGOA) passed in the United States in 2000 – offering preferential access for certain African exports in 37 sub-Saharan African countries as part of the policy of 'trade not aid' (Bahadur, 2004: 39) – and sweat-shop conditions. One of the consequences is a switching of predominant exports from Malawi, for example, which previously went to South Africa, to the US. In a number of cases working conditions have deteriorated, for example, increased overtime up to 27 hours weekly in Lesotho, repression of trade union rights and little enforcement of labour laws with high unemployment in sub-Saharan Africa. The bargaining power of unions in this sector is compromised. In South Africa, over 20,000 retrenchments have occurred in the clothing industry, a result largely of cheap imports from lower cost producers in Asia. A well-organised and soundly led union, the South African Clothing and Textile Workers Union (Sactwu) has struggled to fight this trend. One of its initiatives which has some employer support is a 'buy South Africa' campaign – this to try and preserve jobs.

These industry examples reflect the increasingly precarious nature of employment and flexible labour markets in most African countries. Even in South Africa, arguably with a strongly protective Labour Relations Act (1995) institutionalised Labour Court, and the Commission for Conciliation Mediation and Arbitration, as well as minimum standards legislation in the form of the Basic Conditions of Employment Act (1997) and arguably the strongest union movement on the continent, precarious, non-standard work has increased while formal standard work has declined. The combined effects of globalisation, trade policies, new technology, capital mobility, new managerial practices, in some cases hostile labour market policies, and poorly implemented labour relations legislation, have served to place trade unions in Africa largely on the defensive. This even as ILO initiatives to establish dispute resolution machinery are occurring in several African countries. Kalula (2003) argues in this regard that labour laws in Southern Africa do not take into account the social realities of countries in the region, with their changing labour markets. He submits that labour law reflects Western models 'borrowing and bending' legal reforms seeking adherence to ILO standards, sometimes transplanting inappropriate legal precepts focussing on formal sector standard employment, whilst ignoring the bigger reality of a dramatically increasing informal sector. He states that 'the vast majority are left out', arguing that 'labour law is a sharp instrument of social policy. Labour market regulation must strive to influence work beyond the formal sector narrowly defined. Mutual rights and obligations in the workplace remain important, but labour law must be part of an agenda for alleviating poverty.' (ibid.: 57). Traditional trade union contestation and power-conflict models may be inappropriate as are traditional distributive forms of collective bargaining based on an adversarial tradition. In Africa, union and employer strategies will need to focus increasingly on human resource development. Continuing challenges of poverty and civil strife such as in Darfur, Sudan, present enormous challenges at a most basic level of human need. In more developed and stable political economies in Africa, joint collaboration in the work place will be vital for effective competition in the market place. In Africa the employment relations agenda will have increasingly to concern itself not only with managerial–working class relations and global competitiveness but with a growing and socially excluded underclass.

References

Anstey, M. (2004), 'African Renaissance – Implications for Labour Relations in South Africa', *South African Journal of Labour Relations*, 28, 1: 54–5, 58–60.
Aryee, S. (2004), 'Human Resource Management in Ghana', in Kamoche, K., Debrah, Y., Horwitz F.M., and Muuka, G. (eds), *Managing Human Resources in Africa*. London: Routledge.
Bahadur, A. (2004), 'Taking the Devil's Rope – AGOA', *South African Labour Bulletin*, 28, 1: 39–42.
Buegre, C.D. (2004), 'Human Resource Management in Ivory Coast', in Kamoche, K., Debrah, Y., Horwitz, F.M. and Muuka, G. (eds), *Managing Human Resources in Africa*. London: Routledge.
Debrah, Y. (2004). 'Human Resource Management in Tanzania', in Kamoche, K., Debrah, Y, Horwitz, F.M. and Muuka, G. (eds), *Human Resource Management in Africa*. London: Routledge.

Fashoyin, T. (2000), 'Management in Africa', in Warner M. (ed.), *Management in Emerging Countries*. London: Thomson Learning.

Fashoyin, T., Matanmi, S. and Tawase, A. (1994), 'Reform Measures, Employment and Labour Market Processes in the Nigerian Economy', in Fashoyin, T. (ed.), *Economic Reform Policies and the Labour Market in Nigeria*. Lagos: Friedrich Ebert Foundation/ Nigerian Industrial Relations Association.

Gwiyo, C. (2004), 'ZCTU Leader Talks about his Role', *South African Labour Bulletin*, 28, 4: 67.

Horwitz, F.M., Nkomo, S,M., and Rahah, M. (2004), 'Human Resource Management in South Africa', in Kamoche, K., Debrah, Y., Horwitz, F.M. and Muuka, G. (eds), *Managing Human Resources in Africa*. London: Routledge.

ILO (1997), *World Labour Report 1997–8: Industrial Relations Democracy and Social Stability*. Geneva: ILO.

Jackson, T. (2002), 'Reforming Human Resource Management in Africa, A Cross-Cultural Perspective', *International Journal of Human Resource Management*, 13, 7: 999.

Kalula, E. (2003), 'Labour Laws Need a Dash of Reality', *South African Labour Bulletin*, 27, 4: 56–9.

Kalula, E and Madhuklu, L. (1997). *Public Sector Labour Relations in Southern Africa: Developments and Trends*. Cape Town: Institute of Development and Labour Law, University of Cape Town.

Kamoche, K., Muuka, G., Horwitz, F.M. and Debrah, Y.A. (2004a), *Managing Human Resources in Africa*. London: Routledge.

Kamoche, K., Nyambegerd, S. and Mulinge, M. (2004b), 'Human Resource Management in Kenya', in Kamoche, K., Debrah, Y., Horwitz, F.M. & Muuka, G (eds), *Managing Human Resources in Africa*. London: Routledge.

Koen, M. (2004), 'A Tale of Four Unions: The State of Clothing Unions in Four African Countries', *South African Labour Bulletin*, 28, 1: 53–6.

Matanmi, S. (2000), 'Industrial relations in emerging countries', in Warner, M. (ed.), *Management in Emerging Countries – International Encyclopedia of Business and Management*. London: Thomson Learning.

Mekonnen, S. and Mammon, A. (2004), 'Human Resource Management in Ethiopia', in Kamoche, K., Debrah, Y., Horwitz, F.M. and Muuka, G. (eds), *Managing Human Resources in Africa*. London: Routledge.

Levy, S. (2004), 'Mozambique – Legal Framework for Labour Relations', *South African Labour Bulletin*, 28, 3: 57–8.

Muhandin, V.H. (2000), 'Management in Zambia', in Warner, M. (ed.), *Management in Emerging Countries*. London: Thomson Learning.

Muhandin, V.H. (2000), 'Management in Zambia', in Warner, M. (ed.), *Management in Emerging Countries*. London: Thomson Learning, p. 239.

Muuka, G and Mwenda, K. (2004), 'Human Resource Management in Zambia', in Kamoche, K., Debrah, Y., Horwitz, F.M. and Muuka, G. (eds), *Managing Human Resources in Africa*. London: Routledge.

Musonda, J. 2004. 'African Round-up – Zimbabwe', *South African Labour Bulletin*, 28, 4: 68.

Nyambegera, S.M. 2002. 'Ethnicity and Human Resource Management Practice in Sub-Saharan Africa', *International Journal of Human Resource Management*, 13, 7: 1077–90.

Ramgutty-Wong, A. (2004), 'Human Resource Management in Mauritius', in Kamoche, K., Debrah,Y., Horwitz, F.M. and Muuka, G. (eds), *Managing Human Resources in Africa*. London: Routledge.

Shelley, S. (2004), *Doing Business in Africa*. Cape Town: Zebra Press.

Siddique, S.A. (1989), 'Industrial Relations in Third World Setting', *Journal of Industrial Relations*, 31: 385–401.
Stiglitz, J. (2002), *Globalisation and its Discontents*. London: Penguin Books.
Tamangani, Z and Muranda, Z. (2000), 'Management in Zimbabwe' in Warner, M. (ed.), *Management in Emerging Countries*. London: Thomson Learning.
Theron, J and Godfrey, S. (2000), 'Protecting Workers on the Periphery', *Development and Labour Law Monograph* 1/2000, Institute of Development and Labour Law, University of Cape Town, pp. 1–51.
Verma, A., Kochan, T. and Wood, S. (2002), 'Union Decline and Prospects for Revival', *British Journal of Industrial Relations*, 40, 3: 373–84.
Webster, E. and Wood, G. (2004), 'Evolving Labour Relations in Mozambique', *South African Labour Bulletin*, 28, 3: 51–6.
Yagocubi, M. (2004), 'Human Resource Management in Tunisia', in Kamoche, K., Debrah, Y., Horwitz, F.M. and Muuka, G. (eds), *Managing Human Resources* in Africa, London: Routledge, pp. 157–8.

Index

'Brain drain' 2, 220
'Brazilianization' 8
Academic Staff Union of Universities (ASUU) (Nigeria) 165-6, 167, 171
Administrative Commissions (Mozambique) 90
African Civil Servants Technical Workers Union (Nigeria) 153
African National Congress (ANC) 112, 113
Agricultural sector 17-18, 37, 39, 40, 47, 50, 54, 56, 66-8, 78, 79, 80, 82, 100, 103, 105, 137, 138, 139, 140, 162, 164, 189, 198, 201, 210, 213, 215, 222, 226; *see also* peasantry
Akpala, A. 149
All Nigeria Trade Union Federation 154
American Centre of International Labour Solidarity 21
Amin, Idi 67
Apartheid 98, 100, 102-3, 105, 113, 126, 220, 221, 223
Appeals Labour Court of Kenya 43
Arbitration 32, 34, 56, 57, 61, 114, 138, 141, 144, 157, 163, 164, 167, 174, 175, 177-8, 183, 184, 188, 190-1, 194, 196n, 220, 229, 231
Association of Local Unions 185-6
Authoritarianism 7, 10, 19, 24, 53-5, 59, 64, 66, 67, 77, 79, 82-4, 86, 100, 101, 164, 219, 223
Automobile industry see motor industry

Bafyou, P. 152
Bahadur, A. 231
Bamangwato Concession Limited 128
Banda, H. 9, 53-5, 59
Bantustans 103
Basic Conditions of Employment Act (South Africa) 115, 231
Bechuanaland Democratic Party 126, 132n; *see also* Botswana Democratic Party
Bechuanaland Protectorate Union 125

Bechuanaland Trade Union Congress 125
Botswana 6, 11, 77, 125-33, 220, 222, 225, 229
Botswana Banking Employees Union 125
Botswana Construction Workers Union 125
Botswana Council and General Workers Union 125
Botswana Democratic Party 132n
Botswana Federation of Trade Unions (BFTU) 125, 127, 129
Botswana Mining Union 125
Botswana Mining Workers Union 129, 131
Botswana National Front 127, 129
Botswana Railway Workers Union 125
Botswana Teachers Union 129, 131
Botswana Trade Union 125
Bretton Woods 222
Britain 17, 18, 19, 28, 31-3, 45, 55, 126, 148, 149, 153, 163, 165, 183, 199, 219
Budhwar, P. 1
Buhlungu, S. 122, 122n
Building, Construction, Civil Engineering and Allied Workers Union (Malawi) 56
Burawoy, M. 98-9
Busia Progress Party (PP) 185

Central Labour Organization Law (Nigeria) 155
Central Organization of Trade Unions (Kenya) 34, 39, 43, 48, 50
Central Personnel Administration of Eritrea 22
Centrale Dignite (Ivory Coast) 229
Chemmuttat, C. 34
Chissano, J. 89
Civil Servants Association (Ghana) 190, 192
Civil Service Union (CSU) (Nigeria) 149
Civil society 9, 18, 24, 45-6, 119, 127, 156, 158, 178, 198, 221

235

Civil war 3, 66, 88, 89, 154, 164, 169, 222, 232
Cockar, S. 34
Collective bargaining 21–2, 29, 33–4, 36, 37, 39, 41–2, 45, 46–8, 53, 56–61, 63, 70, 71, 77, 81, 84, 88, 91, 94, 95, 98, 100, 103, 106–7, 108, 113, 114, 129, 130, 131, 141–2, 143–4, 150, 153, 159, 166–74, 184, 186–90, 196n, 198, 211, 212, 220–6, 228, 230–2
Colonialism 6, 11, 12, 17–20, 28–32, 39, 53, 55, 66, 88, 89, 98–104, 125, 126, 127, 130, 137, 147–50, 154, 155, 159, 160, 163, 183–4, 199–200, 201, 204, 219, 221, 223, 229
Commercial African Trade Union (Malawi) 55
Commercial and General Workers Union (Botswana) 127
Commission for Conciliation, Mediation and Arbitration (South Africa) 114, 231
Commonwealth Trade Union Council 58
Confederation Nigerien du Travail (CNT) 201
Confederation of Ethiopian Trade Unions (CETU) 227
Confederation of Free and Independent Trade Unions of Mozambique (CONSLIMO) 91
Confederation of Free Trade Unions (Uganda) 72
Congress for Malawi Trade Unions 59
Congress of South African Trade Unions (COSATU) 7, 83, 111–22
Constitution of Ghana (1982) 186
Constitution of Ghana (1992) 187
Constitution of Kenya 41
Constitution of Morocco 140
Convention Peoples Party 183–4
Corruption 79–80, 89, 147, 148, 177, 179, 185
Court of Appeal (Niger) 202
Court of First Instance (Morocco) 140
Cross, J. 213

De Beers 129; *see also* Debswana
Debrah, Y. 1
Debswana Mining Company 128, 129, 131

Debt 3, 54, 222
Deleanne, R. 200
Democratic Confederation of Labour (CDT) (Morocco) 140–1, 143
Democratic Federation of Labour (FDT) (Morocco) 141
Democratic Peoples Party (Malawi) 54
Democratic Republic of Congo 78
Democratic Union 89
Democratization 6–7, 10, 11, 21, 45, 47, 53, 61, 63–4, 86, 87, 88, 91, 92, 95, 112, 126, 131, 155, 176, 185, 186, 201, 211, 212, 219, 221, 223, 228, 230
Department of Labour of Eritrea 21
Department of Labour of Malawi 55
Dynamizing Groups (Mozambique) 90

East Africa Association 45
Eastern Europe, Economic Transitions in 211
Economic Recovery Programme (Uganda) 68
Education and training 2, 3, 18, 21, 23, 33, 43, 54, 57, 58, 67, 68, 72, 74, 82, 89–90, 104, 107, 108, 115, 117, 126, 130, 139, 140, 141, 143, 149, 162, 166, 167, 168, 173, 175, 178, 185, 189, 202, 211, 213, 215, 220, 226, 228
Egypt 228
Employer Associations 25, 44–5, 50, 71–2,143, 151, 152–3, 164, 173, 188, 193, 225, 227, 228
Employers 5–6, 7–8, 20–5, 33–7, 55–62, 68, 81, 91, 94, 95, 96, 98, 100–2, 105–8, 113, 114–15, 117, 122n, 128, 129, 130–2, 139, 141–5, 147–53, 155, 157, 160, 163–5, 168–76, 179, 184–94, 198, 202, 210–12, 214, 221, 223, 225, 229, 230–1
Employers Consultative Association of Malawi 56, 59–60
Employers Federation of Eritrea 22
Employment Act (Malawi) 56, 58
Employment Act (Uganda) 71
Employment Equity Act (South Africa) 115, 223
Eritrea 9, 17–27
Ethiopia 17–22, 24, 25, 221, 227, 228
Ethopia Trade Union (AETU) 227

Export Processing Zones (EPZs)   41, 46, 231
Ezeife, T.   167

Factory Act (Nigeria)   163, 164
Factory Act (Uganda)   69
Federal Office of Statistics of Nigeria   162
Federation of Rhodesia and Nyasaland   53
Federation of Uganda Employers   70–1
First Instance Labour Court   23
Fishing industry   100, 189, 215
Flexibility   10, 100, 104–7, 108, 112, 131, 194, 225, 230, 231
FNV/Mondiaal (Netherlands)   203, 212
Food and Beverage Industry   5
France   137, 199–204, 219
France Telecom   203–4
Francophone Africa   1, 9, 11–12, 135–46
Freeman, R.   6
Frelimo   88, 89, 90, 96n
Freund, B.   149
Frynas, G.   198, 211

General Agricultural Workers Union (Ghana)   213
General Union of Moroccan Workers (UGTM)   141
General Union of Workers of Ivory Coast (UGTCI)   229
George, S.   2
GEPATU   216
Germany   19, 100
Ghana   11, 12, 182–97, 209–18, 220, 225, 228
Ghana Employers Association   188–9, 193
Ghana Federation of Labour (GFL)   187, 189, 192
Ghana National Association of Teachers   190, 192, 193
Ghana Private Road Transport Union (GPTRU)   213–14, 215, 216
Ghana Registered Nurses Association   190, 192
Ghana Trades Union Congress see Trades Union Congress of Ghana
Gono, G.   85

Growth, Employment and Reconstruction (GEAR) policy (South Africa)   112
Guebaza, A.   89
Gwiyo, C.   227–8

Hassan II, King of Morocco   137
Health and safety   81, 130, 143, 215, 216, 226, 230
Heavily Indebted Poor Countries Initiative   54
HIV/AIDS   25, 54, 71, 127, 226, 229, 230
Honneyer, G.   100
Hoogevelt, A   3
Hotel industry see tourism and hotel industry
Hut Tax   29

Indian Communist Party   30
Indian Self-Employed Women's Association   216
Indian Trade Union, The   30
Industrial and Commercial Workers' Union (Ghana)   187
Industrial Arbitration Panel (Nigeria)   163, 174
Industrial Commission of Australia   32
Industrial Councils (Malawi)   61
Industrial Court (National) of Nigeria   163, 174, 178
Industrial Court of Botswana   130–1
Industrial Court of Kenya   32–7, 41, 43, 49
Industrial policy   5, 37, 41, 89, 231
Industrial Relations Act (Ghana)   185–7, 194
Industrial Relations Act (Mauritius)   228
Industrial Relations Charter (Kenya)   32, 41, 42–4, 48, 50
Industrial Relations Court (Malawi)   57, 60–1
Informal networks of support   4, 6, 148, 214
Informal sector   4, 7–8, 11, 12, 21, 40–1, 43, 80, 86, 95, 112, 113, 121, 122n, 145, 162, 163, 193, 195, 198, 202–4, 209–18, 222, 223, 224, 230, 232
Informal traders associations   8, 95
Interim Management Committees   186, 212, 215

International Confederation of Free Trade Unions (ICFTU)   21, 30, 83, 140, 143, 150, 154, 158, 204, 231
International Labour Organization (ILO)   21, 28, 41, 42, 58, 68, 83, 105, 106, 125, 128, 130, 131, 132, 139, 140–5, 165, 166, 175, 178, 187, 189, 204, 209, 210, 212, 213, 216, 220, 223, 231, 232
International Monetary Fund (IMF)   3, 5, 38, 40, 54, 60–1, 67, 85, 88, 89, 95, 137, 164, 185, 219, 230
Istiqlal Party   141
Italy   17, 18, 19
Ivory Coast   229

Japan   1
Joint Consultative Committees   167–8
Joint Disputes Commission (Kenya)   33
Joint Industrial and Commercial Consultative Committee (Kenya)   50
Joint Industrial and Commercial Consultative Council (Kenya)   45
Joint Industrial Committees (Nigeria)   167–8
Joint Industrial Councils (Nigeria)   168–9
Justice and Development Party (PJD) (Morocco)   141

Kadoma Declaration of Intent   84
Kamoche, K.   1
Kaufman, B.   6
Kaunda, B.   61
Kaunda, K.   227
Kenya   2, 7, 28–38, 39–52, 73, 221, 223, 228, 229, 230
Kenya African National Union (KANU)   33, 49
Kenya Association of Manufacturers   45
Kenya Business Consultative Forum   45
Kenya Business Council   45
Kenya Federation of Employers/ Federation of Kenya Employers   33, 41, 44, 47–8
Kenya Federation of Labour   32, 33
Kenya Federation of Trade Unions   32
Kenya National Chambers of Commerce and Industry   45
Kenya Union of Commercial, Food and Allied Workers   43–4

Kenyatta, J.   32
Kibaki, M.   47
Koen, M.   230

Labour Act (Namibia)   105–6
Labour Acts (Ghana)   187–8, 193–4
Labour Advisory Council (Namibia)   105
Labour Code (Morocco)   140, 143
Labour Code (Niger)   198, 200
Labour Court (Namibia)   105, 106
Labour Court (South Africa)   231
Labour Department/Ministry of Labour (Ghana)   187–8
Labour Inspectorate (Morocco)   139–40, 143, 144
Labour Law (Mozambique)   91
Labour legislation   4, 5, 10, 11, 20, 22–3, 25, 29, 32–8, 41–3, 46–51, 53, 56–8, 60–1, 63, 71, 80–1, 91, 94, 105–6, 111, 113–15, 116, 122, 128–31, 132, 137–45, 149, 150, 155–8, 163–5, 168, 171, 173, 174, 179n, 182, 186–9, 193–5, 199–200, 202, 204, 226, 228, 230, 231–2
Labour process   98–9, 103
Labour Proclamation (Eritrea)   20, 23
Labour Relations Act (Malawi)   57
Labour Relations Act (South Africa)   113, 114, 231
Labour Relations Act (Zimbabwe)   81
Labour Relations Board   23
Labour Trade Union of East Africa   30, 31
Labour Trade Union of Kenya   30
Labour Unity Front (Nigeria)   154
Labour/Employment Act (Nigeria)   163, 172
League of Nations   28
Lesotho   77, 225
Libya   228
Local Government Workers Union (Malawi)   56
Lockouts   34, 61, 174, 190; see also strikes
LO-Denmark   21, 204
LO-Norway   21

Maghreb   1; *see also* Morocco
Malawi   9–10, 53–65, 225
Malawi Congress of Trade Unions   58, 59

Malawi Congress Party 53, 55
Malawi Railway Workers Union 56
Manufacturers Association of Nigeria 164
Manufacturing sector 5, 6, 37, 39, 45, 50, 68, 78, 80, 82, 85, 88, 91, 103, 107, 163, 164, 166, 172, 173, 179, 189, 221, 223, 224
Master and Servant Proclamation (Namibia) 102
Masters and Servants Ordinance (Kenya) 29
Matanmi, S. 219, 222
Mauritius 225, 228
Mbonini, E. 127
Mboya, T. 31–3
Medoff, J. 6
Mexico 213
Middle East 9, 19
Migrancy 80–1, 99–104, 106, 138, 198, 231
Millennium Council (South Africa) 220
Mines Employees Union (Ghana) 183
Minimum wage 5, 30, 48, 56, 71, 80, 81, 102, 139, 153, 191, 227
Minimum Wages (Miscellenous Provisions) Act (Malawi) 56
Mining sector 5, 80, 82, 100, 102, 126, 129, 130,138, 162, 164, 182, 183, 189, 201, 221, 222, 224, 226
Minister for labour of Morocco 138
Minister of Labour, Productivity and Employment of Nigeria 150, 156, 163
Ministry of Employment, Social Affairs and Solidarity 139
Ministry of Labour of Malawi 56, 61–2
Ministry of Labour of Namibia 104, 105
Modernization theory 8
Mogalakwe, M. 127
Moi, D. 47
Monopsony 6, 101
Moroccan Labour Union (UMT) 140, 143
Morocco 11, 137–46
Motor industry 5, 138, 162, 223
Mozambique 10, 53, 77, 87–96
Multinational Corporations (MNCs) 5, 44, 143, 153, 160, 163, 198, 223
Multi-partyism 7, 11, 45, 54, 59, 61, 63–4, 71, 88, 90, 126, 131, 176, 229

Museveni, J. 67
Mutharika, Bingu wa 54

Nairobi Local Government Servants' Association 31, 33
Namibia 10, 77, 98–108, 220, 221, 225
National Agricultural Research Organization (Uganda) 67
National Amalgamated Local and Central Government and Parastatal Manuel Workers Union (Botswana) 127
National Association of Chambers of Commerce, Industrial, Mines and Manufacture (Nigeria) 164
National Association of Graduate Teachers (Ghana) 192
National Confederation of Eritrean Workers 17, 20–1, 23, 25
National Congress of Nigerian Citizens (NCNC) 153
National Constitution of Malawi 57
National Council of Trade Unions of Nigeria (NCTUN) 154
National Council on Establishments 167
National Economic Consultative Forum (Zimbabwe) 84
National Economic Empowerment and Development Strategy (NEEDS) (Nigeria) 147
National Employment Councils (Zimbabwe) 81
National Inland Canoe Fishermen's Association (Ghana) 215
National Labour Commission (Ghana) 190–1, 194
National Labour Union of Morocco (UNTM) 141
National Liberal Council (Ghana) 184–5
National Organization of Trade Unions (Uganda) 72
National Policy on Labour and Manpower Development (Namibia) 105
National Public Service Negotiating Councils 166–7, 170
National Research and Higher Education Union (SYNARES) (Ivory Coast) 229
National Tripartite Consultative Committee (Kenya) 50

National Tripartite Negotiating
    Committee (Kenya)   49
National Union of Eritrean Women   17
National Union of Eritrean
    Workers   19, 20
National Union of Eritrean Workers for
    Independence   19
National Union of Eritrean Youth and
    Students   17
National Union of Mineworkers (NUM)
    (South Africa)   121
National Union of Nambian Workers
    (NUNW)   102, 107, 108
National Union of Tanganyika
    Employees   229
Nationale des Travailleurs du Niger
    (UNTN)   200–1
Neo-liberalism   2–5, 25, 39–40, 54, 61,
    63, 67, 81, 87, 88, 95, 104, 105, 108,
    113, 127, 179, 185, 202, 203, 204, 211;
    see also structural adjustment
New Partnership for African
    Development (NEPAD)   221
Niger   11–12, 198–205
Niger Delta   148
Nigeria   2, 11, 147–61, 162–81, 211–12,
    220, 225, 228
Nigeria Civil Servants Union
    (NCSU)   154
Nigeria Labour Congress (NLC)   151,
    152, 154, 155, 156, 164, 165
Nigeria Police   159, 167, 169, 178
Nigeria Social Insurance Trust Fund   174
Nigeria Trade Union Congress   154,
    164, 165
Nigerian Employers Consultative
    Association (NECA)   152, 164
Nigerian National Federation of Labour
    (NNFL)   153
Nigerian National Petroleum
    Corporation (NNPC)   168, 171, 176
Nigerian Union of Teachers (Nigeria)
    149, 154
Nigerian Workers Council   154
Nkrumah, K.   183, 184
Non-Governmental Organizations
    (NGOs)   45–6, 71, 179, 212, 229
NUPENG   157, 166
Nyasaland African Congress   53
Nyasaland Employers Association   56

Obasanjo, O.   147, 150, 160, 164
Obasi, I.   126
Oil Producers Trade Sectors (OPTS)
    (Nigeria)   152
Oil sector see petroleum sector
Organicao de Trabalhadores de
    Mozambique (OTM)   90, 91, 95
Organization of African Trades Union
    Unity   150
Organized Private Sector (OPS) (Nigeria)
    153, 163, 164, 172
Oshiomhole, A.   156

Pan African Organization of Trade
    Union Unity   212
Patriarchal management   6, 95, 149, 198
Peasantry   8, 68, 100, 103, 198, 210
Penal Code (Morocco)   142
PENGASSAN   157
Peoples Defense Committees
    (Ghana)   185–6
Peoples Democratic Party (PDP)
    (Nigeria)   148
Peoples National Party (Ghana)   185
Petroleum and Natural Gas Employers
    Association   152
Petroleum sector   148, 149, 152, 157,
    158, 159, 162, 166, 168, 171, 172, 173,
    176, 179n, 189
Picketing   29–30, 107
Plantation and Agricultural Workers
    Union   56
Political parties   33, 53–4, 63, 70, 79,
    83, 88–9, 140–1, 148, 150, 154, 155,
    156, 162, 176, 183, 211, 227, 229;
    see also under individual party names
Poll tax (Kenya)   29
Portugal   90, 200, 219
Poverty Reduction Strategy Papers   3
*Presidential Powers (Temporary Measures)
    Act*   82
Prices and Incomes Stabilization
    Protocol   84
Privatisation   5, 20, 25, 38, 54, 61, 62,
    66, 89–90, 137–8, 162, 164, 179, 185,
    195, 196, 203–4, 220, 222, 223, 226,
    227, 229, 230
Production Councils (Mozambique)   90
Productivity   23, 54, 92, 107, 108, 127,
    167, 169, 171, 175, 191, 222, 227

Protective tariffs 8–9, 35, 89, 137, 222
Provisional National Defence Council (PNDC) (Ghana) 185–6, 195
Public sector 3, 11, 18, 23, 38, 40–2, 43, 54, 58, 60, 61, 62, 67, 71, 79, 80, 82, 105, 117, 130, 140–1, 142, 145, 149, 153, 162–4, 166–71, 175–7,182, 183, 185, 186, 190, 191, 192, 193, 195, 196n, 198, 201–2, 222, 225–6, 229; *see also* State, The
Public Service Negotiating Committees Law (Ghana) 186

Railway Workers Union (Nigeria) 149, 153
Rawlings, J. 185
Redundancies 3–4, 6, 9–10, 11, 12, 18, 42, 48, 50, 61, 62, 88, 90, 111, 131, 152, 178, 179, 195, 196n, 229, 231
Regional Labour Court Tribunals (Kenya) 20
Registrar of Trade Unions (Nigeria) 166
Regulation of Wages and Conditions of Employment Act (Kenya) 42
Renamo 88, 89, 90, 96n
Reserve Bank of Zimbabwe 83, 85
Resident Natives Ordinance (Kenya) 29
Retrenchments see redundancies
Rhodesia *see* Zimbabwe
Roberts, B. 1
Rossignotti, G. 213
Royal Air Maroc 137
Russia 202

Sauvy, A. 211
Secondary Teachers' Union of Ivory Coast (SYNESCI) 229
Segmented business system 211
Senior Staff Consultative Council of Nigeria (SESCAN) 152
Seretse, L. 125
Shagari, S. 175
Shell/BP of Nigeria 167, 168, 171, 173
Shop stewards 91–2, 108, 118, 228
Siddique, S. 224
Singh, M. 30–1
Skills Development Act (South Africa) 115
Skills Development Levies Act (South Africa) 115

Small and Medium Sized Enterprises (SMEs) 45–6, 108, 114, 130–1, 153, 162–3, 165, 223; *see also* informal sector
Social Justice Unionism 111–13, 116–18, 120–2
Social movements 111, 116, 119, 221, 227
Social partnership see tripartism
Socialist Union of Popular Forces (USFP) (Morocco) 140–1
Somalia 219, 228
South Africa 2, 5, 6, 7, 10–11, 88, 89, 100–4, 111–24, 131, 220–1, 223–6, 228–31
South African Clothing and Textile Workers Union (SACTWU) 121, 231
South African Communist Party (SACP) 113
South West Africa Native Labour Association (SWANLA) 101, 102
Southall, R. 7
Southern African Development Community (SADC) 222
Spain 137
State socialism 88, 89
State, The. 4–5, 9–12, 20, 24, 29, 38, 41–3, 48–51, 53–6, 58, 59–63, 68, 71, 72, 77, 79, 81–6, 88–90, 95, 98–102, 105–6, 107, 108, 119, 121, 126, 129, 131, 137–8, 140, 143, 145, 147, 149, 151, 153, 155–7, 159, 160–8, 170–4, 176–9, 182–8, 190–5, 198–202, 204, 210–11, 213–16, 219–23, 227–31; *see also* public sector
Stiglitz, J. 211
Street Net Ghana Alliance (SGA) 214–15, 216
Strikes 9, 11, 19, 23, 24, 30–3, 34, 42, 48–9, 53, 55, 56–8, 60, 61–2, 68, 69, 71, 74, 81–2, 87, 94, 99–103, 106–7, 114, 118–19, 129, 130–1, 138, 142, 145, 148, 153, 157–9, 165–8, 170, 174–7, 183–5, 186, 188, 190–3, 200, 201, 202, 227, 229
Structural Adjustment Programmes 2–3, 6, 9–10, 11–12, 37–8, 40, 54, 66, 79, 83, 85, 87–91, 137, 164, 185, 195, 199, 201, 202–3, 204, 211, 219, 221, 222, 230; *see also* neo-liberalism

242 Index

Sudan   232
Supreme Military Council (Ghana)   185
SWAPO (South West Africa Peoples Organization)   101–4, 106
Syndicat National des Travailleurs de l'Industrie du Niger (SNTIN)   204

Taiwan   231
Tanganyika Federation of Labour   229
Tanzania   53, 228, 229
Taylor, I.   126
Taylorism   6, 100
Tewolde, M.   17, 18
Textile sector   5, 61, 162, 187, 192, 195, 211, 221, 223, 224
Textile, Garment, and Leather Employees Union (Ghana)   187, 192
Theories of the Failure of the State   4
Tourism and hotel industry   39, 138, 189
Trade Disputes (Arbitration and Settlement) Act (Malawi)   56
Trade Disputes (Arbitration and Settlement) Act (Uganda)   69
Trade Disputes (Essential Services) Act (Nigeria)   168–9, 175
Trade Disputes Act (Botswana)   128, 130
Trade Disputes Act (Kenya)   33–4, 41, 42, 48
Trade Disputes Acts (Nigeria)   156, 163, 168, 174, 175, 177
Trade Union Act (Nigeria)   156, 158, 163, 165
Trade Union Congress of Malawi   58; see also Trades Union Congress of Nyasaland
Trade Union Congress of Nigeria   153, 154, 164
Trade Union Ordinance (Ghana)   183
Trade Union Ordinance (Nigeria)   149, 153
Trade unions   3–4, 6–7, 9–12, 17–24, 29–37, 39, 41–51, 53, 55–60, 63, 68–73, 77, 79, 82–5, 87–8, 90–6, 98–9, 101, 103, 105–8, 111–22, 124–32, 138, 140–4, 147–60, 163–6, 174–9, 183–96, 199–205, 209–16, 221–32
Trade Unions Act (Kenya)   33
Trade Unions Act (Malawi)   56
Trade Unions and Employers Organization Act (Botswana)   128

Trade Unions and Labour Relations Act (Mauritius)   228
Trade Unions Decrees (Uganda)   71
Trades Union Congress of Ghana   182, 183, 187, 189, 190–2, 195, 196n, 209, 213, 214, 215, 216
Trades Unions Congress of Nyasaland   55
Training see Education and training
Transnational Corporations (TNCs) see Multinational Corporations (MNCs)
Transport and General Workers Union (Malawi)   55, 56
Tribunal of First Instance (Morocco)   138
Tripartism   12, 21, 40–3, 45, 46, 48–51, 59, 83–5, 104, 105, 106, 126, 164, 174, 178, 191, 220, 225, 226, 230
Tsvangirai, M.   83
Tunisia   226–7
Tunisia Général Employment Union (UGTT)   226–7

Uganda   10, 66–73, 222
Unemployment   3–4, 6, 9–10, 29, 72, 80, 86, 103, 104, 112, 114–16, 126–7, 138, 145, 166, 183, 192, 214, 219, 226, 227, 231
Unemployment Insurance Act (South Africa)   115
Union Generale de Travailleurs de l'Afrique Noir   200
Union of Kenya Civil Servants   42
United Democratic Front (Malawi) (UDF)   54
United Gold Coast Convention   183
United States of America   32, 33, 45, 137, 139

Van Donge, J.   61
Victimization   62, 71, 82, 83, 107, 131, 143, 202
Voice   6, 94, 128, 186, 211, 225

Wage Councils (Kenya)   48, 51
Wages Advisory Councils (Malawi)   56
Wages Board (Malawi)   56
Wages Board (Nigeria)   172
War on Want   213
Waterman, P.   122n

Webb, S. and B. 210
Wiehahn Commission 113
Workers Compensation Act (Uganda) 69
Workers Defense Committee 185–6
Workmen's Compensation Act (Nigeria) 163, 164
World Bank 38, 40, 54, 60, 63, 85, 89, 126, 137, 164, 185, 219, 222, 230
World Federation of Trade Unions (WFTU) 30, 150, 154

Zambia 7, 53, 77, 220, 221, 225, 226, 227, 228
Zimbabwe 10, 77–86, 88, 89, 220, 225, 227–8, 231
Zimbabwe Congress of Trade Unions 79, 82–84, 227–8, 231
Zimbabwe Federation of Trade Unions 79, 83